Lecture Notes in Computer Science   10971

Commenced Publication in 1973
Founding and Former Series Editors:
Gerhard Goos, Juris Hartmanis, and Jan van Leeuwen

Editorial Board

More information about this series at http://www.springer.com/series/7409

Jing Xiao · Zhi-Hong Mao
Toyotaro Suzumura · Liang-Jie Zhang (Eds.)

Cognitive Computing – ICCC 2018

Second International Conference
Held as Part of the Services Conference Federation, SCF 2018
Seattle, WA, USA, June 25–30, 2018
Proceedings

 Springer

Editors
Jing Xiao
Big Data Platform Division
Peking
China

Zhi-Hong Mao
University of Pittsburgh
Pittsburgh, PA
USA

Toyotaro Suzumura
IBM Thomas J. Watson Research Center
Yorktown Heights, NY
USA

Liang-Jie Zhang
Kingdee International Software Group
  Co., Ltd.
Shenzhen
China

ISSN 0302-9743   ISSN 1611-3349   (electronic)
Lecture Notes in Computer Science
ISBN 978-3-319-94306-0   ISBN 978-3-319-94307-7   (eBook)
https://doi.org/10.1007/978-3-319-94307-7

Library of Congress Control Number: 2018947329

LNCS Sublibrary: SL3 – Information Systems and Applications, incl. Internet/Web, and HCI

Printed on acid-free paper

This Springer imprint is published by the registered company Springer International Publishing AG
part of Springer Nature
The registered company address is: Gewerbestrasse 11, 6330 Cham, Switzerland

Preface

The International Conference on Cognitive Computing (ICCC) was created to cover all aspects of sensing intelligence (SI) as a service (SIaaS). Cognitive computing is a sensing-driven computing (SDC) scheme that explores and integrates intelligence from all types of senses in various scenarios and solution contexts. It is well beyond the traditional senses of human beings: four major senses (sight, smell, hearing, and taste) located in specific parts of the body, as well as a sense of touch located all over a body.

This volume presents the accepted papers for the ICCC 2018, held in Seattle, USA, during June 25–30, 2018. The major topics of ICCC 2018 included but were not limited to: cognitive computing technologies and infrastructure, cognitive computing applications, sensing intelligence, cognitive analysis, mobile services, cognitive computing on smart home, cognitive computing on smart city.

We accepted 15 papers, including ten full papers and five short papers. Each was reviewed and selected by at least three independent members of the ICCC 2018 international Program Committee. We are pleased to thank the authors whose submissions and participation made this conference possible. We also want to express our thanks to the Organizing Committee and Program Committee members, for their dedication in helping to organize the conference and reviewing the submissions. We owe special thanks to the keynote speakers for their impressive speeches.

May 2018

Jing Xiao
Zhi-Hong Mao
Toyotaro Suzumura
Liang-Jie Zhang

Organization

General Chair

Xuan Wang   Harbin Technology University, Shenzhen, China

Program Chairs

Zhi-Hong Mao   University of Pittsburgh, USA
Toyotaro Suzumura   IBM T. J. Watson Research Center, USA
Jing Xiao   Ping An Group, China

Program Vice Chair

Jianzhong Wang   Ping An Group, China

Application and Industry Track Chairs

Jing He   Victoria University, Australia
Ashish Kundu   IBM T. J. Watson Research Center, USA
Shaochun Li   IBM Research, China

Short Paper Track Chair

Yung Ryn (Elisha) Choe   Sandia National Laboratories Livermore, USA

Publicity Chair

Raju Vatsavai   North Carolina State University, USA

Services Conference Federation (SCF 2018)

General Chairs

Wu Chou   Essenlix Corporation, USA
Calton Pu   Georgia Tech, USA

Program Chair

Liang-Jie Zhang   Kingdee International Software Group Co., Ltd, China

Finance Chair

Min Luo   Huawei, USA

Panel Chair

Stephan Reiff-Marganiec   University of Leicester, UK

Tutorial Chair

Carlos A. Fonseca   IBM T. J. Watson Research Center, USA

Industry Exhibit and International Affairs Chair

Zhixiong Chen   Mercy College, USA

Organizing Committee

Huan Chen (Chair)   Kingdee Inc., China
Sheng He (Co-chair)   Tsinghua University, China
Cheng Li (Co-chair)   Tsinghua University, China
Yishuang Ning (Co-chair)   Tsinghua University, China
Jing Zeng (Co-chair)   Tsinghua University, China

Steering Committee

Calton Pu   Georgia Tech, USA
Liang-Jie Zhang (Chair)   Kingdee International Software Group Co., Ltd, China

Program Committee

Rui Andr Cisuc   University of Coimbra, Portugal
Luca Cagliero   Turin Polytechnic, Italy
Tao Chen   University of Birmingham, UK
Rik Eshuis   Eindhoven University of Technology, The Netherlands
Yen-Hao Hsieh   Tamkang University, China
Eleanna Kafeza   Athens University of Economics and Business, Greece
Nagarajan Kandasamy   Drexel University, USA
Nuno Laranjeiro   University of Coimbra, Portugal
ShaoChun Li   IBM Research (China), China
Wenjia Li   New York Institute of Technology, USA
Min Luo   Huawei, USA
Yutao Ma   Wuhan University, China

Contents

Short Paper Track: Cognitive Modeling

Research: Cognitive Modeling

A Set-Associated Bin Packing Algorithm with Multiple Objectives in the Cloud

Fei Luo[⊠] and Chunhua Gu

School of Information and Engineering,
East China University of Science and Technology, Shanghai, China
luof@ecust.edu.cn

Abstract. The bin packing problem (BPP) is NP-hard and it is widely studied due to its various applications, where the initial sole object is to find a minimum number of bins for the items. This paper applies the BPP in the cloud, and tries to attain multiple objectives, such as minimum used bins, minimum packing time and load balance for the bins. Therefore, a set-associative bin packing algorithm is proposed, where the item set is first divided into two sets with descending order, and then a two-way set-associative mapping process is used to combine the elements in divided sets and pack them into a suitable bin. The packing process is iterated until all the items are resolved. With different performance indicators, experiments and analysis are carried out by the comparison with the traditional typical packing algorithms, which verifies the efficiency of the algorithm.

Keywords: Bin packing · Set-associative · Load balance · Multiple objectives

1 Introduction

The Bin Packing Problem (BPP) appears as a NP-hard [1] combinatorial grouping problem. It often occurs in real life and has been widely studied due to its various applications in computer network design, job scheduling on uniform processors, industrial balancing problem, aircraft container loading, etc. [2].

In this paper the BPP is focused on the scheduling in the cloud. Therein, the workloads are represented as items, while the virtual machines are regarded as bins. There are numerous classical heuristics, such as *next fit* (NF), *first-fit* (FF) and *best-fit* (BF) algorithms, etc. [3]. However, those algorithms normally consider one objective to minimize the bins used. Unlike the traditional solutions for just one objective, this paper tries to attain other objectives, such as load balance of each bin, subject to a number of practical constraints.

There are many evolutional or meta-heuristic algorithms to solve multi-objective BPP with pareto solutions, such as Particle Swarm Optimization (PSO), NSGAII, etc. [4]. However, the final decision needs to be made by the user to get a practical solution. Furthermore, the time complexity of such algorithms are affected by the parameters used in the algorithm, which incurs uncertainty for the deadline-limited scheduling in the cloud. On the other side, the packing time affects the performance of the scheduling. Therefore, the meta-heuristics are not considered in this paper.

© Springer International Publishing AG, part of Springer Nature 2018
J. Xiao et al. (Eds.): ICCC 2018, LNCS 10971, pp. 3–17, 2018.
https://doi.org/10.1007/978-3-319-94307-7_1

We propose a novel set-associative heuristic algorithm to resolve the scheduling in the cloud. In this algorithm, the item set is divided into two, and then a two-way set-associative mapping process is used to combine the elements and pack them into a suitable bin. Specially, the set-associative process considers both the load balance, packing efficiency and packing fill-level, as well the number of used bins.

The main contribution of the paper is that a heuristic one-dimensional algorithm is presented to achieve multiple objectives, such as minimum bins used, minimum packing time and load balance among bins. Also experiments are carried out with classical datasets and randomly generated datasets, which tried to verify the performance and efficiency of the proposed algorithm.

The rest of the paper is organized as follows. Related works are summarized in Sect. 2. The scheduling problem is formulized as a BPP in Sect. 3, where different objectives are presented. The proposed algorithm is detailed and implemented in Sect. 4. To illustrate the performance of the algorithm, the evaluation strategy is defined, and experiments and analysis are carried out Sect. 5. The final conclusions are drawn in Sect. 6.

2   Related Works

As NP-hard, it is unlikely that efficient (i.e., polynomial-time) optimization algorithms can be found for the BPP's solution. Then researchers have thus turned to the study of approximation algorithms, which do not guarantee an optimal solution for every instance, but attempt to find a near-optimal solution within polynomial time [5].

There is a large body of literature concerning the one-dimensional bin packing problem. the well-known online algorithms are Next Fit (NF), First Fit (FF), Best Fit (BF), Worst Fit (WF), and so on [6]. In addition to meet the basic goal of minimizing the number of bins, the algorithms try to reduce the time complexity. The time complexity of NF is clearly $o(n)$ and it has a relatively poor *asymptotic performance ratio* (APR). By adopting appropriate data structures for representing packing, it is easy to verify that the time complexity of these algorithms is $o(n \log n)$, such as FF, BF and WF.

Both exact and heuristic methods have been applied for solving the problem. Martello and Toth [7] proposed a branch-and bound procedure (MTP). Scholl et al. [8] developed a hybrid method (BISON) that combines a tabu search with a branch-and bound procedure based on several bounds and a new branching scheme. Schwerin et al. [9] offered a new lower bound for the BPP based on the cutting stock problem, then integrated this new bound into MTP and achieved high-quality results. Valerio de Carvalho [10] proposed an exact algorithm using column generation and branch-and-bound.

Gupta and Ho [11] introduced a *minimum bin slack* (MBS) constructive heuristic. At each step, a set of items that fits the bin capacity as tightly as possible is identified and packed into the new bin. Fleszar and Hindi [12] developed a hybrid algorithm that combines a modified version of the MBS and the variable Neighborhood Search. Their hybrid algorithm performed well in computational experiments, by producing and optimal solution for 1329 out of 1370 instances considered. Gambosi et al. [13] gave two algorithms via repacking.

Although the heuristic algorithms above can be applied in the practical applications, they are focused on one objective to minimize the used bins.

Also meta-heuristics are also used to solve the BPP. Alvim et al. [14] presented a hybrid improvement heuristic (HI_BP) that uses tabu search to move the items between bins. In their algorithm, a complete yet infeasible configuration is to be repaired through a tabu search procedure.

In recent years, several competitive heuristics have been presented with results similar to those obtained by HI_BP. Singh and Gupta [15] proposed a compound heuristic (C_BP) which combines a hybrid steady-state grouping genetic algorithm with an improved version of Fleszar and Hindi's Perturbation MBS. Loh et al. [16] developed a weight annealing (WA) procedure, by relying on the concept of weight annealing to expand and accelerate the search by creating distortions in various parts of the search space. The proposed algorithm is simple and easy to implement; moreover, the authors reported high-level performances, exceeding those obtained by HI_BP.

Fleszar and Charalambous [17] offered a modification to the Perturbation-MBS method where a new sufficient average weight (SAW) principle is introduced to control the average weight of items packed in each bin (referred to as Perturbation-SAWMBS). This heuristic outperformed the best state-of-the-art HI_BP, C_BP and WA algorithms.

Quiroz-Castellanos et al. [18] involves a grouping genetic algorithm (GGA-CGT) that outperforms all previous algorithms with regard to the number of optimal solutions found, particularly for the most difficult set of instances hard28.

Brandão and Pedroso [19] devised an exact approach for solving the bin packing and cutting stock problems based on an Arc-Flow Formulation of the problem which is then solved with the commercial Gurobi solver. They were able to optimally solve all standard bin packing instances within a reasonable computation times, including those instances that were not solved to optimality by any heuristic method.

The performance of those meta-heuristics depend on the parameters set in the algorithm, which result in uncertainty for the application in the cloud.

3 Problem Description

The load balance requirement of the bin packing is first described, and then the optimizing objectives are mathematically modeled.

It is the assumption that there is one scheduling center in the cloud, where the workloads are sequentially received from users and dispatched into virtual computing resources (VMs). Therein, workloads can be represented as workflows with dependent tasks and jobs with independent tasks, which are both commonly used in distributed scientific computations. In this paper, we focus on the scheduling issues on workload model with jobs, which considers non-preemptible and non-migratable independent tasks with a hard deadline. Then a job J is denoted as formula 1, which consists of n tasks T_j and a deadline d. Therein, the quantity of the computing demand for each task T_j is denoted as w_j.

$$J = \{T_j, d | 0 \leq j < n\} \tag{1}$$

Users submit jobs to cloud systems to accommodate and schedule them to computer resources, e.g., the virtual machines (VM), for further execution. Currently, it is considered that a task at most occupies one VM. Then the scheduling process needs m VMs for the job J, and $m \leq n$. Here the capacity of each VM VM_i is denoted as c_i.

There are two basic requirements necessary to be considered. From the cost point of view, the scheduling process can be looked as a bin packing process, where the tasks are regarded as items, and the VMs are set as bins which are assumed to be sufficient. It means the number of used VMs should be as small as possible.

From the point of view of the scheduling efficiency, the tasks should be computed as soon as possible. It is assumed that the scheduling process is launched at time 0. Through the bin packing scheduling process, the finish time t_i for the scheduled tasks in the ith VM VM_i is shown in formula 2, which meets the condition in formula 3. Therein, the amount of calculation in T_j is also represented as w_j, and x_{ij} represents that whether the task T_j is assigned to the VM VM_i, denoted as formula 4. Then the time t for the job J is the computing time in the VM which finally completes the calculation of the dispatched tasks, denoted as formula 4.

$$t_i = \frac{\sum_{i,i=1}^{n} w_j \times x_{ij}}{c_i} \tag{2}$$

$$t_i \leq d \tag{3}$$

$$x_{ij} = \begin{cases} 1 & \text{if } T_j \text{ is assigned to } VM_i \\ 0 & \text{otherwise.} \end{cases} \tag{4}$$

$$t = \max\{t_i\} \tag{5}$$

Based on the above analysis, the scheduling efficiency, i.e., minimizing t in formula 4, can be improved from two aspects. On the one hand, each t_i should be minimized. When the VMs are homogeneous, i.e., $c_i = c$ (a constant), the direction is to reduce the dispatched tasks in VM_i. It conflicts with the object of bin packing scheduling, and it will not be considered in the following. On the other hand, according to formula 4, the values in the set $\{t_i | 1 \leq i \leq n\}$ should be consistent as much as possible. It should be comprehensively considered with the bin packing scheduling.

From the above analysis, the bin packing scheduling can be modeled as follows. There are two formulized objectives for the bin packing scheduling, represented as formula 6 and 7, which are subject to formula 8–11, where y_i and x_{ij} are explained as formula 12 and 4, respectively.

$$\text{minimize} \quad z = \sum_{i=1}^{n} y_i \tag{6}$$

$$\text{minimize} \quad d = |w_k - w_i|, \quad i, k \in N = \{1, 2, \ldots, n\} \tag{7}$$

Subject to:

$$\sum_{j=1}^{n} w_j x_{ij} \leq c y_i, \quad i \in N \tag{8}$$

$$\sum_{i=1}^{n} x_{ij} = 1, \quad j \in N \tag{9}$$

$$y_i = 0 \; or \; 1, \quad i \in N \tag{10}$$

$$x_{ij} = 0 \; or \; 1, \quad i, j \in N \tag{11}$$

$$y_i = \begin{cases} 1 & \text{if VM}_i \text{ is used,} \\ 0 & \text{otherwise.} \end{cases} \tag{12}$$

For example, there is a item set s = {1, 2, 4, 5, 8, 9, 10}, and the bin size is c = 11. Then there are several packing pattern, and two of them are shown as follows, where [] represents a packed bin with items.

$$P1 : [1, 8], [9], [10], [2, 4, 5]$$
$$P2 : [8], [4, 5], [2, 9], [1, 10]$$

Although the number of used bins in P1 and P2 are the same, the load balances are different, i.e., d1 > d2 (di represents the shaking distance of the ith packing). Then the packing P2 is the expected packing.

4 Design of the Algorithm

To meet the objective in formula 6 and 7, we propose a set-associative bin packing algorithm as shown in Algorithm 1.

To help the packing process, there are three sets used, SmallSet, BigSet and FinSet. Therein, SmallSet consists of the items which are less than half of the bin size, $c/2$, while BigSet consists of the items which are no less than $c/2$. FinSet consists of the items which will not participate in the set-associative packing process.

First, SmallSet, BigSet, FinSet are set to be empty. And then the original set w will be divided into SmallSet and BigSet through divide(), where each item of w will be checked and inserted into one of the two sets.

Afterwards, through the set-associative mapping, launched by *setAssociativeMapping()*, all the items will be put into FinSet. Finally, each item or compound item will be packed into one bin, and it will be iterated when all the items in FinSet are processed by the function of finish(), which will results in the final bins.

Algorithm 1. Set-Associative Bin Packing Algorithm

Input : item set $w = \{w_i \mid 1 \leq i \leq n\}$

Output: bins with items
SmallSet = {}; BigSet = {}; FinSet = {};
SmallSet, BigSet = divide(w);
FinSet = setAssociativeMapping(SmallSet, BigSet, FinSet);
  bins = finish(FinSet);

The key procedure in Algorithm 1 is the function of *setAssociativeMapping()*, which is a two-way set-associative mapping process between SmallSet and BigSet depicted in Algorithm 2.

The set-associative mapping is an iterated packing process. In Algorithm 2, the terminal condition for the iteration is first checked, where there is no element in SmallSet, or all the elements have been moved into FinSet except one left in SmallSet. Then the left elements will be further moved into FinSet by the function of *moveElement()*.

Afterwards, when BigSet is empty and there is more than 2 elements in SmallSet, the biggest two elements will be extracted from SmallSet by getRmElement(). Then they make up a compound element through compound(). Here the weight of the compound element is the sum of the original elements' weight. The compound element will be further added into the BigSet or SmallSet based on its weight. And then the iteration will be continued.

Algorithm 2. SetAssociativeMapping

Input   : SmallSet, BigSet, FinSet
Output: FinSet
small_length = len(SmallSet);
bin_length = len(BigSet);
if small_length ≤0 **then**
 moveElement(BigSet, FinSet);
 return FinSet;
end
if big_length ==0 and small_length == 1 **then**
   moveElement(SmallSet, FinSet);
 return FinSet;
end
if big_length == 0 and small_length > 1 **then**
 sort(SmallSet);
   minIndex = small_length – 1;
   secondIndex = minIndex -1;
   elemMin = getRmElement(minIndex, SmallSet);
   elemSecond = getRmElement(secondIndex,
SmallSet);
   compElem = compound(elemMin, elemSecond);
   if weight(compElem) < c/2 **then**
     addElement(compElem, SmallSet);
   else
     addElement(compElem, BigSet);
   end
   return SetAssociativeMapping(SmallSet, BigSet,
FinSet);
 end

 minBigElem = getMinimalElement(BigSet);
 return matchDescending(minBigElem, SmallSet,
BigSet, FinSet);

If both of SmallSet and BigSet are not empty, the minimal element in BigSet will be attempted to be compounded with the elements in SmallSet in descending order, as shown in Algorithm 3. If one of the elements in SmallSet is found to be compounded, the new compound element will be added into BigSet, and the iteration will continue. Otherwise, all the elements in BigSet will be moved into FinSet by moveElement(), and the iteration will also continue.

Algorithm 3. matchDescending

Input   : minElem, SmallSet, BigSet, FinSet
  Output: FinSet
  sort(SmallSet);
  small_length = len(SmallSet);
  for index := small_length − 1 to 0 step -1 **do**
    elem := getElement(index, SmallSet);
    if (elem + minBigElem) ⩽ c **then**
      compElem = compound(elem, minBigElem);
      removeElement(SmallSet, elem);
      removeElement(BigSet, minElem);
      addElement(compElem, BigSet);
      return SetAssociativeMapping(SmallSet, BigSet,
FinSet);
    end
  end
  moveElement(BigSet, FinSet);
  return SetAssociativeMapping(SmallSet, BigSet,
FinSet);

---

5   Experiments and Evaluation

Because there are multiple objectives in this paper, the formulized two objectives shown in formula 6 and 7, as well as the packing efficiency of the proposed algorithm will be evaluated respectively. On the one hand, the minimal used bins, i.e., represented in formula 6, will be first analyzed based on the typical datasets. On the other hand, to evaluate the load balance in formula 7, new evaluating indicators are devised. All the evaluation is processed by the comparison between the proposed algorithm with the typical bin packing algorithms.

5.1   Configuration of Experiments

To carry out the experiments, there are three issues to be resolved. First, the algorithms to be compared are focused on polynomial-time approximation algorithms. Because the environment for the proposed algorithm is the scheduling in the cloud, the high performance demand for the scheduling requires the utilized algorithms to have the character of polynomial-time approximation. In the scope of heuristics, the most well-known and efficient heuristic packing algorithms are selected to be compared with the proposed algorithm, such as NF, NFD, WFD, BFD.

Second, the performance indicators should be set for the algorithms' comparison. To pack a set of items, the used indicators including the Packing Time (PT), the Competitive Ratio (CR), the average fill-level (AVF) and the standard deviation of the fill-levels (SDF). The PT is the time used to packing a the specified set of items. The CR is defined as the ratio of the number of bins used in the algorithm's solution (denoted as SOL) to the lower-bound of the problem instance's optimal solution (denoted as OPT), as shown in formula 13.

$$CR = SOL/OPT \tag{13}$$

The fill-level of the packed bin is defined as ratio of the sum of the packed items to the capacity of the bin, the AVF is the average value of the fill-levels for the used bins, and the SDF is the standard deviation of the fill-levels for the bins.

Finally, there are two types of datasets are used in the experiments. One is from a common set of one-dimensional bin packing instances, i.e., a class developed by Falkenauer, and the other is a randomly generated dataset. Therein, the instances of Falkenauer is made of two sets, uniform and triplets (denoted by U and T respectively in the tables of results) each with 80 instances. Optimal solutions (OPT) for the instances are known. The inputs of the randomly generated dataset meet the uniform distribution between 0 to the capacity of the bin, while the number of the inputs is 1500. It is known that the value of SOL has a lower bounding for all possible input items as shown in formula 14. Then the lower bounds of SOL, i.e., L, is set as the value of OPT for the random inputs.

$$SOL \geq L = \left\lceil \frac{\sum_{i=1}^{n} w_i}{C} \right\rceil \tag{14}$$

The implemented algorithms are executed in a personal computer with an Intel-i5 CPU and 8 GB memory.

5.2   Results

For the U datasets the results are shown in Figs. 1, 2, 3 and 4, including the packing time, the Competitive Ratio (CR), the average fill-level (AVF) and the standard deviation of the fill-levels (SDF). Therein, the proposed algorithm is represented as SP, while NF, NFD, BFD and WFD are used for comparison. Then the results with the same indicators are shown in Figs. 5, 6, 7 and 8 for all the U and T datasets, and they are presented in Figs. 9, 10, 11 and 12 for the random datasets.

The results show that NF and NFD are the fastest packing algorithms, while their CR and SDF are much more than the other algorithms'. It indicates that although NF and NFD can get are almost the fastest algorithms, the number of bins used are much more and they cannot assure the load balance.

Although The packing time cost in SP is a bit more than that in BFD and WFD, the cost in BFD, SP and WFD is almost in the same order of magnitude. However, for the U datasets, the AVF of those three algorithms are almost the same, and the CR and the SDF in SP is less that those in BFD and WFD. It means that SP can use less bins for the U datasets with better load balance. It can be further verified for the random datasets. But for the U and T datasets, the results are not very clear. Both of these three algorithms almost achieve the same values of the indicators. It can be depicted that the performance of the packing algorithms can be affected by the selection of datasets.

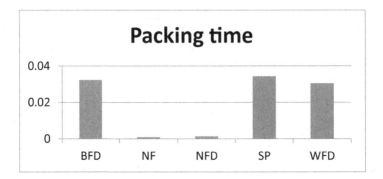

Fig. 1. Packing time for the U datasets

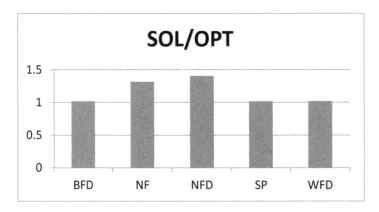

Fig. 2. Competitive Ratio for the U datasets

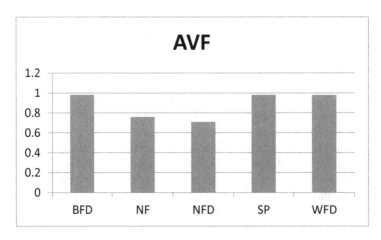

Fig. 3. Average fill-level for the U datasets

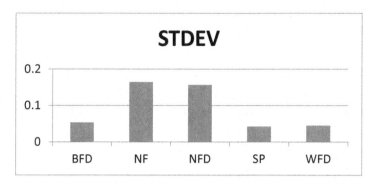

Fig. 4. Standard deviation of the fill-levels for the U datasets

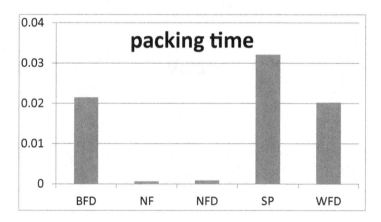

Fig. 5. Packing time for the U and T datasets

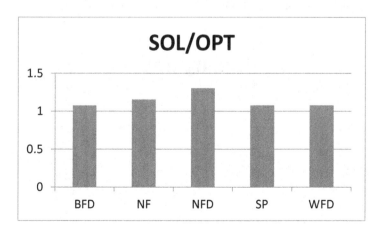

Fig. 6. Competitive Ratio for the U and T datasets

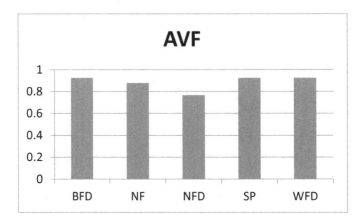

Fig. 7. Average fill-level for the U and T datasets

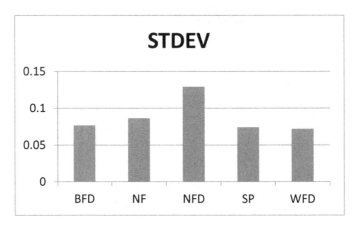

Fig. 8. Standard deviation of the fill-levels for the U and T datasets

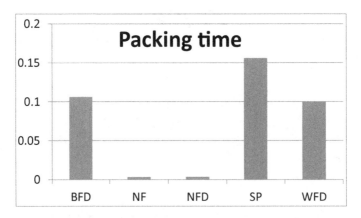

Fig. 9. Packing time for the random datasets

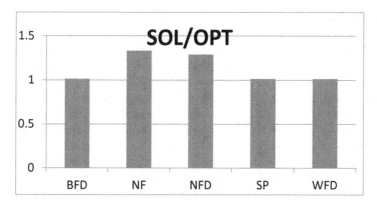

Fig. 10. Competitive Ratio for the random datasets

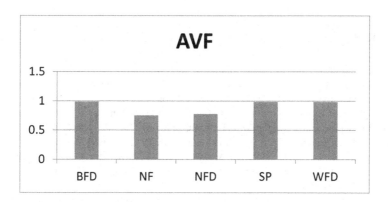

Fig. 11. Average fill-level for the random datasets

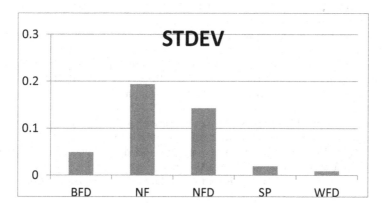

Fig. 12. Standard deviation of the fill-levels for the random datasets

6 Conclusions

Bin Packing has been widely studied due to its industrial applications. In this paper, the concern is focused on not only the number of used bins, but also the packing efficiency and the load balance of used bins. Then by applying the concerns on task scheduling in the cloud computing, a multiple objective bin packing problem is mathematically modeled. Afterwards a novel set-associative bin-packing algorithm is proposed. Therein, a two-way set-associative mapping process is used to combine the elements in divided sets and pack them into a suitable bin. Through experiments, the proposed algorithm perform well with comprehensive consideration of the packing time, the number of used bins and the load balance of used bins.

Acknowledgments. This paper is supported by China Ministry of Education Online Education Research Center Online Education Fund (pervasive education) (No. 2017YB122), the Nature Science Fund of China (NSFC) (No. 61472139).

References

1. Coffman Jr., E.G., Csirik, J., Galambos, G., Martello, S., Vigo, D.: Bin packing approximation algorithms: survey and classification. In: Handbook of Combinatorial Optimization, pp. 455–531. Kluwer Academic Publishers (2013)
2. Dokeroglu, T., Cosar, A.: Optimization of one-dimensional bin packing problem with island parallel grouping genetic algorithms. Comput. Ind. Eng. **75**, 176–186 (2014)
3. Garey, M.R., Johnson, D.S.: Approximation algorithms for bin packing problems: a survey. In: Ausiello, G., Lucertini, M. (eds.) Analysis and Design of Algorithms in Combinatorial Optimization. ICMS, vol. 266, pp. 147–172. Springer, Vienna (1981). https://doi.org/10.1007/978-3-7091-2748-3_8
4. Naderi, B., Yazdani, M.: A real multi-objective bin packing problem: a case study of an engine assembly line. Arab. J. Sci. Eng. **39**(6), 5271–5277 (2014)
5. Boyar, J., Favrholdt, L.M.: The relative worst order ratio for online algorithms. ACM Trans. Algorithms **3**, 1–24 (2007)
6. Boyar, J., Epstein, L., Levin, A.: Tight results for next fit and worst fit with resource augmentation. Theor. Comput. Sci. **411**, 2572–2580 (2010)
7. Martello, S., Toth, P.: Knapsack Problems: Algorithms and Computer Implementations. Wiley, Chichester (1990)
8. Scholl, A., Klein, R., Jurgens, C.: Bison: a fast hybrid procedure for exactly solving the one-dimensional bin packing problem. Comput. Oper. Res. **24**(7), 627–645 (1997)
9. Schwerin, P., Wscher, G.: A new lower bound for the bin-packing problem and its integration into MTP and bison. Pesqui. Op. **19**, 111–129 (1999)
10. de Valerio Carvalho, J.M.: Exact solution of bin-packing problems using column generation and branch-and-bound. Ann. Oper. Res. **86**, 629–659 (1999)
11. Gupta, J.N.D., Ho, J.C.: A new heuristic algorithm for the one-dimensional bin packing problem. Prod. Plann. Control **10**, 598–603 (1999)
12. Fleszar, K., Hindi, K.S.: New heuristics for one-dimensional bin-packing. Comput. Oper. Res. **29**, 821–839 (2002)

13. Masson, R., Vidal, T., Michallet, J., Penna, P.H.V., Petrucci, V., Subramanian, A., et al.: An iterated local search heuristic for multi-capacity bin packing and machine reassignment problems. Expert Syst. Appl. **40**(13), 5266–5275 (2013)
14. Alvim, A.C.F., Ribeiro, C.C.: A Hybrid bin-packing heuristic to multiprocessor scheduling. In: Ribeiro, C.C., Martins, S.L. (eds.) WEA 2004. LNCS, vol. 3059, pp. 1–13. Springer, Heidelberg (2004). https://doi.org/10.1007/978-3-540-24838-5_1
15. Singh, A., Gupta, A.K.: Two heuristics for the one-dimensional bin-packing problem. OR Spectr. **29**(4), 765–781 (2007)
16. Loh, K.H., Golden, B., Wasil, E.: Solving the one-dimensional bin packing problem with a weight annealing heuristic. Comput. Oper. Res. **35**(7), 2283–2291 (2008)
17. Fleszar, K., Charalambous, C.: Average-weight-controlled bin-oriented heuristics for the one-dimensional bin-packing problem. Eur. J. Oper. Res. **210**, 176–184 (2011)
18. Quiroz-Castellanos, M., Cruz-Reyes, L., Torres-Jiménez, J., GomezSantill, C., Huacuja, H.J.F., Alvim, A.C.F.: A grouping genetic algorithm with controlled gene transmission for the bin packing problem. Comput. Oper. Res. **55**, 52–64 (2015)
19. Brando, F., Pedroso, J.P.: Bin Packing and Related Problems: General Arc-flow Formulation with Graph Compression, Technical Report DCC-2013-08, Faculdade de Ciênciasda Universidadedo Porto, Portugal (2013)

A Pair-Wise Method for Aspect-Based Sentiment Analysis

Gangbao Chen$^{(\boxtimes)}$, Qinglin Zhang, and Di Chen

Harbin Institute of Technology Shenzhen Graduate School,
Shenzhen 518055, Guangdong, China
gbchen0823@gmail.com, ieqinglinzhang@gmail.com, chandichn@gmail.com

Abstract. Aspect-based sentiment analysis aims at identifying the sentiment polarity of specific target in its context. Researches mainly focus on the ways for exploring the sentiment polarity based on explicit aspect of different products. The existing approaches have realized the sentiment classification with given targets and developed various methods with the goal of precisely polarity classification. However, there are no given explicit aspects in most practical scenarios. In this paper, we propose a pair-wise method which merges aspect-sentiment pair extraction and polarity classification in an unified framework. We convert the aspect-sentiment pairs detection process into a pairs binary classification problem correspondingly. Meanwhile, we construct a feature system applied to opinion mining. The experimental results on CCF BDCI 2017 aspect-based sentiment analysis shared task dataset show that our proposed pair-wise method obtained good performance with a 0.718 F1 score which outperforms most proposed methods.

Keywords: Aspect-based sentiment analysis (ABSA) · Pair-wise
Ensemble

1 Introduction

Sentiment analysis, also known as opinion mining, is a fundamental task and a popular domain in text mining. Sentiment analysis is crucial to understanding user generated text in social networks or product reviews, and thus it has drawn a lot of attentions from both industry and academic communities. In this paper, we focus on aspect-based sentiment (ABSA) classification without given aspect term or entity, which is a fundamental and extensively studied subtask in the field of sentiment analysis. Given a sentence, this task calls for inferring the aspect-sentiment pairs and polarity of each pair. Aspect-based sentiment analysis method receives a set of review texts as the input, each of which discussing a particular entity (e.g. a new series of a mobile phone). For each given review text, the method attempts first to detect the main aspects(the most frequently discussed) of the entity (e.g. 'battery life', 'screen', 'sound quality', etc.) and then to estimate the sentiment of the text wrt. every detected aspect (e.g. how positive or negative the opinions are for an aspect).

© Springer International Publishing AG, part of Springer Nature 2018
J. Xiao et al. (Eds.): ICCC 2018, LNCS 10971, pp. 18–29, 2018.
https://doi.org/10.1007/978-3-319-94307-7_2

Aspect-based sentiment analysis aims to identify the aspects of entities and the sentiment expressed for each aspect. The ultimate goal is to generate summaries including all the aspects, sentiment expression and their overall polarity. For many exist applications, classifying review texts at the document level or the sentence level is often insufficient for applications because they do not identify opinion targets or assign sentiments to such targets (aspects). Most of the existing approaches on aspect-based sentiment analysis are based on word-level analysis of texts and require predefined aspect as part of input.

In this study, we proposed a pair-wise method for aspect-based sentiment analysis which takes review text as input and outputs a set of triad tuples which contain aspect, sentiment expression and their polarity. Our proposed approach extracts the aspect, sentiment expression as pairs and then determine their polarities. Statistical features, semantic features, similarity features and negation words are utilized in our approach. These features are incorporated in a supervised boost learning based classifier. The experimental results on CCF BDCI 2017 aspect-based sentiment analysis task dataset show that the proposed method outperforms most proposed methods.

The rest of this paper is organized as follows. Section 2 briefly reviews the related works on ABSA, Sect. 3 presents our proposed method and Sect. 4 gives the experimental results with corresponding discussions. Finally, Sect. 5 concludes this paper.

2   Related Works

Aspect based sentiment classification is a fundamental task in the field of sentiment analysis [14]. Given a sentence and an aspect occurring in the sentence, this task aims at inferring the sentiment polarity (e.g. positive, negative, neutral) of the aspect. Many methods concerning the ABSA have been proposed. Some of them are based on supervised learning while others are in unsupervised manner. Hu and Liu [8] proposed the work on aspect detection from on-line reviews which used association rule mining based on Apriori algorithm to extract frequent noun phrases as product features. They used two seed sets of 30 positive and negative adjectives. Meanwhile, Word-Net [6] was employed to expand the seed words with their synonyms. Infrequent aspects had been processed by finding the noun related to an opinionated word. Opinion Digger [17] also used Apriori algorithm to extract the frequent aspects then filtered out the non-aspects text by applying a constraint-learned from the training data - on the extracted aspects. Some unsupervised methods based on LDA (Latent Dirichlet allocation) were proposed. Brody and Elhadad [1] used LDA to find the aspects. The determination of the number of topics is based on a clustering method. They used a similar method proposed by Hatzivassiloglou et al. [7] to extract the conjunctive adjectives but not the disjunctive due to the specificity of the domain. The seed sets were used and weighted. The weighted scores were propagated by using propagation method through the aspect-sentiment graph building from the pairs of aspect and related adjectives.

HASM, which was proposed by Kim et al. [11], discovered a hierarchical structure of aspect-based sentiments from unlabeled online reviews. Normally, the supervised based methods uses CRF (Conditional random fields)' or HMM (Hidden Markov Model) models. Wei et al. [23] applied a lexicalized HMM model to extract aspects by using the words and their part-of-speech tags in order to learn a base model. Then, the unsupervised algorithm used the nearest opinion word to the aspect and took the polarity negation words(such as not) into account. CRF based model was used by Jakob and Gurevych [9] with the features of tokens, POS tags, syntactic dependency (if the aspect has a relation with the opinion word), word distance (the distance between the word in the closest noun phrase and the opinionated word), and opinion sentences (each token in the sentence containing an opinionated expression is labeled by this feature). The input opinionated expressions are utilized to predict the aspect sentiment by using the dependency parsing results for retrieving the pair aspect-expression.

In the recent years, deep learning based model have been applied to the aspect-based sentiment analysis, and they have achieved good performance. Nguyen et al. [18] presented to identify sentiment of an aspect of an entity by employing an extension of RNN (Recursive Neural Network) which takes both dependency and constituent trees of a sentence into account. Dong et al. [5] proposed Adaptive Recursive Neural Network (AdaRNN) for target-dependent Twitter sentiment classification. AdaRNN adaptively propagates the sentiments of words to target depending on the context and syntactic relationships between them. It modeled the adaptive sentiment propagations as distributions over these composition functions. Vo et al. [21] show that competitive results can be achieved without the use of syntax, by extracting a rich set of automatic features. Specially, they split a tweet into a left context and a right context according to the given target. The distributed word representations and neural pooling functions are employed to extract features. Tang et al. [19] proposed to integrate the connections between target word and context words for building a learning system. They develop two target dependent long short-term memory (LSTM) models, where target information is automatically taken into account. Unlike feature-based SVM or sequential neural models such as LSTM, Tang and Liu [20] proposed an approach explicitly captures the importance of each context word for inferring the sentiment polarity of an aspect. Such importance degree and text representation are calculated with multiple computational layers, each of which is a neural attention model over an external memory. Ma et al. [15] argued that both targets and contexts deserve special treatment and need to be learned their own representations via interactive learning. They proposed an interactive attention networks (IAN) to interactively learn attentions in the contexts and targets, and to generate the representations for targets and contexts separately. With this design, the IAN model may represent a target and its collocation pattern, which are helpful to sentiment classification. Wang et al. [22] revealed that the sentiment polarity of a Sentence is not only determined by the content but is also highly related to the respect aspect. They proposed an Attention-based Long Short-Term Memory Network (ATAE-LSTM) for aspect-level sentiment classification. This mechanism concentrated on different parts of a sentence when different aspects are taken as input.

3   Our Method

3.1   Task Analysis

The task of Aspect-based Sentiment Analysis focus on identifying the aspects of a given entity and the sentiment expressed towards each aspect, then determining the polarity of aspect term and sentiment expression pair (aspect-sentiment pair) for the target entity. The CCF BDCI 2017 aspect-based sentiment analysis shared task (in short BDCI 2017 ABSA) dataset consists of customer reviews from E-commerce platform with manually-annotated aspects with sentiment expression and corresponding polarity. A data sample was shown in Fig. 1, in this sample, the aspect-sentiment pairs are "null, Affordable", "delivery speed, fast" and "service, good". It means that for a input review text, the number of aspect terms in a review text is uncertain and the number of words in an aspect term is uncertain too. So it is difficult to detect all of the aspects from a review text precisely through tagging model such as CRF and Bi-LSTM network.

Fig. 1. A data sample (aspect-sentiment pairs are red colored) (Color figure online)

To overcome these difficulties, we divided the whole ABSA task into two sub-tasks:

sub-task-1: Training a model to identify all aspect term and sentiment expression pairs in the input sentence and return a list of distinct identified aspect-sentiment pairs.

sub-task-2: Given a set of aspect term and sentiment expression pairs within a review, determine the polarity of each pair condition to current review is positive, negative or neutral (neither positive nor negative).

For sub-task-1, We convert the aspect-sentiment pair identification problem into a candidate pair classification problem. We construct a set of candidate aspect terms and sentiment expressions after the statistical analysis of the training dataset. This set is established by duplicating all aspect terms and sentiment expressions in training label. As shown in Fig. 2, given a sentence from review text with word segmentation, we pick up all common terms in aspect terms set and sentiment expressions set, separately. The results are list of 'null', 'delivery

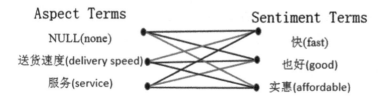

Fig. 2. A data sample (candidate aspect-sentiment pairs constructed from aspects and sentiment expressions) (Color figure online)

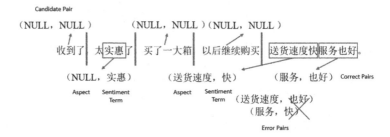

Fig. 3. A training data sample (positive and negative samples are red colored) (Color figure online)

speed', 'service' and list of 'Affordable', 'fast', 'good' for aspect and sentiment, respectively. We combine the terms between all terms from two common terms sets. The candidate pairs consist of $9\,(3*3=9)$ samples, in which 3 samples (sign in red) in them are correct and the rest (sign in black) are wrong. In this way, we train a binary classification model by using those positive(red) and negative(black) pair samples.

3.2 Framework

Our proposed method are based on supervised learning with linguistic knowledge and feature engineering. The main idea is to investigate and develop a method to create a features learning based approach for aspect based sentiment analysis. To extract aspect and sentiment terms pairs, this method incorporates several relevant techniques in opinion mining and sentiment analysis. Meanwhile, some new methods for features extraction are proposed. As a result, this method is expected to archive high precision, recall and F-Measure with a high degree of scalability and stability.

The proposed method consists of three main modules:

- Features Extractor
- Aspect-sentiment pairs identification
- Pairs polarity classification

They are shown in Fig. 4.

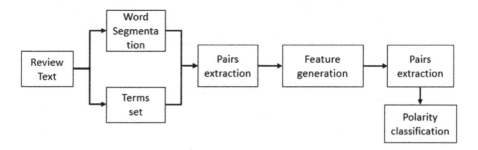

Fig. 4. The framework of our proposed method

Our proposed method concentrates on how to extract the aspect-sentiment pairs from a sentence in order to understand the sentiment expressed in the reviews. Original natural language sentences are the inputs for sentiment analysis, but they always contain malformed and incomplete text because of the less restricted, free format when users generating the content. Thus, we need normalize each input sentence by delete some invalid characters and emoji emoticons which are irrelevant of task.

3.3 Data Preprocessing

To minimize interference and irrelevant information, we applied the sentence compression model proposed by Che et al. [3] to reduce sentence complexity and standardize sentences. We use training data and features provided in [3]. As shown in Fig. 5, in the sample sentence, the upper line is the case before compression, we can extract two pairs ('sense- good' and 'screen-good') by following the extraction rules. After compression process, we can extract only one pair ('screen- good'). In practical, this sentence compression model can improve accuracy of extraction through refine the process of candidate pairs extraction.

With motivation of creating a high-coverage aspect and sentiment terms vocabulary, we expand the base vocabulary, which is built from labeled aspect and sentiment terms in training dataset, to improve the quality and coverage of candidate pairs. Based on CRF [13] tagging model with BIO and TSN tagging schema, we tag aspect terms and sentiment words under the CRF's partial generalization ability to discovery new words (aspect or sentiment expression) and extract candidate pairs features simultaneously. In Fig. 6, we show the labeled tags for one sample sentence with CRF model, several new aspects ('delivery' and 'speed') were discovered from aspect ('delivery speed').

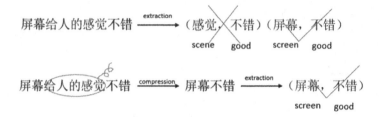

Fig. 5. Comparison with or without Sentence Compression

			BME	TSN
BIO	收到了	送货速度快服务也好	O-Other	O-Other
	O O O	B I I I B B I B I	B-Begin	T-Theme
			I-Inner	S-Sentiment
TSN	收到了	送货速度快服务也好		N-Number
	O O O	$T_1 T_1 T_1 T_1 \, S_1 \, T_2 T_2 \, S_2 S_2$		

Fig. 6. Vocabulary Expansion with CRF

3.4 Feature Extractor

As discussed in Sect. 3.1, we construct the training samples including the sentences from review and the pairs extract from them. In Fig. 3, the training samples from this sentence consist of 3 positive and 6 negative samples. In this way, we obtained 8 times more training samples compared with number of sentences.

Before feature training, converting sentences and pairs into feature vectors is a focal task of supervised learning based sentiment analysis method. The features for aspect-sentiment pair are listed in Table 1, which can be divided into 3 parts. The first part is the features used in common sentence classification, including statistic features (TF, IDF, word length, position, distance), semantic features (sentence vector, word2vec, POS tagging) and similarity features (the similarity based on VSM, LSI, LDA, word2vec [16] between aspect and sentiment terms). We have designed the extraction-related features in the second part (pair number of sentence, sub-string) to distinguish pairs which are similar in construction but different in semantic and generalize semantic features. Lastly, we add the negation words based features (negative words, distance between negation word and sentiment terms) in the third part, which are specially used to correct the mistake caused by negation expression in polarity classification.

Table 1. Features of sentiment sentences

Statistic features	1. TF(w) 2. IDF(w)	TF and IDF of the words
	3. len(w)	Length of aspect and sentiment terms
	4. posi(w) 5. distance(w1, w2)	Position index of aspect and sentiment terms distance = posi(sentiment)-posi(aspect)
Semantic features	6. sent2vec and word2vec	Trained by gensim
	7. POS tagging	POS tag using LTP [2]
Similarity features	8. The similarity based on VSM, LSI, LDA	Cosine distance between sentence and pairs
	9. word2vec between aspect and sentiment terms	Cosine distance
Extraction-related features	10. Number of pairs in sentence	Predict by textCNN [12]
	11. Sub-string	One term is sub-string of another term
Negation words based features	12. Negative words, 13. Distance between negation word and sentiment terms	Words like not, never

3.5   Aspect-Sentiment Pair Identification

The goal of Aspect-sentiment pair identification module is to detect whether the pairs binding with a sentence can match the sentence or not, so, we may regard the sub-task as a binary classification problem.

The output of this module is a binary label namely True or False against a single input binding pair (sentence and aspect-sentiment pair). Here, we apply the XGBoost [4] model with binary logistic kernel to ensure high classification precision. In order to obtain better generalization performance, we use cross-validation and bagging technique to reduce variance of model.

3.6   Polarity Classification

After aspect-sentiment pair identification step, we obtain the result pairs binding with the sentence. To determine sentiment polarity of aspect-sentiment pairs, the fasttext [10] model was used instead of multiple complex classifiers. Under the condition of aspect-sentiment pairs classification precisely, the polarity classification is expected to achieve competitive effect.

4   Experimental Results and Discussion

We use the datasets and the evaluation standards provided by CCF BDCI2017 (http://www.datafountain.cn/projects/2017CCF/) aspect-based sentiment analysis shared-task.

4.1   Experimental Settings

Dataset: The dataset consists of multi-domain product review text from several Chinese e-commerce website. The statistic details of data are listed in Table 2. The training set consists of 20000 reviews. Meanwhile, 3019 aspect terms and 4206 sentiment expressions are extracted from manually annotated answer tuple. The polarity label consists of 1,0 and −1 corresponded to positive, neutral and negative. After the steps of pairs constructing, the number of candidate pairs are 577819 and 494265 in train and test set, respectively. From training data labels, we extract 53374 pairs with manual annotation as positive samples.

Table 2. Statistic of Dataset

dataset	review	pairs	ans_pair	aspect terms	sentiment terms
train	20000	577819	53374	3019	4206
test	20000	494265	-	-	-

Normally, the performance of ABSA are estimated by accuracy. In this paper, consider the imbalance between positive and negative samples, we use the F-score metrics of prediction labels to estimate the performance of the aspect-based sentiment analysis. The evaluation functions are defined as below.

$$P = \frac{tp}{tp + fp + fn_2} \tag{1}$$

$$R = \frac{tp}{tp + fp + fn_1} \tag{2}$$

$$F = 2 * \frac{P * R}{P + R} \tag{3}$$

In the above equation above, tp is the number of correctly identified aspect-sentiment pairs, fp is the number of wrongly identified aspect-sentiment pairs, $fn1$ is the number of missing match and $fn2$ is the number of aspect-sentiment pairs more than truth label.

4.2 Experimental Results on Aspect Identification and Polarity Classification

In this section, we list the experimental results of the pair-wise method for ABSA with different model in Table 3, to illustrate the performance of our proposed method. Meanwhile, we compare the proposed method with some top submitted systems in BDCI2017 ABSA sub-task. They are named as Gripen, MOMO, and Out Of Memory teams. All of those teams are developed and evalauted using the same dataset and metrics.

In Table 3, F1-A represents F-score in A stage, which didn't take polarity classification into account, so the result used to compute F-score are aspect-sentiment pairs only. F1-B represents F-score in B stage, the result used to compute F-score are aspect-sentiment pairs and corresponding polarity. Compared to F1-A, F1-B is a more strict metric.

Table 3. Results of our proposed model against top submitted systems

Baselines	F1-A	F1-B
Gripen	0.7090	0.7210
Ours	0.7050	0.7180
MOMO	0.6877	0.7168
Out Of Memory	0.6750	0.7159

From Table 3, it is observed that our method performs consistently and obviously better than MOMO and Out Of Memory teams. Meanwhile, the performance of our method is just a little lower than Gripen which using many threshold generated from lots of data analysis manually. Noted here that Gripen system has lower scalability compared to our method.

4.3 Experimental Results on Polarity Classification

To discover the contribution of each features set (i.e., Basic Features (BF), Extraction-related Features (ER), Negatiion-words based Features (NWF)) to the final classification performance, we conduct an experiment by add features set one by one at a time in our method. Specifically, Basic Features including statistic features, semantic features and similarity features, which are widely used in other models.

From Table 4, it is shown that ER features set has the major impact to the final performance. In order to further improve accuracy and robustness, we also compute an ensemble model by averaging 7 models that trained independently on different features and parameters according to the bagging algorithm. It is shown that the bagging based ensemble algorithm may further improve the classification performance.

Table 4. An study on the contribution of features

Model	F1-B
BF	0.667
BF + ER	0.705
BF + ER + NWF	0.710
BF + ER + NWF(ensemble)	0.718

5   Conclusion

In this paper, we proposed a new pair-wise based method using the ideas of task decomposition. By incorporating sentence features and aspect-sentiment pair features, our proposed method obtains good performance on CCF BDCI2017 ABSA shared-task dataset. With high scalability, our proposed method may be applied to aspect-level sentiment analysis without prepared aspect terms.

Acknowledgements. This work was supported by the National Natural Science Foundation of China U1636103, 61632011, Key Technologies Research and Development Program of Shenzhen JSGG20170817140856618, Shenzhen Foundational Research Funding 20170307150024907.

References

1. Brody, S., Elhadad, N.: An unsupervised aspect-sentiment model for online reviews. In: Human Language Technologies: Conference of the North American Chapter of the Association of Computational Linguistics, Proceedings, 2–4 June 2010, Los Angeles, California, USA, pp. 804–812 (2010)
2. Che, W., Li, Z., Liu, T.: LTP: A Chinese language technology platform. J. Chin. Inf. Process. **2**(6), 13–16 (2010)
3. Che, W., Zhao, Y., Guo, H., Su, Z., Liu, T.: Sentence compression for aspect-based sentiment analysis. IEEE/ACM Trans. Audio Speech Lang. Process. **23**(12), 2111–2124 (2015). https://doi.org/10.1109/TASLP.2015.2443982
4. Chen, T., Guestrin, C.: XGBoost: A Scalable Tree Boosting System, pp. 785–794 (2016)
5. Dong, L., Wei, F., Tan, C., Tang, D., Zhou, M., Xu, K.: Adaptive recursive neural network for target-dependent twitter sentiment classification. In: Meeting of the Association for Computational Linguistics, pp. 49–54 (2014)
6. Fellbaum, C., Miller, G.: WordNet: An Electronic Lexical Database. MIT Press, Cambridge (1998)
7. Hatzivassiloglou, V., Mckeown, K.R.: Predicting the semantic orientation of adjectives. In: Proceedings of the ACL, pp. 174–181 (1997)
8. Hu, M., Liu, B.: Mining and summarizing customer reviews. In: Tenth ACM SIGKDD International Conference on Knowledge Discovery and Data Mining, Seattle, Washington, USA, August, pp. 168–177 (2004)
9. Jakob, N., Gurevych, I.: Using anaphora resolution to improve opinion target identification in movie reviews. In: Meeting of the Association for Computational Linguistics (2010)

10. Joulin, A., Grave, E., Bojanowski, P., Mikolov, T.: Bag of Tricks for Efficient Text Classification, pp. 427–431 (2016)
11. Kim, S., Zhang, J., Chen, Z., Oh, A., Liu, S.: A hierarchical aspect-sentiment model for online reviews. In: Twenty-Seventh AAAI Conference on Artificial Intelligence, pp. 526–533 (2013)
12. Kim, Y.: Convolutional Neural Networks for Sentence Classification. Eprint Arxiv (2014)
13. Lafferty, J.D., Mccallum, A., Pereira, F.C.N.: Conditional random fields: probabilistic models for segmenting and labeling sequence data. In: Eighteenth International Conference on Machine Learning, pp. 282–289 (2001)
14. Liu, B.: Sentiment Analysis and Opinion Mining. Morgan Publishers, San Rafael (2012)
15. Ma, D., Li, S., Zhang, X., Wang, H., Ma, D., Li, S., Zhang, X., Wang, H.: Interactive attention networks for aspect-level sentiment classification. In: Twenty-Sixth International Joint Conference on Artificial Intelligence, pp. 4068–4074 (2017)
16. Mikolov, T., Chen, K., Corrado, G., Dean, J.: Efficient estimation of word representations in vector space. Computer Science (2013)
17. Moghaddam, S., Ester, M.: Opinion Digger: An Unsupervised Opinion Miner from Unstructured Product Reviews, pp. 1825–1828 (2010)
18. Nguyen, T.H., Shirai, K.: PhraseRNN: phrase recursive neural network for aspect-based sentiment analysis. In: Conference on Empirical Methods in Natural Language Processing, pp. 2509–2514 (2015)
19. Tang, D., Qin, B., Feng, X., Liu, T.: Target-dependent sentiment classification with long short term memory. Computer Science (2015)
20. Tang, D., Qin, B., Liu, T.: Aspect Level Sentiment Classification with Deep Memory Network, pp. 214–224 (2016)
21. Vo, D.T., Zhang, Y.: Target-dependent twitter sentiment classification with rich automatic features. In: International Conference on Artificial Intelligence, pp. 1347–1353 (2015)
22. Wang, Y., Huang, M., Zhu, X., Zhao, L.: Attention-based LSTM for aspect-level sentiment classification. In: Conference on Empirical Methods in Natural Language Processing, pp. 606–615 (2017)
23. Wei, J., Ho, H.H.: A novel lexicalized hmm-based learning framework for web opinion mining. In: International Conference on Machine Learning, pp. 465–472 (2009). note from acm: A joint acm conference committee has determined that the authors of this article violated acm's publication policy on simultaneous submissions. therefore acm has shut of

Forum User Profiling by Incorporating User Behavior and Social Network Connections

Di Chen[✉], Qinglin Zhang, Gangbao Chen, Chuang Fan, and Qinghong Gao

Harbin Institute of Technology Shenzhen Graduate School, Shenzhen 518055, China
chandichn@gmail.com, ieqinglinzhang@gmail.com, gbchen0823@gmail.com,
fanchuanghit@gmail.com, gaoqinghong1994@gmail.com

Abstract. With the rapid development of social media in recent years, user profile inferring becomes crucial to many practical application such as recommendation and customized service. In this paper, we propose an ensemble learning based model, which incorporates user behavior embedding and social network connection embedding, for user profile inference. In which, post content features and user behavior statistics are employed to learn the user behavior embedding. LINE and PUHE are incorporated to learn the user social network connection embedding. The proposed method is evaluated on SMP CUP 2017 user profiling competition dataset. The experiment results demonstrate that leveraging both user behavior embedding and social network connection embedding improves the user profiling efficiently.

Keywords: User profiling · User behavior · Social network
Ensemble learning

1 Introduction

User Profiling in social network are critical for many practical task such as accurate recommendation and customized service. Especially, online forum provides a platform for many users to share their ideas by posting rich contents and to build a social network through interaction. With abundant user-generated data, including historical record of user behaviors and content, automatically inferring user profile has attracted much interest in recent years.

Generally speaking, user profile inference is a challenging task. Firstly, the user-generated data is complex. Besides the posted blogs with diverse topics, users may participate in browsing, upvoting and downvoting blogs, whose records comprise implicit information about users' interest. How to construct features from these information is important for user modeling. Secondly, with the follower-followee mechanism, the social network among users contains crucial attributes of users. Different users should have different representation according to their status. How to conduct user representation based on the network structure is another difficulty.

J. Xiao et al. (Eds.): ICCC 2018, LNCS 10971, pp. 30–42, 2018.
https://doi.org/10.1007/978-3-319-94307-7_3

To address these challenges, in this paper, we propose an ensemble learning based model for inferring forum user profile. Specifically, we leverage information related to user behavior and social network connections. The user behavior features track user by integrating temporal behavior and aggregated statistics. As for the user social network features, LINE (Large-scale Information Network Embedding) and PUHE (Post-User Heterogeneous Embedding) are used for user embedding learning to obtain low-dimension continuous representation. Evaluation on the SMP CUP 2017 dataset implies our model is efficient for user profiling.

2 Related Work

User Profiling has been brought into focus with the development of social media. Much work has been reported for inferring various attributes of a user, and they have primarily paid attention to the construction of sophisticated featured-based classifiers. Tang et al. [18] proposed a three-step scheme including finding, extracting, integrating the user profiles, and built a probabilistic topic model to model the extracted user profiles to capture users interests. Rosenthal et al. [14] constructed a model for age prediction in blogs which combines the style, content and online behavior features in pre- and post-social media. Rao et al. [13] developed a hierarchical Bayesian model for predicting the ethnicity and gender of Facebook users from Nigeria by using letter n-grams from user names and word n-grams from user content as features. Tu et al. [20] analyzed users' tweets and extracted emoticons features, Web abbreviation features, word unigrams and bigrams features for Support Vector Machines (SVM) classifier to predict the profession of Twitter users.

User behaviors as the foundation of user dynamic profiling, have been analyzed and discussed for many years. Sin [15] developed a PIE (Person-in-Environment) framework to model individuals behavior, which takes the impacts of socio-structural and individual factors into consideration. Gomes et al. [6] analyzed the social interactions in group of Facebook users by leveraging a human-readable technique to identify the most symmetric social interactions. Lee et al. [8] presented a model based on the goal-directed and experiential behaviors, in order to better understand users search behaviors on Internet. Radinsky et al. [12] constructed a temporal model based on users Web search activities with current and past behavioral data, for enhancing the performance of Web search and information retrieval. Achananuparp et al. [1] proposed a framework to model the behaviors for information propagation based on Twitter users retweeting activities.

Besides user-generated data (behavior and content), fusing the content of social network in which users stay is equally critical for user profile inference. Fire et al. [5] constructed a set of features to build a machine learning classifier to identify the missing links between individuals, by using the datasets from DBLP, Facebook and so on. Perozzi et al. [11] proposed a DeepWalk model that used local information obtained from truncated random walks to learn latent representations by treating walks as an equivalent of sentences. Tang et al. [17] proposed a node embedding model named Large-scale Information Network Embedding (LINE), in which edge-sampling algorithm was used to address the limitation of the classical stochastic gradient descent for improving both the effectiveness and the efficiency of the inference. Sun et al. [16] proposed a content-enhanced network embedding (CENE) method, which is capable of jointly leveraging the social network structure and the content in an unsupervised way.

3   Our Approach

3.1   The Framework

Generally speaking, in this paper, we employed **Two** main categories of features for user profiling. The first one is user behavior embedding. Here, the contribution of user behavior is represented by a set of **Behavior Features**, concentrating on user-generated data, which consists of Post Content Statistics, Post Content Semantics and User Behavior Statistics. These features are the foundation of user representation. Besides that, to capture the users' context of social network, we construct a set of **Social Network Connection Features**, proposing similar users should have similar network representation. Contrary to the statistic feature, user node in social network is embedded into low-dimensional continuous vector space. Figure 1 shows the framework of our proposed user profiling approach.

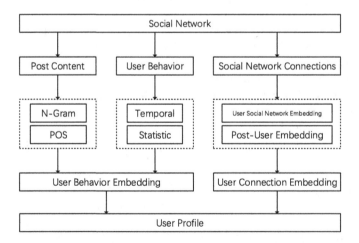

Fig. 1. The framework of our proposed user profiling approach

3.2   User Behavior Embeddings

Post Content Statistics. To predict user profile, firstly, we consider the statistics of post content. There are two kinds of user-generated content, namely blog and message. Considering different users have various contents, intuitively, statistics like the *max length*, *min length* and *mean length* of these content can be the corresponding representation. Besides, the content from users' followers and users' followees is another important aspect.

User Content Semantics. User-generated content provides abundant information of users' interests. Here, lexical features are generated for users' content. We utilize Unigram, Bigram and Trigram features and Part of Speech (POS) tag features [19] in the blog. In this study, LTP[1] is used for Chinese word segmentation. In addition, we also generate small lists of users' interests terms, resulting in a binary feature which indicates that whether users' posts have one of the terms from the list.

User Behavior Statistics. Online Forum is a platform for many users to share their ideas, thus user historical behavior records such as browsing, upvoting and downvoting are the foundation of user profiling. Specifically, we derive each user's behavior from his last 12 months records, including #posting blogs, #browsing blogs, #posting comments, #upvoting blogs, #downvoting blogs, #favorite blogs, and #message. To capture the tendency of activity in each month, all of these records are converted into sparse representation as shown in Fig. 2. Furthermore, we take the statistics of records into account as well, consisting of *maximum*, *minimum*, *sum* and *mean*.

Fig. 2. Sparse representation of behaviors.

3.3   Social Network Connection Embeddings

User Network Statistics. In Online Forum, each user may follow other users to establish social connection, and vice versa. The resulting graph, or social network connections, regards each user as a node and following connection as an edge between two nodes. We define the network as $G = (U, E)$, where U is the set of nodes representing users and E is the set of edges, where for any $e \in E$ is an ordered pair $e = (u_i, u_j)$ representing user u_i is followed by u_j. Then, basic

---

[1] https://pyltp.readthedocs.io/zh_CN/latest/.

social network connection features of user are generated from the attributes of corresponding node, which denote users' influence in network. The main features [2,9] are listed and described as below.

- **Degree.** The degree of a node is defined as the number of its neighboring edges. Considering a directed network, the degree of a node $d(u)$ comprise indegree $d^-(u)$ and outdegree $d^+(u)$, indicating that #user's followers and #user's followees respectively, such that:

$$d(u) = d^-(u) + d^+(u) \tag{1}$$

- **Clustering Coefficient.** For a node u, the clustering coefficient $c(u)$ represents the likelihood that any two neighbors of u are connected. More formally, the clustering coefficient of a node u is defined as:

$$c(u) = \frac{\lambda(u)}{\tau(u)} \tag{2}$$

$$\tau(u) = \frac{d(u)^2 - d(u)}{2} \tag{3}$$

where $\lambda(u)$ is #triangles (complete graph with three nodes) of a node u and $\tau(u)$ denotes #triples a node u has. Alternatively, the clustering coefficient for node u can be defined as the ratio of #actual edges between the neighbors of u to #possible edges between them (Fig. 3).

- **Effective Eccentricity.** The eccentricity of a node u is defined as:

$$e(u) = \max\{dis(u,v), u, v \in U\} \tag{4}$$

where the distance $dis(u,v)$ is the length of the shortest path from u to v. For effective eccentricity we take the maximum length of the SP from u, so that u can reach at least 90% of nodes in the graph. When taking noise into account, effectiveness is a more robust measure.

- **Closeness Centrality.** The closeness centrality of a node u is defined as the reciprocal of the averaged total path length between node u and every other that is reachable from node u, i.e.

$$closeness(u) = \frac{|U| - 1}{\sum_{v \in U, v \neq u} d(u,v)} \tag{5}$$

- **Ego-Network Based Embedding.** The ego-network of a node u centers on u and extends with u's one-hop and two-hop away neighbors. To generate a more specific context for u, we compute *average degree of neighbors, average clustering coefficient of neighbors, #edges in ego-network, #outgoing edges of ego-network* and *#neighbors of ego-network* (Fig. 4).

User Social Network Representation. For mining useful information from social network, network embedding, which aims at learning low-dimension continuous vector representation of users in networks, has been propose as a critical

Fig. 3. A triangle with its three triples.

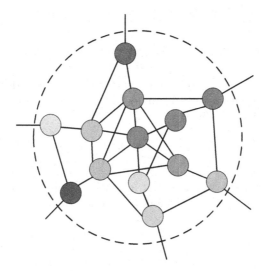

Fig. 4. Ego-network.

technique for network analysis. Given a network, we need to find an arbitrary mapping function $f : u_i \rightarrow \boldsymbol{u_i} \in \mathbb{R}^d$, where $\boldsymbol{u_i}$ is the vector representation of node u_i. The mapping function need to preserves some proximity measure on original network and reduce the dimensionality of nodes' representation $d \ll |U|$.

Here, we apply two node embedding methods. The first one uses Large-scale Information Network Embedding (LINE) [17] to approximate the first- and second- order proximities of the following network. The second one uses Post-User Heterogeneous Embedding (PUHE) which incorporates the linguistic information of post to improve the learning of node embedding.

– **Large-scale Information Network Embedding**. It preserves both the first-order and second-order proximities between users to learn the representation of nodes in network. The first-order proximity refers to the local pair-wise proximity between the nodes in the network. To model the first-order proximity, for each edge (u_i, u_j), the joint probability $p_1(u_i, u_j)$ between u_i and u_j and its objective function O_1 are defined as follows:

$$p_1(u_i, u_j) = \frac{1}{1 + \exp(-\boldsymbol{u}_i^T \cdot \boldsymbol{u}_j)} \tag{6}$$

$$O_1 = - \sum_{(u_i, u_j) \in E} \log p_1(u_i, u_j) \tag{7}$$

The second-order proximity assumes that nodes which share similar neighbors have similar representation. It specifies the following objective function for each edge (u_i, u_j). The probability of context u_j generated by u_i is defined by:

$$p_1(u_j \mid u_i) = \frac{\exp(-\boldsymbol{u}_j^T \cdot \boldsymbol{u}_i)}{\sum_{k=1}^{|V_c|} \exp(-\boldsymbol{u}_k^T \cdot \boldsymbol{u}_i)} \tag{8}$$

where $|V_c|$ is #nodes in context. To preserve the second-order proximity, the conditional probability $p_2(\cdot \mid u_i)$ should be close to the empirical distribution. The object function is defined as:

$$O_2 = - \sum_{(u_i, u_j) \in E} \log p_2(u_j \mid u_i) \tag{9}$$

To avoid computation of summation over the whole set of nodes, negative sampling is used to optimize the following objective:

$$\log \sigma(\boldsymbol{u}_j'^T \cdot \boldsymbol{u}_i) + - \sum_{i=1}^{K} E_{v_n \sim P_n(v)} \left[\log \sigma(-\boldsymbol{u}_n'^T \cdot \boldsymbol{u}_i) \right] \tag{10}$$

where $\sigma(x) = \frac{1}{1+\exp(-x)}$ is the sigmoid function. The first term models the observed edges. The second term models the negative edges drawn from the noise distribution. K is #negative edges and $P_n(V) \propto d^+(u)^{\frac{3}{4}}$. To preserve both first- and second-order proximities, we train both O_1 and O_2 to attain $\boldsymbol{u}_i^{1st}$ and $\boldsymbol{u}_i^{2nd}$ and then concatenate these embeddings by:

$$\boldsymbol{u}_i = \boldsymbol{u}_i^{1st} \oplus \boldsymbol{u}_i^{2nd} \tag{11}$$

– **Post-User Heterogeneous Embedding.** Inspired by [7], we construct a post-user heterogeneous network which treats the similar word preferences between the users as links. Denote vocabulary used in all posts as $V = \{v_1, v_2, \cdots, v_m\}$ and the set of users is $U = \{u_1, u_2, \cdots, u_m\}$. We create a link from user u_i to word v_j if v_j appears in the post of u_i. The weight of link is computed by the ratio of occurrence of specific word appearing in users' posts. For example, #v_j appearing in u_i's posts is denoted as n_i^j, if $n_i^j \geq 1$, the weight w_i^j of link between u_i and v_j is:

$$w_i^j = \frac{n_i^j}{\sum_{k=1}^{m} n_i^k} \tag{12}$$

where m is the size of vocabulary. We get user embedding by optimizing an objective for modeling the probability of adjacent nodes in post-user hetero-geneous network. Similarly, for each edge (u_i, v_j), the conditional probability of v_j generated by u_i is:

$$p(v_j \mid u_i) = \frac{\exp(\boldsymbol{v}_j^T \cdot \boldsymbol{u}_i)}{\sum_{k=1}^m \exp(-\boldsymbol{v}_k^T \cdot \boldsymbol{u}_i)} \tag{13}$$

Therefore, the corresponding objective function is:

$$O = - \sum_{(u_i, v_j) \in E} w_i^j \log p(v_j \mid u_i) \tag{14}$$

Since optimizing the objective above directly is computation expensive, we leverage negative sampling which is used to train word embedding [10]. Specif-ically, we sample N negative edges according to each edge (u_i, v_j) and convert this problem to binary classification (Fig. 5).

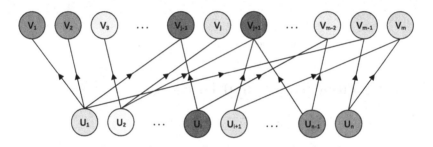

Fig. 5. Post-user heterogeneous network.

3.4   Ensemble Learning

Ensemble learning plays an important role in the research field of data min-ing and machine learning, whose basic idea is to construct a strong learner by combining a set of weak learners. Also, ensemble methods are well known for overcoming over fitting problems and enhancing generalization performance. An overview of various ensemble methods can be found in [4].

It is usually time consuming to find an optimal way to ensemble. Since we formulate our task as a regression problem. In this study, we use a simple but turns out to be efficient way: we split the training data into 10 folds, 9 of them are utilized for training XGBoost [3] model while left one for avoiding over-fitting. As show in Fig. 6, after 10 rounds, we obtain 10 different models and final prediction on testing data is the average prediction outputs of 10 models.

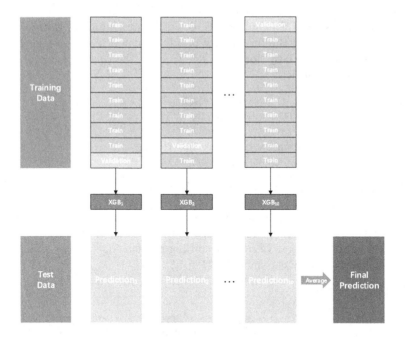

Fig. 6. Ensemble learning framework.

4   Experimental Results and Discussion

4.1   Datasets and Metrics

The dataset used in this paper is released by SMP CUP 2017 User Profiling Competition[2]. The dataset is collected from Chinese Software Developer Network[3] (CSDN). CSDN is the largest service platform for software developer in China as well as the largest Chinese IT Forum all over the world, consisting of more than 50 million users, where hundreds of thousands of users communicate, consult and share with others every day.

The statistics of the dataset is listed in Table 1. It is worthy to notice that the dataset with few labeled data make the prediction of growth value much more challenging. Also, as shown in Fig. 7, the distribution of users' interests is quite sparse, which motivates to extract features in multi-dimension for better user representation.

According to official rules, the evaluation metrics for the prediction is defined as below, and larger Relative Error indicates better performance:

$$\text{Relative Error} = 1 - \frac{1}{N}\sum_{i=1}^{N} \begin{cases} 0 & v_i = v_i^* = 0 \\ \frac{|v_i - v_i^*|}{\max\{v_i, v_i^*\}} & \text{otherwise} \end{cases} \tag{15}$$

---

[2] https://www.biendata.com/competition/smpcup2017/.
[3] https://www.csdn.net.

Table 1. Detail of datasets

Data type	Data content	Amount
User content	Blog documents	1,000,000
User behavior	Post records	1,000,000
	Browse records	3,536,444
	Comment records	182,273
	Upvote records	95,668
	Downvote records	9,326
	Favorite records	104,723
Social networks	Following relations	667,037
	Message records	46,572
Labeled data	Blogs with topic words	3,000
	Users with interests	3,000
	Users with growth value	3,000

where N is #test samples, v_i is the prediction of growth value for user i, whose corresponding ground truth of growth value is v_i^*.

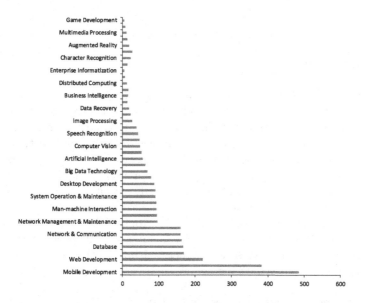

Fig. 7. The distribution of users' interests.

4.2   Experiment Results

Table 2 lists the results of proposed user profiling model. In this table, larger value of relation error indicates better performance. To discover the contribution of different features, we further conduct our experiments by adding one kind of feature at a time. The baseline contains Behavior Features only. It is observed that, the network embeddings of users impacts significantly on the performance of our user profiling. With the help of ensemble learning, our approach has a further improvement. The proposed approach achieved the second place among nearly 900 participant systems in the SMP 2017 User Profiling Competition which shows the effectiveness of our proposed approach.

Table 2. Detail of datasets

Model	Relative error (%)
Baseline	72.82
Baseline + network statistics	73.16
Baseline + network statistics + LINE	74.42
Full architecture (single)	74.93
Full architecture (ensemble)	75.22

5   Conclusion

In this paper, we present an ensemble learning based approach for inferring forum user profile. Our framework jointly models two main categories of features for user profiling, namely User Behavior Features and Social Network Connection Features. The former one is employed to track user according to their historical record with sparse representation. By integrating temporal behavior and aggregated statistics, we find it a better way for user modeling. As for Social Network Connections Features, LINE and PUHE algorithm are incorporated to learn the user relationship in forum, which describes users' context more sufficiently. Experimental results show that the proposed approach achieves good performance on SMP 2017 User Profiling Competition dataset. In the future, we will investigate more diverse user-generated information and embrace deep learning methods for user profiling.

Acknowledgements. This work was supported by the National Natural Science Foundation of China U1636103, 61632011, Key Technologies Research and Development Program of Shenzhen JSGG20170817140856618, Shenzhen Foundational Research Funding 20170307150024907.

References

1. Achananuparp, P., Lim, E.P., Jiang, J., Hoang, T.A.: Who is retweeting the tweeters? Modeling, originating, and promoting behaviors in the twitter network. ACM Trans. Manag. Inf. Syst. **3**(3), 1–30 (2012)
2. Berlingerio, M., Koutra, D., Eliassi-Rad, T., Faloutsos, C.: Netsimile: a scalable approach to size-independent network similarity. Comput. Sci. **12**(1), 28(1–28) (2012)
3. Chen, T., Guestrin, C.: XGBoost: a scalable tree boosting system. In: ACM SIGKDD International Conference on Knowledge Discovery and Data Mining, pp. 785–794 (2016)
4. Dieterich, T.G.: Ensemble methods in machine learning. In: Kittler, J., Roli, F. (eds.) MCS 2000. LNCS, vol. 1857, pp. 1–15. Springer, Heidelberg (2000). https://doi.org/10.1007/3-540-45014-9_1
5. Fire, M., Tenenboim-Chekina, L., Puzis, R., Lesser, O., Rokach, L., Elovici, Y.: Computationally efficient link prediction in a variety of social networks. ACM Trans. Intell. Syst. Technol. **5**(1), 10 (2013)
6. Gomes, A.K.: Measuring media-based social interactions provided by smartphone applications in social networks. In: ACM Workshop on Social and Behavioural Networked Media Access, pp. 59–64 (2011)
7. Gui, L., Xu, R., He, Y., Lu, Q., Wei, Z.: Intersubjectivity and sentiment: from language to knowledge. In: International Joint Conference on Artificial Intelligence, pp. 2789–2795 (2016)
8. Lee, J., You, M.: Research on website usage behavior through information search perspective: a comparison of experiential and goal-directed behaviors. In: Yamamoto, S. (ed.) HIMI 2013. LNCS, vol. 8016, pp. 456–464. Springer, Heidelberg (2013). https://doi.org/10.1007/978-3-642-39209-2_52
9. Li, G., Semerci, M., Zaki, M.J.: Effective graph classification based on topological and label attributes. Stat. Anal. Data Min. **5**(4), 265–283 (2012)
10. Mikolov, T., Sutskever, I., Chen, K., Corrado, G., Dean, J.: Distributed representations of words and phrases and their compositionality, vol. 26, pp. 3111–3119 (2013)
11. Perozzi, B., Alrfou, R., Skiena, S.: Deepwalk: online learning of social representations, pp. 701–710 (2014)
12. Radinsky, K., Svore, K.M., Dumais, S.T., Shokouhi, M., Teevan, J., Bocharov, A., Horvitz, E.: Behavioral dynamics on the web:learning, modeling, and prediction. ACM Trans. Inf. Syst. **31**(3), 1–37 (2013)
13. Rao, D., Paul, M., Fink, C., Yarowsky, D., Oates, T., Coppersmith, G.: Hierarchical bayesian models for latent attribute detection in social media. In: International Conference on Weblogs and Social Media, Barcelona, Catalonia, Spain, July (2011)
14. Rosenthal, S., Mckeown, K.: Age prediction in blogs: a study of style, content, and online behavior in pre- and post-social media generations. In: Proceedings of the Conference on The Meeting of the Association for Computational Linguistics: Human Language Technologies, Portland, Oregon, USA, 19–24 June, 2011, pp. 763–772 (2011)
15. Sin, S.C.J.: Modeling individual-level information behavior: a person-in-environment (PIE) framework. Proc. Am. Soc. Inf. Sci. Technol. **47**(1), 14 (2010)
16. Sun, X., Guo, J., Ding, X., Liu, T.: A general framework for content-enhanced network representation learning (2016)

17. Tang, J., Qu, M., Wang, M., Zhang, M., Yan, J., Mei, Q.: Line: large-scale information network embedding, vol. 2, no. 2, pp. 1067–1077 (2015)
18. Tang, J., Yao, L., Zhang, D., Zhang, J.: A combination approach to web user profiling. ACM Trans. Knowl. Disc. Data 5(1), 2 (2010)
19. Toutanova, K., Klein, D., Manning, C.D., Singer, Y.: Feature-rich part-of-speech tagging with a cyclic dependency network, pp. 173–180 (2003)
20. Tu, C., Liu, Z., Luan, H., Sun, M.: PRISM: profession identification in social media. ACM Trans. Intell. Syst. Technol. 8(6), 81 (2017)

Adversarial Training for Sarcasm Detection

Qinglin Zhang$^{(\boxtimes)}$, Gangbao Chen, and Di Chen

Harbin Institute of Technology Shenzhen Graduate School, Shenzhen 518055, China
ieqinglinzhang@gmail.com, gbchen0823@gmail.com, chandichn@gmail.com

Abstract. Adversarial training has shown expressive performance in image classification task. However, there are few applications in natural language processing domain. In this paper, we propose to apply adversarial training strategy to sarcasm detection with small labeled samples. Several different neural network architectures are adopted including Convolutional Neural Networks (CNN) and Hierarchical Recurrent Neural Networks (HRNN). The experimental results on three datasets show that adversarial training is effective to improve the performance on sarcasm detection.

Keywords: Adversarial training · Sarcasm detection
Neural networks

1 Introduction

Deep neural networks have achieved state-of-the-art performance in many tasks, but normally the training of neural networks requires a large amount of labeled data. Lacking of labeled data may lead to over fitting of the model. In the past years, various data augmentation techniques were proposed [8] to generate more synthetic samples, while various training techniques such as batch normalization [10], dropout [26] were proposed to reduce the influence of this problem. Adversarial examples [27] are examples generated by adding noise in the form of small perturbations to the original data. The generated samples can be correctly predicted by humans without any extra difficulty, but can fool a trained neural network to output a wrong label prediction with high confidence [7]. Goodfellow made the distinction between adversarial learning and common data augmentation techniques such as transformations: adversarial examples are not naturally occurring examples that need to realistically happen in the world.

Adversarial Training [18] is a technique for regularizing deep neural network models by training the model to correctly classify both raw examples and perturbed ones. In practice, adversarial training not only enhances the robustness of the neural network but also improves the generalization performance. Previous work has largely used adversarial training to classification tasks, including image classification [7] and text classification [18]. But the goals of these tasks are not sensitive to perturbation and in most cases enough labeled examples are

© Springer International Publishing AG, part of Springer Nature 2018
J. Xiao et al. (Eds.): ICCC 2018, LNCS 10971, pp. 43–54, 2018.
https://doi.org/10.1007/978-3-319-94307-7_4

provided. It remains uncertainty whether adversarial training is effective to the tasks sensitive to semantic perturbation with less labeled examples, e.g., sarcasm detection [6], or a different evaluation metric other than prediction accuracy (e.g. F1 score).

This paper focuses on the task of sarcasm detection, which is regarded as a document classification task. One popular way to this task is to use discrete features to represent the input text, which takes a lot of time and effort to design and create features manually. There are also some work investigating the use of neural network for sarcasm detection [29]. However, those neural network models are limited in performance due to the lack of labeled training samples. In this study, we propose to apply the adversarial training framework to sarcasm detection in order to improve the performance of neural network models. Three different neural network architectures are adopted including Convolutional Neural Networks (CNN), recurrent neural network (RNN) and Hierarchical Recurrent Neural Networks (HRNN). The experimental results on three different satiric corpus show that our proposed adversarial training framework achieves better performance compared to traditional training strategy on sarcasm detection task. The achieved the F-value performance on these three corpus outperforms the state-of-the-art methods.

2   Related Work

2.1   Adversarial Training

Adversarial training is a training strategy, which use both raw examples and adversarial examples to train a model [7] in order to improve the generalization performance. Adversarial examples are small perturbation to an example that is negligible to humans but can fool a computer system to make an incorrect prediction. Adversarial training was firstly applied to computer vision research [27] and later to natural language processing domain as well [11].

Goodfellow et al. proposed a simple and fast method for generating adversarial examples [7]. By using this method to provide examples for adversarial training, the trained model reduced the test set error of the MNIST dataset. Samanta and Mehta [25] proposed a method to generate adversarial samples in the domain of text processing by preserving the semantic meaning of the sentences as much as possible. Fast Gradient Sign Method (FGSM) is the most popular method of generating adversarial samples from existing ones. It generate the adversarial noise by considering the gradient of the cost function of the classifier with respect to the raw input training samples. FGSM is shown fast and effective in some applications.

There are also some other ways of producing adversarial examples. Jin et al. [12] generated adversarial examples with respect to random Gaussian noise, which are used to train a forward convolutional neural network. They demonstrated that the adversarial examples generated with FGSM mainly concentrates in the decision boundary, thus the model is more vulnerable to be attacked. Miyato et al. [19] proposed the concept of local distributional smoothness and virtual adversarial training. They proved that adversarial training is equal to a regularization term in the objective function. Meanwhile, the complex pattern in data may be found with the help of adversarial training. Their model achieved the best performance on three standard image datasets.

2.2 Sarcasm Detection

In the past decades, sarcasm detection attracted more interest in the area of sentiment analysis and opinion mining [22]. The target of one sentiment analysis system is to automatic identify the sentiment expressions in the text and determine their polarity. However, sarcastic or ironic expressions transform the polarity of a text message into its opposite.

Usually, sarcasm detection was treated as a binary document classification problem. Given a piece of text, the goal of detection model is to predict whether there exists sarcasm expression. Furthermore, Joshi et al. [13] defined sarcasm detection for dialogue as a sequence labeling task. Each round of conversation was treated as one unit of the sequence, and the existence of irony was the hidden states. Ghosh et al. [5] modeled sarcasm detection as a sense disambiguation task. They assumed each word has two senses, one is literal sense and another one is ironic sense. In this paper, we regarded sarcasm detection as a text classification task.

Most traditional research work on sarcasm detection were based on manually established features. Kreuz and Caucci [15] proposed a sarcasm detection method based on lexical features, such as words and phrases, especially the interjections and punctuations. Carvalho et al. [3] proposed an algorithm to detect sarcasm from oral or gestural expressions represented by using emoji and special characters as features. Reyes et al. [24] proposed to apply Naive Bayes and Decision Tree to sarcasm detection which were organized according to four types of conceptual features, namely signatures, unexpectedness, style, and emotional scenarios. More recently, some researchers have also designed their model which leverages contextual information regarding the author or tweet. Davidov et al. [2] designed a deep learning-based model which exploiting features not only from the local context of the message itself but also using the information related to the authors. There has been some comprehensively studies on the effect of various features to sarcasm detection [1,13]. Zhang et al. [29] constructed a deep neural network model for tweet sarcasm detection, and achieved a better performance.

However, most deep learning-based model were all trained on hashtag-based labeling data, and the quality of the dataset may become doubtful. To mitigate this problem, most of those work train their deep learning-based model by using a large dataset of hashtag-annotated tweets, but use a testing set of manually annotated tweets. This solution brings data shift problem. Thus, in the work, we aims to investigate to train and test the deep learning-based model only on manually labeled datasets, but avoid the over-fitting caused by limited data size. The adversarial train strategy should be one of the alternative solutions.

3   Our Approach

In this section, we present the design of our approach for sarcasm detection based on adversarial training. We first describe the base neural network models in our adversarial training framework: Convolutional Neural Networks (CNN) [30], Long Short-term Memory (LSTM) [9] and Hierarchical Recurrent Neural Network (HRNN) [16]. We also apply the self-attention mechanism [17] to various models. Then, the adversarial training approach is presented at the end of this section.

3.1   Base Neural Networks Model

In this part, we will introduce the base neural networks model in the adversarial training framework.

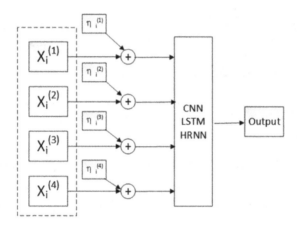

Fig. 1. Base model architecture

Convolutional Neural Networks
The convolutional neural network we used here contains four layers: input layer, two convolution layers, pooling layer and output layer. We feed the data into the model through input layer. And two convolutional layers deal with "quotes" and "responses", respectively. The features outputted by convolutional layers are feed to a max-pooling layer, and produce the output that indicates whether the input is satiric. The convolutional neural network used is shown in the Fig. 1.

Long Short-Term Memory
Recurrent neural network is used to process the serialized information and capture the temporal characteristics of the text. In this paper, we use Long Short-term Memory Networks proposed by Hochreiter et al. [9] as our recurrent neural networks. LSTM has three gates which are input gate i_t, forget gate f_t and output gate o_t. These gates co-decide how to update the current memory cell c_t

and current hidden state h_t. While processing time-series data, it looks at the current word x_t as well as the previous output of hidden state h_{t-1} at each time step. The LSTM transition functions are defined as follows:

$$i_t = \sigma(W_i \cdot [h_{t-1}, x_t] + b_i) \tag{1}$$

$$f_t = \sigma(W_f \cdot [h_{t-1}, x_t] + b_f) \tag{2}$$

$$q_t = \tanh(W_q \cdot [h_{t-1}, x_t] + b_q) \tag{3}$$

$$o_t = \sigma(W_o \cdot [h_{t-1}, x_t] + b_o) \tag{4}$$

$$c_t = f_t \odot c_{t-1} + i_t \odot q_t \tag{5}$$

$$h_t = o_t \odot \tanh(c_t) \tag{6}$$

Here, σ is the logistic sigmoid function, $tanh$ denotes the hyperbolic tangent and $\odot$ denotes the element-wise multiplication.

Hierarchical Recurrent Neural Networks

For the hierarchical recurrent neural networks, we use two LSTM layers to deal with word-level and sentence-level semantic representation, respectively. The raw embedding of words-series is modeled by the first recurrent layer, and the sentence-level of representation is obtained by hidden states of the first layers with sentence boundary. The obtained embedding of sentence-series is then model by second recurrent layers. The final representation of "quotes" or "responses" is the output of second layer.

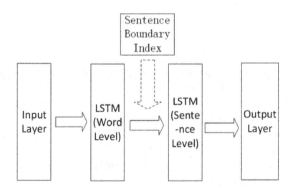

Fig. 2. Hierarchical recurrent neural networks

3.2   Attention Mechanism

Recently, attention mechanism [20] has been widely employed in various tasks of natural language processing. With the intensive study of attention mechanism, self-attention [28] has become a research hotspot. Self-attention mechanism can partially solve the long-term dependency problem in the text field. The impressive performance has been achieved on various tasks. In this paper, we use the self-attention mechanism proposed by Lin et al. [17]. For simplicity, we note the output features map of convolutional layers or all hidden states of recurrent layers as H, who have the size $n - by - m$. For recurrent layers, n is the number of time steps, and m is the size of hidden vectors. Our idea is to encode a variable length of sentence n into a fixed size embedding. The attention computation module takes H as input, and outputs a vector of attentive weights a:

$$a = softmax(w_2 tanh(W_1 H^T)) \tag{7}$$

Here W_1 is a weight matrix with a shape of $d - by - m$, and W_2 is a vector of parameters with size d, where d is a hyperparameter we should manually set. The $softmax()$ ensures all the computed weights sum up to 1. This attention computation module can be simply implemented through two linear layers without bias items. After obtain the above attentive weights, the sentence or doc representation e is calculated as follows:

$$e = a * H \tag{8}$$

3.3   Adversarial Training

Adversarial training [7] first employed in image processing domain, where the heavy use of neural networks have shown powerful ability across various computer vision task. Adversarial noise is computed with respect to target labels. Such noise is undetectable by human but significantly increase the loss incurred by a machine learning model. Adversarial training aims to help the model to correctly classify original examples and adversarial examples. Goodfellow's claim is that training neural networks with such mechanism will make model more robust and forces the model to capture the real semantics behind the task.

Without the loss of generality, we define our sarcasm detection task as a binary classification task. Obviously, if our classifier can classify an example with high confidence, it does not make any sense if we add a very small perturbation to the example. We define the process formally as follows:

$$\tilde{x} = x + \eta \wedge \|\eta\|_\infty < \epsilon \Rightarrow class(\tilde{x}) = class(x) \tag{9}$$

where ϵ is the hyper-parameter of our method, which means the intensity of perturbation we add.

In this study, for add random noise as perturbations, we regard the standard variance of the Gaussian distribution as ϵ as follows:

$$\tilde{x} = x + \eta \, , \ \eta \sim Gaussian(0, \ \epsilon^2) \tag{10}$$

In the adversarial perturbations generation, we use an arbitrary small number to control the perturbations added to a word vector. At each step, we compute the worst case perturbations η with backpropagation, and then train the model to be robust to the adversarial attack by Stochastic Gradient Descent (SGD). The adversarial perturbations generation process is as follows:

$$\eta_{adv} = -\epsilon g / \|g\|_2 \ \ where \ g = \nabla_x L(y, \ \tilde{y}) \tag{11}$$

In the above equation, g means the gradient of our input x (word embedding) with respect to current loss. In the forward computation of our model, adversarial training is equal to adding the follow regularization term to our raw objective function.

$$Loss_{adv}(y, \ \tilde{y}) \ \ where \ \tilde{y} = F(x + \eta_{adv}) \tag{12}$$

$$Loss_{raw}(y, \ \tilde{y}) \ \ where \ \tilde{y} = F(x) \tag{13}$$

$$Loss = \alpha * Loss_{adv} + (1 - \alpha)Loss_{raw} \tag{14}$$

where F represents our model forward prediction process.

4   Experimental Results and Discussion

We evaluate the effectiveness of adversarial training with six models: CNN, CNN with attention (CNN_attention), RNN, RNN with attention (RNN_attention), HRNN, HRNN with attention (HRNN_attention) on three satiric corpus from Internet Argument Corpus (IAC): Generic Sarcasm, Rhetorical Questions and Hyperbole.

4.1   Datasets

The statistics of the three datasets are listed in Table 1. All of the data samples are organized in "Quote-Response" pairs. The sarcasm annotations relate only to the "response", and the quote text included can be regard as context. Notice here that the datasets shared by Oraby is only a subset of the data. So the benchmarks in the paper [21] are not directly comparable. For each corpus, we randomly sample 20% of data as testing sets, and the rest samples are used as train sets and validation sets. We select hyperparameters of the models with a grid search method in cross-validation.

Table 1. Dataset statistics

Dataset	Size	Mean_Len_Q	Num_of_Sents_Q	Mean_Len_R	Num_of_Sents_R
Generic	3260	56.4	2.8	47.3	3.0
Rhetorical questions	850	63.2	3.8	77.4	5.1
Hyperbole	582	63.4	3.9	63.2	4.1

4.2   Experiment Settings

In this part, we describe all experimental settings in our various models. The part is organized by three different base models: convolutional neural networks, recurrent neural networks and hierarchical recurrent neural networks.

Convolutional Neural Networks

For convolutional neural network, We use fixed length 150 for both quotes and responses in spite of corpus. There are two convolutional component, and "quotes" and "responses" are modeled by their respective component. Each convolutional component has two kernel size (3 and 5 g) followed by a max-pooling layer and a dropout layer. At the end of model, two fully connected layers are used to make predictions. For convolutional neural network with attention mechanism, we replace the max-pooling layer with an attention calculation module, which is composed by two linear layer without bias. Finally, we obtain the representation though attentive weights and features map output by convolutional component.

Long Short-Term Memory

For Long Short-Term Memory Networks, we use two LSTM layers for "quotes" and "responses", respectively. We choose hidden state size $h = 50$ for LSTM. The hidden states of last time step are used to represent semantic of "quotes" and "responses". The dropout layer and fully connected layers are used with the same settings as convolutional network. As for LSTM with attention mechanism, we use an attention calculation module to weight hidden states of every time step. We obtain the representation of "quotes" and "responses" by combining attentive weights and all hidden states.

Hierarchical Recurrent Neural Networks

For hierarchical recurrent neural network, we use two LSTM layers to model the words-level semantics and sentences-level semantics, respectively. The same as the above standard recurrent model, we choose hidden state size $h = 50$ for recurrent layers. Note here that, due to the limited data size, we use the same two recurrent layers for "quotes" and "responses" here. It will reduce the number of parameters and thus it is helpful to avoid the explosion of parameters. The remaining settings of hierarchical recurrent model are the same as convolutional neural networks and recurrent neural networks.

In all of the experiments, the settings of normal training strategy and adversarial training strategy have no difference. We use Glove [23] word embeddings with size $d_w = 300$, batch size $b = 64$ and do a manual search over ϵ. Adam Optimizer [14] with learning rate 0.001 and cross-entropy loss function are the default choices of our models.

4.3   Experimental Results

Table 2 shows the achieved performance on the Generic Sarcasm Corpus, Table 3 for Rhetorical Questions Corpus and Table 4 for Hyperbole Corpus, respectively. It is observed that adversarial training improve the detection performance on all of the base models. All of the best performance on three corpora are achieved by following adversarial training strategy. To ensure the adversarial noise improve the robustness of model, we also train each model with samples perturbed by random noise. The experimental results show that adding random noise to samples can only lead to poor performance. It means that random noise will increase the difficulty of convergence.

The state-of-the-art sarcasm detection approach on generic corpus used a pre-trained deep model with massive external data [4]. Our performance achieved by CNN_attention with adversarial training is slightly better. Besides that, using massive external data to pre-train a deep neural networks is a very complicated thing. The adversarial training for sarcasm detection has shown more valuable way. On the other two corpora, our approach achieves comparable or higher performance compared to the neural network's benchmark proposed by Oraby [21]. Note that, because the full datasets is unavailable, the performance may not be compared directly. Even so, adversarial training can achieve comparable or better performance, which is powerful evidence of the effectiveness of adversarial training.

The comparisons between different models show that, the performance achieved by LSTM is unsatisfactory. Convolutional neural network based system achieves the highest performance on rhetorical questions corpus, hyperbole corpus and generic sarcasm corpus. Hierarchical recurrent neural network based system achieves almost the same level of performance as CNN. The reason why the convolutional and hierarchical recurrent neural networks have better performance than long short-term memory networks would be that, the recurrent neural networks suffer from the problem of the long-range dependency and lacking of data. Compared with convolutional neural networks, LSTM have much more parameters, which will cause worse performance on small datasets. Compared with LSTM, HRNN can get more effective representation for samples, it shows that hierarchical structures make it easier to learn more comprehensive semantic representation.

Table 2. Performance of various model on generic sarcasm corpus

Model	Normal train		Adversarial train		Random noise	
	F1-value	Accuracy	F1-value	Accuracy	F1-value	Accuracy
CNN	0.716	0.720	0.743	0.745	0.686	0.689
CNN_attention	0.731	0.732	0.750	0.752	0.664	0.671
RNN	0.684	0.686	0.678	0.678	0.651	0.660
RNN_attention	0.659	0.663	0.676	0.676	0.653	0.659
HRNN	0.734	0.736	0.750	0.751	0.657	0.659
HRNN_attention	0.738	0.740	**0.751**	**0.753**	0.646	0.646

Table 3. Performance of various model on rhetorical questions corpus

Model	Normal train		Adversarial train		Random noise	
	F1-value	Accuracy	F1-value	Accuracy	F1-value	Accuracy
CNN	0.672	0.672	0.701	0.707	0.636	0.638
CNN_attention	0.681	0.681	**0.711**	**0.711**	0.620	0.621
RNN	0.641	0.647	0.647	0.653	0.603	0.603
RNN_attention	0.647	0.649	0.633	0.641	0.595	0.594
HRNN	0.672	0.672	0.697	0.701	0.621	0.620
HRNN_attention	0.686	0.690	0.707	0.707	0.611	0.612

Table 4. Performance of various model on hyperbole corpus

Model	Normal train		Adversarial train		Random noise	
	F1-value	Accuracy	F1-value	Accuracy	F1-value	Accuracy
CNN	0.606	0.607	0.641	0.642	0.583	0.586
CNN_attention	0.629	0.635	**0.654**	**0.654**	0.585	0.586
RNN	0.589	0.603	0.591	0.595	0.576	0.578
RNN_attention	0.576	0.578	0.559	0.560	0.576	0.586
HRNN	0.617	0.621	0.636	0.638	0.610	0.612
HRNN_attention	0.609	0.612	0.646	0.647	0.611	0.612

5   Conclusion

In this paper, we propose to apply adversarial training to sarcasm detection. CNN, LSTM and HRNN are adopted as base neural networks, respectively. They are employed in an adversarial training framework. The experiments results on three datasets shows that adversarial training can improve the performance compared to the same models with normal training strategy. In addition, we also propose an more effective hierarchical recurrent neural network for sarcasm detection task. Our approach is show outperforms state-of-the-art methods on three sarcasm corpora.

Acknowledgements. This work was supported by the National Natural Science Foundation of China U1636103, 61632011, Key Technologies Research and Development Program of Shenzhen JSGG20170817140856618, Shenzhen Foundational Research Funding 20170307150024907.

References

1. Amir, S., Wallace, B.C., Lyu, H., Carvalho, P., Silva, M.J.: Modelling context with user embeddings for sarcasm detection in social media. In: Proceedings of the 20th SIGNLL Conference on Computational Natural Language Learning, CoNLL 2016, Berlin, Germany, 11–12 August 2016, pp. 167–177 (2016). http://aclweb.org/anthology/K/K16/K16-1017.pdf
2. Bamman, D.: Contextualized sarcasm detection on Twitter (2015)
3. Carvalho, P., Sarmento, L., Silva, M.J., De Oliveira, E.: Clues for detecting irony in user-generated contents: oh...!! it's "so easy";-) pp. 53–56 (2009)
4. Felbo, B., Mislove, A., Søgaard, A., Rahwan, I., Lehmann, S.: Using millions of emoji occurrences to learn any-domain representations for detecting sentiment, emotion and sarcasm. In: Proceedings of the 2017 Conference on Empirical Methods in Natural Language Processing, EMNLP 2017, Copenhagen, Denmark, 9–11 September 2017, pp. 1615–1625 (2017). https://aclanthology.info/papers/D17-1169/d17-1169
5. Ghosh, D., Guo, W., Muresan, S.: Sarcastic or not: word embeddings to predict the literal or sarcastic meaning of words. In: Proceedings of the 2015 Conference on Empirical Methods in Natural Language Processing, EMNLP 2015, Lisbon, Portugal, 17–21 September 2015, pp. 1003–1012 (2015)
6. González-Ibáñez, R.I., Muresan, S., Wacholder, N.: Identifying sarcasm in Twitter: a closer look. In: Proceedings of the Conference on the 49th Annual Meeting of the Association for Computational Linguistics: Human Language Technologies - Short Papers, Portland, Oregon, USA, 19–24 June 2011, pp. 581–586 (2011). http://www.aclweb.org/anthology/P11-2102
7. Goodfellow, I.J., Shlens, J., Szegedy, C.: Explaining and harnessing adversarial examples. CoRR abs/1412.6572 (2014). http://arxiv.org/abs/1412.6572
8. Guo, J., Gould, S.: Deep CNN ensemble with data augmentation for object detection. CoRR abs/1506.07224 (2015). http://arxiv.org/abs/1506.07224
9. Hochreiter, S., Schmidhuber, J.: Long short-term memory. Neural Comput. 9(8), 1735–1780 (1997)
10. Ioffe, S., Szegedy, C.: Batch normalization: accelerating deep network training by reducing internal covariate shift. In: Proceedings of the 32nd International Conference on Machine Learning, ICML 2015, Lille, France, 6–11 July 2015, pp. 448–456 (2015). http://jmlr.org/proceedings/papers/v37/ioffe15.html
11. Jia, R., Liang, P.: Adversarial examples for evaluating reading comprehension systems. In: Proceedings of the 2017 Conference on Empirical Methods in Natural Language Processing, EMNLP 2017, Copenhagen, Denmark, 9–11 September 2017, pp. 2021–2031 (2017). https://aclanthology.info/papers/D17-1215/d17-1215
12. Jin, J., Dundar, A., Culurciello, E.: Robust convolutional neural networks under adversarial noise. arXiv:Learning (2015)
13. Joshi, A., Tripathi, V., Bhattacharyya, P., Carman, M.J.: Harnessing sequence labeling for sarcasm detection in dialogue from TV series 'friends'. In: Proceedings of the 20th SIGNLL Conference on Computational Natural Language Learning, CoNLL 2016, Berlin, Germany, 11–12 August 2016. pp. 146–155 (2016). http://aclweb.org/anthology/K/K16/K16-1015.pdf
14. Kingma, D.P., Ba, J.: Adam: a method for stochastic optimization. CoRR abs/1412.6980 (2014), http://arxiv.org/abs/1412.6980
15. Kreuz, R.J., Caucci, G.M.: Lexical influences on the perception of sarcasm. In: The Workshop on Computational Approaches to Figurative Language (2009)

16. Lin, R., Liu, S., Yang, M., Li, M., Zhou, M., Li, S.: Hierarchical recurrent neural network for document modeling. In: Proceedings of the 2015 Conference on Empirical Methods in Natural Language Processing, EMNLP 2015, Lisbon, Portugal, 17–21 September 2015, pp. 899–907 (2015). http://aclweb.org/anthology/D/D15/D15-1106.pdf

17. Lin, Z., Feng, M., dos Santos, C.N., Yu, M., Xiang, B., Zhou, B., Bengio, Y.: A structured self-attentive sentence embedding. CoRR abs/1703.03130 (2017), http://arxiv.org/abs/1703.03130

18. Miyato, T., Dai, A.M., Goodfellow, I.: Adversarial training methods for semi-supervised text classification (2016)

19. Miyato, T., Maeda, S., Koyama, M., Nakae, K., Ishii, S.: Distributional smoothing with virtual adversarial training. In: International Conference on Learning Representations (2016)

20. Mnih, V., Heess, N., Graves, A., Kavukcuoglu, K.: Recurrent models of visual attention. In: Advances in Neural Information Processing Systems 27: Annual Conference on Neural Information Processing Systems 2014, Montreal, Quebec, Canada, 8–13 December 2014, pp. 2204–2212 (2014), http://papers.nips.cc/paper/5542-recurrent-models-of-visual-attention

21. Oraby, S., Harrison, V., Reed, L., Hernandez, E., Riloff, E., Walker, M.A.: Creating and characterizing a diverse corpus of sarcasm in dialogue. CoRR abs/1709.05404 (2017), http://arxiv.org/abs/1709.05404

22. Pang, B., Lee, L.: Opinion mining and sentiment analysis. Found. Trends Inf. Retr. **2**(12), 1–135 (2008)

23. Pennington, J., Socher, R., Manning, C.D.: Glove: global vectors for word representation. In: Proceedings of the 2014 Conference on Empirical Methods in Natural Language Processing, EMNLP 2014, A meeting of SIGDAT, a Special Interest Group of the ACL, Doha, Qatar, 25–29 October 2014, pp. 1532–1543 (2014). http://aclweb.org/anthology/D/D14/D14-1162.pdf

24. Reyes, A., Rosso, P., Veale, T.: A multidimensional approach for detecting irony in Twitter. Lang. Resour. Eval. **47**(1), 239–268 (2013). https://doi.org/10.1007/s10579-012-9196-x

25. Samanta, S., Mehta, S.: Generating adversarial text samples. In: Pasi, G., Piwowarski, B., Azzopardi, L., Hanbury, A. (eds.) ECIR 2018. LNCS, vol. 10772, pp. 744–749. Springer, Cham (2018). https://doi.org/10.1007/978-3-319-76941-7_71

26. Srivastava, N., Hinton, G.E., Krizhevsky, A., Sutskever, I., Salakhutdinov, R.: Dropout: a simple way to prevent neural networks from overfitting. J. Mach. Learn. Res. **15**(1), 1929–1958 (2014). http://dl.acm.org/citation.cfm?id=2670313

27. Szegedy, C., Zaremba, W., Sutskever, I., Bruna, J., Erhan, D., Goodfellow, I.J., Fergus, R.: Intriguing properties of neural networks. CoRR abs/1312.6199 (2013). http://arxiv.org/abs/1312.6199

28. Vaswani, A., Shazeer, N., Parmar, N., Uszkoreit, J., Jones, L., Gomez, A.N., Kaiser, L., Polosukhin, I.: Attention is all you need. CoRR abs/1706.03762 (2017). http://arxiv.org/abs/1706.03762

29. Zhang, M., Zhang, Y., Fu, G.: Tweet sarcasm detection using deep neural network. In: COLING 2016, 26th International Conference on Computational Linguistics, Proceedings of the Conference: Technical Papers, Osaka, Japan, 11–16 December 2016, pp. 2449–2460 (2016). http://aclweb.org/anthology/C/C16/C16-1231.pdf

30. Zhang, X., Zhao, J.J., Lecun, Y.: Character-level convolutional networks for text classification. In: Neural Information Processing Systems, pp. 649–657 (2015)

Reinforcement Learning with Monte Carlo Sampling in Imperfect Information Problems

Jiajia Zhang[(✉)] and Hong Liu

Shenzhen Graduate School, Peking University, Shenzhen 518055, China
zhangjiajia@pkusz.edu.cn

Abstract. Artificial intelligence is an approach that analyzes, studies, optimizes human strategies in challenging domains. Unlike perfect information problems, imperfect information problems usually present more complexity because the accuracy of conditions estimation cannot be effectively guaranteed. Thus, imperfect information problems need much more training data or much longer learning process when using supervised and unsupervised learning systems. This paper presents and evaluates a novel algorithm that based on Monte Carlo sampling as terminal states' estimation method in reinforce learning systems. The learning system calculates an adjusted result by novel algorithm in each iterations to smooth the fluctuation of imperfect information conditions. In this paper, we apply the new algorithm to build a deep neural network (DNN) learning system in our Texas Holdem poker game program. The contrast poker program has gained third rank in Annual Computer Poker Competition 2017 (ACPC 2017) and system with new approach shows better performance while convergence much faster.

Keywords: Reinforcement learning · Monte Carlo sampling
Imperfect information

1 Introduction

Game problems can be classified as perfect or imperfect information conditions, which are based on whether or not players have the whole information of the game [1]. In imperfect information problems, certain relevant details are withheld from the players. Thus, they have a myriad of applications such as negotiation, shopping agents, cyber-security, physical security, and so on [2].

Poker is a typical interesting test-bed for artificial intelligence research in this area. It is a game of imperfect knowledge, where multiple competing agents must deal with risk management, agent modeling, unreliable information and deception, much like decision-making applications in the real world [3].

As a recognized approach of building a competitive game system, DNN has been extensively applied that are trained to imitate the strategies of human experts [4]. However, expert data is usually expensive, unreliable and unhelpful for train process of DNN. The shortage of high quality data is much more serious in imperfect information games for their complexity. One solution is using unsupervised system or reinforcement

© Springer International Publishing AG, part of Springer Nature 2018
J. Xiao et al. (Eds.): ICCC 2018, LNCS 10971, pp. 55–67, 2018.
https://doi.org/10.1007/978-3-319-94307-7_5

learning system which has gained success in the study of Go [5]. In the research of DeepMind, Alpha Go Zero system learns from its own experience based a deep neural networks trained by reinforcement learning. The succeed of DeepMind on Go problem shows the hopes of solution about game problems without human expert knowledge.

However, this approach faces more challenge when applied to imperfect information problems. That is because in Alpha Go Zero structure, Monte Carlo Tree Search (MCTS) constructs a search tree to tracing the states progress of the game. The structure self-play randomly to simulate huge amount states until the end of the game which can be evaluated as a triple set $(1, 0, -1)$ means win, draw and lose. However, unlike we can exactly evaluate finial result in Go, states of imperfect information problems cannot be evaluated individually by one simulation result and are generally evaluated by mean values of many Monte Carlo simulations [6]. The accuracy of states estimation cannot be effectively guaranteed when simulation is insufficient. In this condition, the exploration and exploitation of game tree is mislead and the training performance of the reinforcement learning system is degraded.

In fact, the accuracy of states estimation is greatly influenced by simulation time of MCTS. In another words, given sufficient compute and time resources, MCTS can make an infinite approximation of exact value. Anyway, the mean value of Monte Carlo simulations is much better than just a individual outcome in vanilla reinforcement learning. Thus, Monte Carlo sampling is definitely helpful to guarantee the accuracy of states estimation and the efficient distribution of simulation resource becomes a severe problem in estimation process.

In this paper, we provide novel algorithms, MC-SD and MC-KL, to modify the reinforcement learning methods in imperfect information problems which has at least two advantages. First, Monte Carlo sampling is adopt to provide mean estimations of amount of Monte Carlo simulations instead of one individual result of certain state. In our verification experiments, Monte Carlo sampling provides more reasonable results and accelerates the convergence process of reinforcement learning process. Second, novel algorithms can guarantee the accuracy of MCTS estimation in limited time. Monte Carlo sampling is adjusted dynamically with the reliability of current estimation which is decided by current game world scale and grouped estimation variance and KL-divergence. To verify the effectiveness, the new algorithms are applied on our new Texas hold'em poker game system. The contrast is a top-level poker system which gained third rank in Annual Computer Poker Competition 2017 (ACPC 2017) [7]. The new system shows nearly performance while convergence much faster.

2　Related Works

2.1　MCTS and UCT Approach in Imperfect Information Problems

The ideal solution of game problems, at least for two-player zero-sum games, is to use a solution technique that can produce Nash equilibrium. However, this is usually computationally infeasible in most imperfect information domains for its precondition about guaranteeing perfect play against perfect opponents.

One popular way of dealing with imperfect information has been to avoid the issue. Instead of solving a full game, perfect information worlds from the game are sampled and solved either exactly or heuristically [8]. Monte-Carlo sampling, also called computer random simulation method, deals with imperfect information problem by a heuristics search method. The main idea is to create a subset of possible conditions by random sampling and to find out the best solution for them. Based on a statistical hypothesis that the optimal solution for a random-sampling subset is comparable to the global optimal solution, the solution is then treated as acceptable for the whole problem. Thus, game tree is searched and extended in this ideology, called MCTS.

MCTS constructs a search tree to tracing the states progress of the game. Figure 1 gives a simple description of the operation process of MCTS algorithm. The algorithm iterates in four stages. In the selection and expansion stage a tree is built and explored. An expansion path is selected from the root node to leaf node basing on the evaluation policy. The evaluation and back propagation stage begins when the end of the game tree is reached. At this point the expanded leaf node is reevaluated and the result will be back propagated to each node of the expansion nodes. The process will recycle many times until the searching time exhausted. The branch selected at the last loop is considered as the best strategy. In this process, the evaluation policy is wildly studied and one of a good choice is UCT [9].

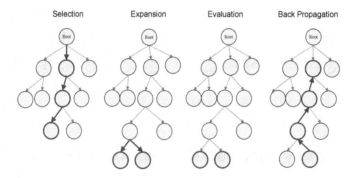

Fig. 1. The process of MCTS algorithm operation for one loop.

2.2 DNN for MCTS Evaluation Policy

In Deepmind gourp's research on Alpha Go system, DNN is employed as the evaluation policy in MCTS structure. The advantage is DNN can be trained with domain expert knowledge [4] or self-play experience for reinforcement learning [5]. Thus, comparing with online mode, the well trained DNN can provide more accuracy states' estimation. In their recent research, Alpha Go system is trained as a reinforcement learning mode, which overcome the drawbacks of reliable of expert data and the ceiling on performance. As the result, we build our imperfect information system as the same manner.

We choose convolutional neural network (CNN) for the main structure of our DNN for its advantage on feature extraction on poker game. Enlightened by the study of Nikolai Yakovenko [10] and Christopher Clark [11], we extend the 4*13 poker matrix, which represents 52 pokers in the game, to a 17*17 matrix with element 0. The 17*17 matrix is used as unit input matrix of DNN. And also, history data, public conditions and actions frequency are extracted as the same manner. Finally, 7 unit input matrix are formed as a 3 dimension matrix which is used as the input layer of DNN, as Fig. 2 shows.

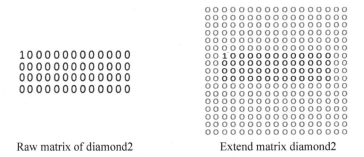

Raw matrix of diamond2   Extend matrix diamond2

Fig. 2. Unit input matrix of endgame generating DNN.

The hidden layer is realized as Fig. 3 shows:

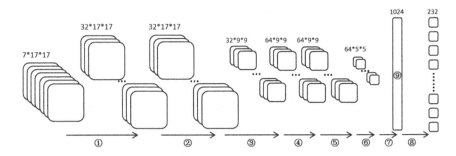

Fig. 3. Hidden layer of endgame generating DNN.

The labels in Fig. 3 means as following:

① 32 convolution kernels (3*3) ② 32 convolution kernels (3*3)
③ 2*2 max-pooling ④ 64 convolution kernels (3*3)
⑤ 64 convolution kernels (3*3) ⑥ 2*2 max-pooling
⑦ fully meshed ⑧ fully meshed ⑨ 50 percent dropout layer

3   Modified Reinforcement Learning in Imperfect Information Problems

In this section, we introduce our application of reinforcement learning with our modifications in imperfect information problems. On the whole, our approach has a similar structure of DeepMind's research while three points' modifications. First, the evaluation about finial states is calculated as a linear value to replace the dispersed "win or lose" value in raw system. Second, differs from the individual evaluation at the end of the game state, Monte Carlo sampling is used to estimate the expected revenue to decrease the fluctuating of feedback value in learning. Third, algorithms are proposed to guarantee the accuracy of Monte Carlo sampling in limited time resource.

3.1 Reinforce Learning with MCTS Approach

In our reinforcement learning poker system, a circulatory control center plays a game from random deal to each step, $s_0, s_1 \ldots s_n \in S$, of a poker game. In Texas Holdem, Set S contains preflop, flop, turn, river and finial result steps. In each step s_i, MCTS method is executed with DNN as its extend policy π_i. Both of the two methods are similar as the realization in Go and have been briefly introduced in preceding section. Figure 4 shows the process of system operation.

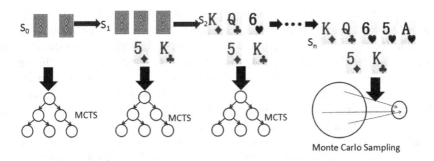

Fig. 4. Reinforcement learning with MCTS in Texas Holdem system.

When game comes to the terminal step S_n, which means the result of certain round can be clearly calculated based on the rules of game, another calculation of result should be executed that differs from perfect information game problems. As Figs. 5 and 6 shows, terminal result in imperfect information problems are determined by both imperfect and perfect information of the state. Individually evaluation cannot effectively represents the exact expected revenue of game progress and will lead to huge fluctuation in learning process of the whole system. Thus, Monte Carlo sampling method is employed again in this step to smooth the expected revenue of terminal state by sample and estimate the revenue of sub set to instead whole possible worlds.

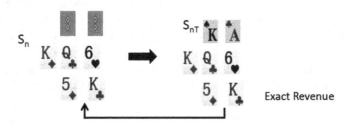

Fig. 5. Terminal states' evaluation with individual condition.

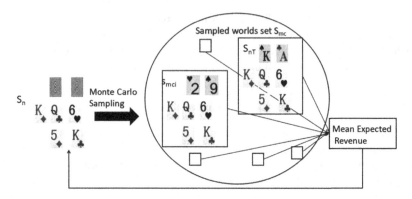

Fig. 6. Terminal state evaluation with Mean estimation of Monte Carlo Sampling.

Figure 5 shows the evaluation method in perfect information problems like Go. When game process comes to terminal state S_{nT}, all factors that influence finial result are clear. A certain value can be calculated based on game rules. Learning system transmit this value to DNN as the trace back value for learning. Generally speaking, this result, whether be a discrete value (win or lose) or a liner interval, reflects the performance of the strategies leads game tree to this state. However in imperfect information problems, individual result of certain state cannot effectively reflects this performance. As Fig. 5 shows in Texas Holdem poker, hidden information "opponent: A, K" means we fail in this round. However, "raise" in former steps is also a very likely good strategy for that "Double K" is bigger enough in most possible conditions. This is the reason that a more effective approach should be employ in this condition.

Figure 6 shows the modified approach of terminal state estimation. Monte Carlo sampling is executed to simulate thousands of other possible conditions that may happens in same trace of game tree progress. Then, each simulated state $s_{mci} \in S_{mc}$ is evaluated individually based on game rules. All of the results are collected and the mean expected revenue is calculated by statistic method.

3.2   Guarantee Accuracy of Monte Carlo Sampling Estimation

In terminal states of our system, Monte Carlo sampling method is employed to smooth the fluctuation of imperfect information estimation. The standard Monte Carlo sampling method is based on the ideology as following. Let S is the whole set of possible worlds of current state. S_{mc} is the sampled set that randomly selected from S, $S_{mc} \subset S$. Attention that, the hidden game information is simulated by certain rules and possibility statistics method in both S and S_{mc}. Thus each factor $s_{mci} : s_{mci} \in S_{mc}$ can be exactly evaluated for its revenue R_i based on game rules. Suppose S is a states set that contributed by N elements, Monte Carlo sampling method estimates the expected revenue E_r of current state as Eq. (1) expresses.

$$E_{rs} = \frac{1}{N} \sum_{i=1}^{N} R_i \qquad (1)$$

Monte Carlo sampling method employs the complete evaluation of sub set to estimate and substitute real evaluation of the whole worlds set. The accuracy of this estimation severely depends on the proportion of S and S_{mc}. In this sense, when S has a huge scale, the accuracy of states estimation cannot be effectively guaranteed when sampling time is insufficient in practice. Weather it is the manner of online calculation or offline learning, the contradiction between Monte Carlo sampling accuracy and time consumption is severe and should be solved.

In our research, subgroup's standard deviation is firstly employed to measure and modify the balance of accuracy and time consumption in Monte Carlo sampling process. The sample process is divided into groups as a dynamic growth manner, and the estimation variance is calculated based a predefined threshold to control the end of sample process. Let $S_i : S_i \subset S_{mc}$ is the subgroups of S_{mc}, which is divided into n groups. When S_i is sampled and E_{rsi} is calculated by Eq. (1), the estimation of standard deviation of S can be calculated as:

$$V_i = \sqrt{\frac{1}{i} \left[(E_{rs} - E_{rs1})^2 + (E_{rs} - E_{rs2})^2 + \ldots\ldots (E_{rs} - E_{rsi})^2 \right]} \qquad (2)$$

The first algorithm of modified Monte Carlo sampling estimation that based standard deviation is provided as following:

Algorithm 1: Modified Monte Carlo based standard deviation: MC-SD

· Parameters: threshold T, subgroup scale n, loop times t, time consumption limit c.
· Initialization: Set $S_{mc} = \emptyset$, $t = 0$.
· Loop:

1. if time consumption c has exhausted, goto End.
2. Simulate n possible states to form subgroup set S_t, $S_{mc} = S_{mc} \cup S_t$.
3. Calculate E_{rs} and E_{rsi} by Eq. (1) where $0 \leqslant i \leqslant t$.
4. Calculate V_t by Eq. (2).
5. If $V_t \leq T$ and $t \neq 0$, go to end step, else go to step 1.

· End: Return E_{rs} as the Monte Carlo estimation of current state.

Based on Algorithm 1, Monte Carlo sampling can serve a likely accurate estimation while time consumption is under control. However, in our poker practice, standard deviation of mean value is not the best method that measure and express the difference of the characters among subgroups S_t, Thus, Kullback-Leibler (KL) divergence is used to exploit a more appropriate expression of Monte Carlo sample and its fluctuation [10].

In probability theory and information theory, Kullback–Leibler divergence is a non-symmetric measure of the difference between two probability distributions P and Q (Kullback and Leibler 1951). Specifically, the KL divergence of Q from P, denoted $D_{KL}(P \| Q)$, is a measure of the information lost when Q is used to approximate P. Formula 3 shows the definition of D_{KL}.

$$D_{\mathrm{KL}}(P\|Q) = \sum_i \ln\left(\frac{P(i)}{Q(i)}\right)P(i) \qquad (3)$$

In words, it is the expectation of the logarithmic difference between the probabilities P and Q, where the expectation is taken using the probabilities P.

For distributions P and Q of a continuous random variable, KL-divergence is defined to be the integral as formula 4 shows.

$$D_{\mathrm{KL}}(P\|Q) = \int_{-\infty}^{\infty} \ln\left(\frac{p(x)}{q(x)}\right)p(x)\mathrm{d}x \qquad (4)$$

In this sense, we can express a subgroups S_t by probability distribution P as Fig. 7 shows. First, possible individual state revenue are divided to m interval. More intervals means more exact expression but more calculate and time resource consumption. Second, P is calculated based on the evaluation of each state in S_t, as Eq. 5 shows. Each p_i donates the probability that states evaluated in its interval in which $p_{i\_}$ and $\hat{p}_i$ means the lower limit and upper limit of interval p_i.

$$P = (p_1, p_2, p_3 \ldots \ldots p_m)$$

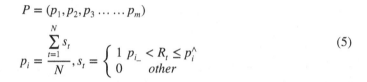

$$p_i = \frac{\sum_{t=1}^{N} s_t}{N}, s_t = \begin{cases} 1 & p_{i\_} < R_t \leq p_i^{\wedge} \\ 0 & other \end{cases} \qquad (5)$$

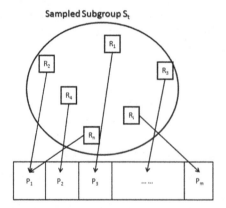

Fig. 7. Expression of sampled subgroup S_t by probability distribution P.

Thus, the D_{KL} between subgroup S_t and sampling set S_{mc} can be calculated as Eq. 6 shows.

$$D_{\mathrm{KL}}(S_t\|S_{mc}) = \sum_{i=0}^{m} \ln\left(\frac{P_{S_t}(i)}{P_{S_{mc}}(i)}\right)P_{S_t}(i) \qquad (6)$$

Now, we provide our modified method of Monte Carlo sampling estimation based on KL divergence.

Algorithm 2: Modified Monte Carlo based KL divergence: MC-KL

· Parameters: threshold T, subgroup scale n, loop times t, time consumption limit c, interval number m.

· Initialization: Set $S_{mc} = \emptyset$, $t = 0$.

· Loop:

1. if time consumption c has exhausted, goto End.
2. Simulate n possible states to form subgroup set S_t, and then $S_{mc} = S_{mc} \cup S_t$.
3. Calculate R_i of each state in S_{mc} and S_t.
4. Calculate P_{Smc} and P_{St} by (5)
5. Calculate $DKL(S_{mc}\|S_t)$ by (6).
6. If $DKL(S_{mc}\|S_t) \leq T$ and $t \neq 0$, go to end step, else go to step 1.

· End: Calculate E_{rs} by (1) and return it as the Monte Carlo estimation of current state.

So far, two modified Monte Carlo sampling estimation algorithms MC-SD and MC-KL have been introduced. We apply them in our Texas Holdem poker to verify their performance, which will introduced in next section.

4   Experiments

In this section, we verify the performance of our novel method MC-SD and MC-KL, compared with classical method that without Monte Carlo estimation. Three reinforcement learning process are parallel running which are build with similar frames but different evaluation methods in terminal states. The experiments are applied on Texas Holdem poker problems, which are based on Heads-up No-Limit rule and pineapple rules.

First, the configuration of parameters in MC-SD and MC-KL should be well set which has been introduced in former chapter. Briefly speaking, the bigger threshold T, subgroup scale n and interval number m is set, the more accuracy states are estimated while more time is consumed which means less training iterations can be operated in certain time. Thus, best configuration should achieve a better balance between effectiveness of each training iteration and time consumption. As the results of this part of work, top three configurations are listed in Fig. 8.

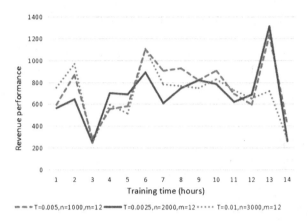

Fig. 8. The performance of top 3 configurations of algorithm MC-KL.

In our course of training, 8400 games are generated for each iteration. Each round are operated three times with a alternating deal order for three agents to guarantee the fairness in this round. Thus, 25200 rounds data is trained for the CNN's update in each iteration. Figure 8 shows the revenue performance of three agents. The fluctuation shows the revenue is severely influenced by not only the agents' strategy but also the "lucky factor" of card deal. Base on this process, we choose "T = 0.005, n = 1000, m = 12" as the best configuration in following experiments.

Second, we observe the performance of Texas Holdem poker system during self-play reinforcement learning. Every iterations are set as same as upper manner, and the performance is judged by accuracy with expert data which is from the strategy of our best system [7] and partially modified by human experts.

Figure 9 shows the training process of MC-SD, MC-KL and basic reinforcement learning in our poker system, 24 days in all. The prediction accuracy on expert strategy, which is counted each 4 h, are observed as criterion of their performance. In this experiment, basic reinforcement learning process shows a relatively bigger fluctuation in its growth curve and finally achieve accuracy of 77%. Compare with it, novel algorithm MC-SD performs much stable and achieves accuracy of 90.35%. Best of all, MC-KL performs most raising stability and finally achieve 97.5%. Figure 10 shows the self-play game among the upper three method. In nearly 17000 rounds games, which are also based on deal alternating mode for fair. MC-KL shows obvious advantage than the other two agents, which wins 6282 chips, 0.3643 chips per round on average. MC-SD wins 1914 chips and 0.111 chips per round. The result is directly proportional to their raising curve in training process in general and verify the advantages of novel algorithms again.

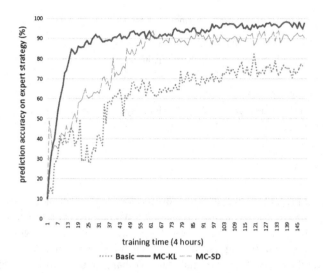

Fig. 9. The performance of strategy accuracy of MC-SD, MC-KL and classic system.

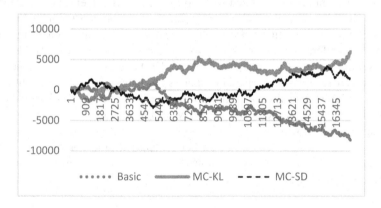

Fig. 10. The performance of chip revenue of MC-SD, MC-KL and classic system.

As Figs. 9 and 10 shows, novel algorithms shows advantages compared with basic reinforce learning on training time and game performance, while MC-KL performs better than MC-SD.

Finally, we present our results that MC-KL system versus professional human player at online poker platform "Tonybet" with rule of pineapple poker [12].

Table 1 shows the online result of new reinforcement learning system and former top level system. In about 150000 rounds game with human player, both of the two agents get a 1 chips per rounds' advantage, while novel agent even performs better. And another side, novel agent which is trained by itself shows a litter different strategy style from former agent which is trained by supervised learning system with human expert data. The efficiency of reinforcement leaning is revealed preliminary.

Table 1. Online result of new reinforcement learning system and former top level system

New reinforcement learning system		Former top level system	
Rounds num	72212	Rounds num	78996
Revenue	78073	Revenue	73623
Average revenue per round	1.0812	Average revenue per round	0.9320
Fantasy rounds percentage	31.11%	Fantasy rounds percentage	38.05%
Lose percentage	24.97%	Lose percentage	28.56%

5   Conclusion

In this paper, we present a novel approaches to improve the accuracy of terminal states estimation in imperfect information problems. Our method, Monte Carlo Estimation with Variance (MC-SD) and Monte Carlo Estimation with KL divergence (MC-KL), employ Monte Carlo sampling estimation to calculate a mean expected revenue to instead individual evaluation in terminal state. To balance the estimation accuracy and time consumption, variance and KL divergence is employed to measure the estimation divergence between sampled set and whole possible set, which reflects the accuracy of estimation. In this sense, the estimation accuracy and time consumption becomes a controllable manner in training process, which means a better configuration can be tested and selected in different problems. We verify our approaches with Texas Holdem poker system. Reinforcement learning system with MC-SD and MC-KL shows much better stability of accuracy raising compared with classical manner in same time consumption of 12 days' training. And also, MC-KL performance better than MC-SD with their best configuration and both of them show a nearly well matched performance in self-play manner against our former best Texas Holdem poker agent and against expert human player on internet. Thus, we can conclude that our approach that combination of Monte Carlo estimation and reinforcement learning method in imperfect information problems is effective and reliable.

References

1. Bampton, H.J.: Solving imperfect information games using the Monte Carlo heuristic, Master dissertation. University of Tennessee, USA (1994b)
2. Brown, N., Sandholm, T.: Safe and nested subgame solving for imperfect-information games (2017)
3. Billings, D., Papp, D., Schaeffer, J. (eds.): Opponent modeling in poker. In: Association for the Advancement of Artificial Intelligence, pp. 493–499. AAAI Press (1998)
4. Silver, D., Huang, A., Maddison, C.J., et al.: Mastering the game of Go with deep neural networks and tree search. Nature **529**(7587), 484 (2016)
5. Silver, D., Schrittwieser, J., Simonyan, K., et al.: Mastering the game of Go without human knowledge. Nature **550**(7676), 354 (2017)
6. Coulom, R.: Efficient selectivity and backup operators in monte-carlo tree search. In: van den Herik, H.J., Ciancarini, P., Donkers, H.H.L.M.J. (eds.) CG 2006. LNCS, vol. 4630, pp. 72–83. Springer, Heidelberg (2007). https://doi.org/10.1007/978-3-540-75538-8_7

7. http://www.computerpokercompetition.org/index.php/competitions/results/125-2017-results

8. Long, J., Sturtevant, N., Buro, M.: Understanding the success of perfect information monte carlo sampling in game tree search. In: Proceedings of AAAI-10, pp. 134–140 (2010)

9. Kocsis, L., Szepesvári, C.: Bandit based monte-carlo planning. In: Fürnkranz, J., Scheffer, T., Spiliopoulou, M. (eds.) ECML 2006. LNCS (LNAI), vol. 4212, pp. 282–293. Springer, Heidelberg (2006). https://doi.org/10.1007/11871842_29

10. Zhang, J., Wang, X., Yao, L., Li, L., Shen, X.: Using Kullback-Leibler divergence to model opponents in poker. In: 28th AAAI Conference on Artificial Intelligence (AAAI 2014) Workshop: Computer Poker and Imperfect Information, QuebecCity, Canada, pp. 50–57 (2014)

11. Van der Kleij, A.A.J.: Monte Carlo Tree Search and Opponent Modeling through Player Clustering in no-limit Texas Hold'em Poker. Master dissertation, University of Groningen, The Netherlands (2010b)

12. https://tonybet.com/sport

Research: System Evaluation

Comparative Evaluation of Priming Effects on HMDs and Smartphones with Photo Taking Behaviors

Naoya Isoyama[1]($\boxtimes$), Tsutomu Terada[1,2], and Masahiko Tsukamoto[1]

[1] Kobe University, 1-1 Rokkodaicho, Kobe, Hyogo 6578501, Japan
isoyama@eedept.kobe-u.ac.jp
[2] PRESTO, JST, Saitama, Japan

Abstract. In this study, we investigated the difference between head-mounted displays (HMDs) and smartphone displays on the priming effects for photo-taking behaviors. HMDs appear to be the successor of mobile displays, including smartphone displays. However, HMDs possibly have their own effects on the human mind and body. It seems that the content shown on displays affect human behavior because users passively see displays frequently. Although the effects of smartphones are not a problem yet, the effects of HMDs are possibly greater than those of smartphones because HMD users see the display anytime, anywhere. It is important that we explore the differences between smartphones and HMDs. This study uses priming effects for comparative research. We focus on application icon images because they are continually seen by users. We experimented on whether users tend to take photographs that are affected by the icon images. We prepared three icon images and confirmed that the participants tend to take photographs that are related to the icon images.

Keywords: Wearable display · HMD · Smartphone · Priming effect

1 Introduction

There are several display devices from which users can get visual information such as smartphones and head-mounted displays (HMDs), and their numbers and models increase annually. One feature of smartphones is that their displays are bigger than those of conventional mobile phones. Many HMDs have been created for daily use, such as Google Glass[1], M100[2], and Telepathy Walker[3]. With HMDs, users can browse information while moving or walking without resorting to hand-held devices.

---

[1] https://www.google.com/glass/.
[2] https://www.vuzix.com/Products/m100-smart-glasses.
[3] http://www.telepathywalker.com.

© Springer International Publishing AG, part of Springer Nature 2018
J. Xiao et al. (Eds.): ICCC 2018, LNCS 10971, pp. 71–85, 2018.
https://doi.org/10.1007/978-3-319-94307-7_6

Our physical and mental behavior are affected by what we see. Unlike real-world scenes in which what we see changes naturally, the content presented on smartphone displays and HMDs can be intentionally changed by others. We think that it is important to investigate how the images shown on smartphone displays and HMDs affect human behavior. Especially, HMD users are presented with information anytime, anywhere. This is called passive browsing. Because users frequently see images on HMDs without consciously considering the images, they are possibly more affected by them.

On the basis of the above idea, we have studied the priming effects on HMDs. Priming is the phenomenon in which a human is unconsciously attracted to a subsequent processing by being given preceding stimuli [1]. We hypothesize that the images shown on HMDs cause priming effects for users and that their attention to real-world objects therefore change. In previous studies, we have examined whether participants changed what they saw in the real world in accordance with the images shown on HMDs [2]. During the experiment, we focused on the effect of the difference in application icon images on the basis of the idea that users have many opportunities to see the icon images during daily use. We evaluated whether there were differences in photos taken by the participants in regard to three icon images. As a result, the participants tended to take many photographs related to the icon images. However, our evaluation only used HMDs, and no comparisons were made with other displays in the experiment. In addition, we had only 15 participants. We need to investigate what the difference in the effects between HMDs and other displays are.

So far, smartphone displays have not been found to problematically affect human behavior. Any possible effects are currently unknown. We now expect an increase in HMD users, who have different display watching habits. If there are any effects by the images presented, we conjecture that there are also problems, e.g., users may have their attention drawn to specific advertisements or develop a negative emotional response to certain content. In addition, we can grasp that there are some concerns that we have to consider when using HMDs in the future.

In this study, we investigate whether there are any changes in what smartphone/HMD users see casually and whether there are any differences in the effects between HMDs and smartphone displays. We assume that the priming effects of HMDs are greater than those of smartphones because HMDs are closer to users' eyes, and users frequently see the display.

The remainder of this paper is organized as follows. In Sect. 2, we explain related work. We then describe the experiment in Sect. 3 and present our considerations in Sect. 4. Finally, we present our conclusion and future work in Sect. 5.

2   Related Work

HMDs are not generally commonplace yet. However, because various uses of HMDs have been studied, they are expected to become commonplace in the near future. Okada et al. have proposed a system that supports masters of ceremonies by using HMD [3]. The masters of ceremonies can smoothly moderate because the system presents speech content, the title of performance, and the time schedule on HMD. A maintenance support system recognizes detailed operations such as using a screwdriver and air pump during the maintenance of a bike and automatically displays the blueprint of a working part or an alert if a user makes an error [4]. A communication support system for talking with foreigners presents foreign language translations on an HMD in real time and automatically displays information related to the conversation [5]. Washington et al. have developed a system for automatic facial expression recognition running on the HMD, delivering real-time social cues to children with Autism Spectrum Disorder (ASD) [6]. They found that children with ASD generally respond well to wearing the system at home and opt for the most expressive feedback choice. Williams et al. have investigated the design of vocabulary prompts on the HMD for individuals with aphasia [7]. They experimented in each of the laboratory and the actual use environment and verified the validity based on the use cases and the interviews for the users. Jain et al. proposed a system to support the localization of sound for hearing impaired persons by presenting the visualization information of the sound on the HMD [8]. They created multiple visualization design proposal for several categories such as the granularity of the direction. There is a problem that deaf and hard of hearing students must constantly switch between several visual sources to gather all necessary information during a classroom lecture (e.g., instructor, slides, sign language interpreter or captioning). Using smart glasses, Miller et al. tested a potential means to reduce the effects of visual field switches, proposing that consolidating sources into a single display may improve lecture comprehension [9].

Additionally, several types of fundamental research have been conducted for daily use of HMDs. Tanaka et al. proposed an information layout method for an optical see-through HMD that considers viewability on the basis of a sight behind the display [10]. The layout for displaying information is dynamically changed to ensure better recognition of the information. Nakao et al. have proposed an information presentation method that takes into account the surrounding environment [11]. They have confirmed that it is difficult to look at HMDs while walking in crowds and up stairs and revealed that the eye movement between an HMD and the surrounding environment leads to eye strain. Profita et al. have focused on use cases for supporting persons with disabilities using HMDs and other wearable devices in everyday life [12]. They revealed that we do not feel discomfort when using such devices for those purposes and showed guidelines for designing HMDs. Haynes et al. conducted a study on visual comfort while reading using an opaque HMD displaced laterally [13]. The results of the study suggested that an HMD displaced laterally up to 10° may be acceptable to casual users without any sacrifice in performance, and an HMD displaced up to 20° may be usable in an industrial setting where preference is less important. Wichrowski et al. conducted a workshop concerning the implementation of applications for the Google Glass platform [14].

Many studies examined how presenting specific information affects humans. The mere-exposure effect is a psychological phenomenon in which the affection for impression of a certain object increases if a person repeatedly has contact with the object [15]. The effect has been reported to increase as the amount of contact increases. If a user is always presented with a specific image on a smartphone or an HMD, it is considered that he/she will favor it after seeing it many times. Shibata et al. confirmed that participants tend to have affection for a face if the activity of the brain's cingulate cortex approaches a state of favor while being shown a specific picture of a face [16]. In the future, if emotion recognition technology advances, and smartphones or HMDs are capable of using it, it becomes possible to change an image on a display and make a user respond to it in a favorable manner when the smartphone or HMD recognizes the users' favorable disposition. Vickery et al. argued that users can quickly find a target by looking at images of the target in advance [17]. When looking at something, it is important to look at and perceive the target. Lupyan et al. used these facts to demonstrate that users can find a target in a shorter time frame by repeating aloud the name of the target [18]. Harris et al. demonstrated that TV food advertising increases snack consumption and may contribute to the obesity epidemic [19]. The Memory Glasses [20] are a wearable, proactive, context-aware memory aid by that presents visual textual priming in wearable displays. Shantz et al. revealed that people who are shown a photo of a woman winning a race performed better on a brainstorming task [21]. In our study, we suspect that presenting such specific information can affect the user and lead him/her to a certain real-world object.

Several types of research have been conducted on the priming effect [22–24]. Jacoby et al. reported that the priming effect persists more than 24 h [25]. Several attempts apply the priming effect to certain situations. The effect is often used for language education because it has been proved that humans tend to use similar sentence patterns to those heard just before speaking [26,27]. For a simulation of a military reconnaissance mission, Luigi et al. utilized the effect to adjust participants' attitudes for the simulation with a virtual environment [28]. Chalfoun et al. designed adaptive Intelligent User Interfaces (IUI) with a subliminal learning technique aimed at enhancing the learner's inductive learning capabilities [29]. The IUI implementing subliminal cuing can indeed be used in both a 2D and 3D learning environment. Ring U [30] is a ring-shaped wearable system aimed at promoting emotional communications between people using vibro-tactile and color lighting expressions. The effect is used for the emotion of a text message as non-verbal stimuli.

3   Experimentation

In the experiment, we investigate the effect of software application icons in the everyday use of smartphones and HMDs. We examine how the images of application icons affect human behaviors by getting participants to take photos.

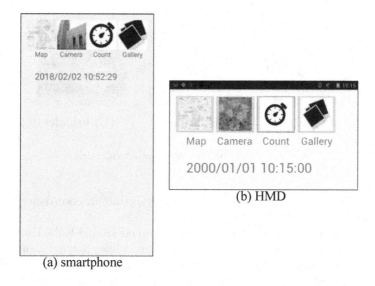

Fig. 1. Screenshots of applications

Although a smartphone/HMD user sets the standby screen by him-self/herself, the application icon image is set by others. In addition, because the user looks at the icon image when starting the application, it is important to study the effect. Hence, we investigate the effect of application icon images in this study. Incidentally, there is a difference between "only turning his/her eyes to something" and "perceiving after turning his/her eyes". It is difficult to record the difference by an eye-tracker. Because we also need to care about influences caused by wearing the eye-tracker, we use the photo-taking application to record the participants' perception. We have assumed that the participants tend to take photos that are related to the presented icon.

It is also important to examine the differences between smartphones and HMDs. If we are affected by the images on smartphones, it is necessary to re-examine the design guidelines of smartphone applications. If the images on HMDs have an effect, it is necessary to set guidelines before HMDs become commonplace. We have hypothesized that the effects from images on HMDs are greater than those of smartphones because users see the images on HMDs anytime, anywhere.

3.1 Experimental Method

For the experimentation, we implemented a software application that works on a smartphone and an HMD. Figure 1 shows the screenshots of the applications. We prepared three images for the icon of "Camera", which were "Building", "Nature", and "Vehicle" (as shown in Fig. 2). We divided participants into six groups for each icon image and smartphone/HMD. We investigated whether

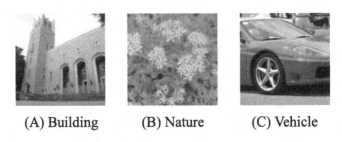

(A) Building   (B) Nature   (C) Vehicle

Fig. 2. Photos for icon image of applications

there was a change in photos taken by the participants in accordance with the icon image of the camera function.

In the experiment, the participants freely strolled around Kobe University or Aoyama Gakuin University (universities in Japan) while carrying a smartphone in their pocket or wearing an HMD. During the stroll, the participants took photos using the application. The shooting targets were what they casually caught sight of.

The application window is like a desktop. The application has four functions. The four icon images for each function of the application are "Map", "Camera", "Count", and "Gallery" from left in Fig. 1. If a user clicks the "Camera" icon, the application activates the camera function, and the user can take a photo.

The application window shows the current time. By indicating the time, we aimed to increase the opportunities in which the participants looked at the display. In addition, we wanted the participants to take several photos at several points. We prepared an interval time for the camera function. Because the application had a one-minute interval for taking the next photo, they could not continuously take photos at the same point. If the participants clicked the "Count" icon, they could check the interval time that they needed to wait until taking the next photo. The application has two other functions. The "Map" function shows a map of the user's surrounding. The "Gallery" function opens the gallery function of Android OS. By using these functions, we aimed to make the participants see the devices' displays naturally.

They used either the smartphone or the HMD, and no participants conducted the experiment using both. The smartphones used for the experiment were the GALAXY NEXUS by SAMSUNG (OS: Android 4.2.2) (as shown in Fig. 3) and the HTC One (OS: Android 5.0.2). The HMD was a Vuzix Corporation M100 (OS: Android 4.0.4) (as shown in Fig. 4). The screen size of the GALAXY NEXUS is 4.65 in., and that of the HTC One is 4.7 in. We can watch the display of the M100 as if it is at a distance of 35 cm from the user's eye, at a size of 4 in.

We told the participants how to operate the application and the experiment principles shown below were explained in advance.

– Stroll more than 30 min.
– Take photos of something the participant casually catches sight of.

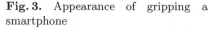

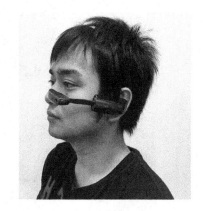

Fig. 3. Appearance of gripping a smartphone

Fig. 4. Appearance of wearing an HMD

- Take more than eight photos.
- Although the participant can activate sleep mode on the smartphone and put it in his/her pocket, leave the experimental application active when using the smartphone.
- When using the HMD, do not activate sleep mode while the display is active.
- Do not open other applications.

They did not know the purpose of the experiment during the experimentation. After the experimentation, we confirmed that all of them had not noticed the true purpose. The participants were 54 people (male: 48, female: 6) whose ages were 21–25. 34 people (smartphone: 15, HMD: 19) conducted the experiment at Kobe University, and 20 people (smartphone: 12, HMD: 8) conducted it at Aoyama Gakuin University. We divided them into six groups (icon images (3) × smartphone/HMD (2)). Each group had nine participants.

3.2 Results

The total number of photos taken was 814. We classified each photo into "Building", "Nature", "Vehicle", or "Other". Then, according to the number of classified photos, we investigated whether the selection of the objects shot had been influenced by the type of the icon image.

For the classification, two people independently and subjectively classified photos taken into four categories. Photos that they individually classified into the same category were used as results. 134 photos were not the same, and 680 photos were used for the evaluation. Each total number of photos classified into each category (Building, Nature, Vehicle, and Other) was 136, 107, 54, and 383 respectively. Figures 5 and 6 show examples of photos taken and the classification.

Building

Nature

Vehicle

Other

Classification by two persons does not match

Fig. 5. Classification example of photos taken by the smartphone

We evaluated the effects by calculating the proportion of each categorized photo taken by each participant. However, there were differences of the situations (e.g., the number of buildings and vehicles encountered) between Kobe University and Aoyama Gakuin University. Therefore, we adjusted the results according to the following procedure. At first, we divided each individual classified number ($T_{category:indiv.}$) by individual total ($T_{indiv.}$) and took the

Fig. 6. Classification example of photos taken by the HMD

number for each participant and multiplied it by 100 (as shown in Formula (1)). This value is I, which is the percentage value. We calculated each total number ($IT_{category:univ.}$) of each category of Kobe University and Aoyama Gakuin University respectively and divided the value of I by the total number (as shown in Formula (2)). This value is II, which is the normalized value. I is the number of photos in each category when it is assumed that each participant takes 100 photos. II is the value that takes into account the ease of taking pictures for each category at each experimental site.

$$I_{category} = T_{category:indiv.}/T_{indiv.} * 100 \qquad (1)$$
$$II_{category} = I_{category}/IT_{category:univ.} \qquad (2)$$

Table 1. Result (smartphone)

Group	Category	Mean	S.D.
Gr.SP-b	Building	0.036	0.038
	Nature	0.039	0.037
	Vehicle	0.027	0.026
	Other	0.044	0.013
Gr.SP-b	Building	0.038	0.045
	Nature	0.043	0.041
	Vehicle	0.040	0.044
	Other	0.038	0.011
Gr.SP-b	Building	0.016	0.018
	Nature	0.018	0.024
	Vehicle	0.058	0.070
	Other	0.056	0.019

Table 2. Result (HMD)

Group	Category	Mean	S.D.
Gr.HMD-b	Building	0.065	0.041
	Nature	0.033	0.028
	Vehicle	0.013	0.019
	Other	0.030	0.016
Gr.HMD-n	Building	0.031	0.020
	Nature	0.051	0.015
	Vehicle	0.048	0.021
	Other	0.030	0.011
Gr.HMD-v	Building	0.036	0.022
	Nature	0.040	0.033
	Vehicle	0.042	0.048
	Other	0.028	0.019

The group with which the participants experimented while watching the "Building" icon with the smartphone is shown as Gr.SP-b, and similarly shown as Gr.SP-n and Gr.SP-v (SP: smartphone, b: "Building", n: "Nature", and v: "Vehicle"). The group with which the participants experimented while watching the "Building" icon with the HMD is shown as Gr.HMD-b and similarly shown as Gr.HMD-n and Gr.HMD-v. Tables 1, 2 and Figs. 7, 8 show the mean and the standard deviation of each category for the value of II in each group. In the HMD groups' results, the proportion of photos classified into the same category as the viewing icon is the largest for each group (e.g. in the result of Gr.HMD-b, the result of the "Building" category is the largest) for all icons. In the smartphone groups' results, the proportion of photos classified into the same category is the largest for each group except Gr.SP-b. In the classification into each category, the proportion for the result of the group that was viewing the same type of icon as each category is the largest (e.g. in the result of the "Building" category, the result of Gr.HMD-b is the largest in the HMD groups) except the smartphone groups' "Building" category and the HMD groups' "Vehicle" category.

For the value of II, we conducted a three-way factorial ANOVA (between-subjects factor) by tools (smartphone or HMD) × icon image groups × classified categories. The interaction between the icon image groups and the classified categories had a significant difference ($F_{(6,144)} = 2.36$, $p < .05$). Additionally, the interaction between the tools and the classified categories had a significant tendency ($F_{(3,144)} = 2.16$, $p < .10$). Other interactions and the main effect of tools did not have significant differences. Then, we tested each simple main effect for the interaction between the icon image groups × the classified categories. As a result, the "Building" icon group has a significant tendency ($F_{(3,144)} = 2.26$, $p < .10$). According to the multiple comparisons with the LSD method, II of the building category is more than that of the vehicle category ($MS_e = 0.0012$, $p < .05$). Next, we tested each simple main effect for the interaction between the tools × the classified categories. As a result, the smartphone groups significantly had taken many photos of the other category ($F_{(1,48)} = 14.55$, $p < .01$).

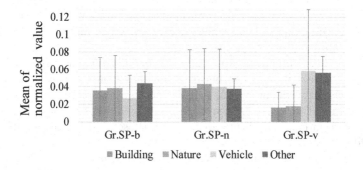

Fig. 7. Results graph (smartphone)

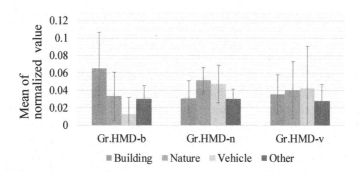

Fig. 8. Results graph (HMD)

4   Considerations

In the HMD groups' results, the proportion of the photos classified into the same category as the viewing icon was the largest. For two results of the smartphone groups, the proportion classified into the same category was the largest. There was a significant difference between the icon image groups and the classified categories for the interaction. From these results, it is possible that icon images affect what users casually turn their eyes toward. In addition, there was a significant tendency between the tools and the classified categories. However, the result showed only that the participants who used the smartphone had significantly taken more "Other" category photos than the HMD users. We could not get the result in which the effects from the images on the HMD were greater than those of the smartphone. The participants who used the smartphone had taken many photos of signage and some roadside and road objects that could be categorized as "Other". Because an HMD's camera lens is on the side of the user's eye, use of the camera is restricted by posture when taking a photo. Therefore, the user may possibly have difficulty taking photos of certain objects. In this study, there were only 54 participants, and we conducted the ANOVA with the between-subjects factor. Hereafter, we need to increase the number of participants and continue the experimentation.

We had a brief interview after the experiment. A participant who used a smartphone while watching the nature icon image said "I saw a convenience store when the experiment began, so I decided to take pictures of convenience stores." He was affected not by the display but by objects in the real world. We need to investigate which effects are greater, those of the displays or those of real-world objects.

In the experiment, we used three photos as the icon images. We assigned the participants to six groups randomly without consideration of their interests. If they are presented with images that are related to their interests, there are both possibilities that the effects are high or low. On the other hand, it is also necessary to investigate the effects of abstract images. If the participants are presented with abstract images such as circles and squares as icons, they might take many photos of round and square objects.

In addition, we will probe the effects on the size of the image because smartphone displays are sometimes large. We will examine whether there is a difference between the icon image and the background image for the effects on user behavior.

We confirmed that the icon image has an effect on the selection of the shooting target. For example, it is possible to take photos of sights or specific attractions by using the images related to them as icons when a user goes sightseeing. Furthermore, it is useful for finding information in the real world. We would often overlook information on a poster or public display even though the information is related to our interests, such as information on a favorite artist or bargain sale. Our findings decrease such oversights by presenting related images on the smartphone or the HMD.

There are also some risks. Smartphones and HMDs can detect a user's position by using GPS. When a device recognizes that a user has approached a convenience store, it is possible to exploit the opportunity for the user to make an impulse purchase by displaying an image of a specific product. While avoiding such adverse use, it is necessary to continue investigating the effects for a future in which HMDs are expected to be commonplace.

5 Conclusion

In this study, we examined how presented visual information (even in the form of a small icon) affected human behaviors. We hypothesized that an image on a smartphone display and an HMD affects a user's mental and physical behavior.

We conducted an experiment in which participants took photos using a smartphone or an HMD. We prepared three icon images for a camera function of the experimentation application. By dividing 54 participants into six groups (smartphone/HMD (2) × icon images (3)), we examined how the photos taken by the participants change in accordance with the icon images. Results showed that the participants tended to take photos that were related to presented information. However, there was no significant difference between the HMD and the smartphones.

In the future, we will extend the experiment to evaluate how users are affected by images such as simple animations, illustrations, and photos. Although we used visual information related to "Building", "Nature", and "Vehicle" in this experimentation, we will evaluate how the system works when users select interests themselves.

Acknowledgements. This research was supported in part by a Grant in aid for Precursory Research for Embryonic Science and Technology (PRESTO) and CREST from the Japan Science and Technology Agency.

References

1. Turving, E., Schacter, D.L.: Priming and human memory systems. Science **247**(4940), 301–306 (1990)
2. Isoyama, N., Terada, T., Tsukamoto, M.: An evaluation on behaviors in taking photos by changing icon images on head mounted display. In: Proceedings of New frontiers of Quantified Self Workshop, UbiComp/ISWC Adjunct 2015, pp. 985–990 (2015)
3. Okada, T., Yamamoto, T., Terada, T., Tsukamoto, M.: Wearable MC system: a system for supporting MC performances using wearable computing technologies. In: Proceedings of the 2nd Augmented Human Conference (AH 2011), no. 25, pp. 1–7 (2011)
4. Stiefmeier, T., Ogris, G., Junker, H., Lukowicz, P., Tröster, G.: Combining motion sensors and ultrasonic hands tracking for continuous activity recognition in a maintenance scenario. In: Proceedings of the 10th International Symposium on Wearable Computers (ISWC 2006), pp. 97–104 (2006)
5. Pham, N.V., Terada, T., Tsukamoto, M., Nishio, S.: An information retrieval system for supporting casual conversation in wearable computing environments. In: Proceedings of the 5th International Workshop on Smart Appliances and Wearable Computing (IWSAWC 2005), pp. 477–483 (2005)
6. Washington, P., Voss, C., Kline, A., Haber, N., Daniels, J., Fazel, A., De, T., Feinstein, C., Winograd, T., Wall, D.: SuperpowerGlass: a wearable aid for the at-home therapy of children with Autism. In: Proceedings of the ACM on Interactive, Mobile, Wearable and Ubiquitous Technologies, vol. 1, issue (3), pp. 1–22 (2017)

7. Williams, K., Moffatt, K., McCall, D.: Designing conversation cues on a head-worn display to support persons with Aphasia. In: Proceedings of the 33rd Annual ACM Conference on Human Factors in Computing Systems (CHI 2015), pp. 231–240 (2015)

8. Jain, D., Findlater, L., Gilkeson, J., Holland, B., Duraiswami, R., Zotkin, D., Gallaudet, C.V., Froehlich, J.E.: Head-mounted display visualizations to support sound awareness for the deaf and hard of hearing. In: Proceedings of the 33rd Annual ACM Conference on Human Factors in Computing Systems (CHI 2015), pp. 241–250 (2015)

9. Miller, A., Malasig, J., Castro, B., Hanson, V.L., Nicolau, H., Brandaõ, A.: The use of smart glasses for lecture comprehension by deaf and hard of hearing students. In: Proceedings of the 2017 CHI Conference Extended Abstracts on Human Factors in Computing Systems (CHI EA 2017), pp. 1909–1915 (2017)

10. Tanaka, K., Kishino, Y., Miyamae, M., Terada, T., Nishio, S.: An information layout method for an optical see-through head mounted display focusing on the viewability. In: Proceedings of the 7th IEEE/ACM International Symposium on Mixed and Augmented Reality (ISMAR 2008), pp. 139–142 (2008)

11. Nakao, M., Terada, T., Tsukamoto, M.: An information presentation method for head mounted display considering surrounding environments. In: Proceedings of the 5th Augmented Human Conference (AH 2014), no. 47, pp. 1–8 (2014)

12. Profita, H., Albaghli, R., Findlater, L., Jaeger, P., Kane, S.K.: The AT effect: how disability affects the perceived social acceptability of head-mounted display use. In: Proceedings of the 34th Annual ACM Conference on Human Factors in Computing Systems (CHI 2016), pp. 4884–4895 (2016)

13. Haynes, M., Starner, T.: Effects of head-worn display lateral position on visual comfort while reading. In: Proceedings of the 21st International Symposium on Wearable Computers (ISWC 2017), pp. 176–177 (2017)

14. Wichrowski, M., Koržinek, D., Szklanny, K.: Google glass development in practice: UX design sprint workshops. In: Proceedings of the Mulitimedia, Interaction, Design and Innovation (MIDI 2015), article no. 11, pp. 1–12 (2015)

15. Zajonc, R.B.: Attitudinal effects of mere exposure. J. Pers. Soc. Psychol. 9(2, Pt. 2), 1–27 (1968)

16. Shibata, K., Watanabe, T., Kawato, M., Sasaki, Y.: Differential activation patterns in the same brain region led to opposite emotional states. PLoS Biol. 14(9), 1–27 (2016)

17. Vickery, T.J., King, L.W., Jiang, Y.: Setting up the target template in visual search. J. Vis. 5(1), 81–92 (2005)

18. Lupyan, G., Swingley, D.: Self-directed speech affects visual search performance. Q. J. Exp. Psychol. 65(6), 1068–1085 (2011)

19. Harris, J.L., Bargh, J.A., Brownell, K.D.: Priming effects of television food advertising on eating behavior. Health Psychol. 28(4), 404–413 (2009)

20. DeVaul, R.W., Pentland, A., Corey, V.R.: The memory glasses: subliminal vs. overt memory support with imperfect information. In: Proceedings of the 7th International Symposium on Wearable Computers (ISWC 2003), pp. 146–153 (2003)

21. Shantz, A., Latham, G.P.: An exploratory field experiment of the effect of subconscious and conscious goals on employee performance. Organ. Behav. Hum. Decis. Process. 109, 9–17 (2009)

22. Zhong, C., Liljenquist, K.: Washing away your sins: threatened morality and physical cleansing. Science 313(5792), 1451–1452 (2006)

23. Kay, A.C., Wheeler, S.C., Bargh, J.A., Ross, L.: Material priming: the influence of mundane physical objects on situational construal and competitive behavioral choice. Organ. Behav. Hum. Decis. Process. **95**, 83–96 (2004)
24. Peña, J., Blackburn, K.: The priming effects of virtual environments on interpersonal perceptions and behaviors. J. Commun. **63**(4), 703–720 (2013)
25. Jacoby, L.L., Dallas, M.: On the relationship between autobiographical memory and perceptual learning. J. Exp. Psychol. General **110**(3), 306–340 (1981)
26. Pickering, M.J., Ferreira, V.S.: Structural priming: a critical review. Psychol. Bull. **134**(3), 427–459 (2008)
27. McDonough, K., Kim, Y.: Syntactic priming, type frequency, and EFL learners' production of Wh-questions. Modern Lang. J. **93**(3), 386–398 (2009)
28. Luigi, D.P., Tortell, R., Morie, J., Dozois, A.: Effects of priming on behavior in virtual environments (2006)
29. Chalfoun, P., Frasson, C.: Subliminal cues while teaching: HCI technique for enhanced learning. Adv. Hum.-Comput. Interact. **2011**(2), 1–15 (2011)
30. Pradana, G.A., Cheok, A.D., Inami, M., Tewell, J., Choi, Y.: Emotional priming of mobile text messages with ring-shaped wearable device using color lighting and tactile expressions. In: Proceedings of the 5th Augmented Human Conference (AH 2014), no. 14, pp. 1–8 (2014)

An Efficient Diagnosis System for Thyroid Disease Based on Enhanced Kernelized Extreme Learning Machine Approach

Chao Ma[1], Jian Guan[2], Wenyong Zhao[1], and Chaolun Wang[3(✉)]

[1] College of Digital Media, Shenzhen Institute of Information Technology,
Shenzhen 518172, China
[2] Computer Application Research Center, Shenzhen Graduate School,
Harbin Institute of Technology, Shenzhen 518055, China
[3] DFH Satellite Co., Ltd., Beijing 100094, China
`carc_2016@outlook.com`

Abstract. In this paper, we present a novel hybrid diagnosis system named LFDA-EKELM, which integrates local fisher discriminant analysis (LFDA) and kernelized extreme learning machine method for thyroid disease diagnosis. The proposed method comprises of three stages. Focusing on dimension reduction, the first stage employs LFDA as a feature extraction tool to construct more discriminative subspace for classification, the system switches from feature extraction to model construction. And then, the obtained feature subsets are fed into designed kernelized ELM (KELM) classifier to train an optimal predictor model whose parameters are adaptively specified by improving artificial bee colony (IABC) approach. Here, the proposed IABC method introduces an improved solution search equation to enhance the exploitation of searching for solutions, and provides a new framework to make the global converge rapidly. Finally, the enhanced-KELM (EKELM) model is applied to perform the thyroid disease diagnosis tasks using the most discriminative feature subset and the optimal parameters. The effectiveness of the proposed system is evaluated on the thyroid disease dataset in terms of classification accuracy. Experimental results demonstrate that LFDA-EKELM outperforms the baseline methods.

Keywords: Kernelized extreme learning machine
Artificial bee colony algorithm · Feature extraction · Medical diagnosis

1 Introduction

The thyroid gland is an important organ located in the front of the neck just below the skin and muscle layers. It takes the shape of butterfly and connects two cone-like lobes, the left lobe (lobus sinister) and the right lobe (lobus dexter) which wrap around the trachea. The primary function of the thyroid gland is to secrete two active thyroid hormones, triiodothyronine (abbreviated T3) and thyroxine (abbreviated T4). These hormones can help control the body temperature, influence the heart rate and regulate the production of protein. As a result, thyroid function influences every cell in the body

© Springer International Publishing AG, part of Springer Nature 2018
J. Xiao et al. (Eds.): ICCC 2018, LNCS 10971, pp. 86–101, 2018.
https://doi.org/10.1007/978-3-319-94307-7_7

and regulates the body's metabolism. In general, thyroid disease can be divided into two types of disorders: Hypothyroidism and Hyperthyroidism. For the former case, the thyroid gland produces too little thyroid hormone. On the contrary, for the latter case, the thyroid is overactive and produces too much thyroid hormone. Both types of disorders are relatively common in the general population. There are many different reasons why either of these conditions might develop. A common method, called the thyroid-stimulating hormone (TSH) test which can be used to identify thyroid disorders even before the onset of symptoms.

In fact, the thyroid function diagnosis can be formulated as an important classification problem. Machine learning techniques are increasingly adopted in this area owing to its strong ability of distinguishing complex information in the medical data. In 1997, Serpen et al. [1] proposed Probabilistic Potential Function Neural Network (PPFNN) classification algorithm and the classification accuracy was 78.14%. In 2002, Ozylimaz et al. [2] adopted three neural network methods including Multi Layer Perceptron (MLP), Radial Basis Function (RBF) and adaptive Conic Section Function Neural Network (CSFNN) to interpret thyroid disease, and the classification accuracies were 86.33%, 89.8% and 91.14% separately. In 2004, Pasi et al. [3] employed Linear Discriminant Analysis (LDA), C4.5 with default learning parameters (C4.5-1), C4.5 with parameter C equal to 5 (C4.5-2), C4.5 with parameter C equal to 95 (C4.5-3) and DIMLP five methods to perform classification, and result accuracies were 81.34%, 93.26%, 92.81%, 92.94% and 94.86% respectively. Polat et al. [4] combined Artificial Immune Recognition System (AIRS) with a developed fuzzy weighted pre-processing to achieve an accuracy of 85%. In 2008, Keles et al. [5] proposed an expert system for thyroid diagnosis called ESTDD, the corresponding accuracy was 95.33%. In 2009, Multi Layer Perception with Levenberg-Marquardt (LM) method was proposed by Temurtas [6] for the diagnosis, whose accuracy was 93.19%. In 2011, 91.86% classification accuracy was obtained by using a Generalized Discriminant Analysis (GDA) and Wavelet SVM (GDA-WSVM) algorithm [7]. In 2011, Chen [8] used particle swarm optimization to optimize SVM with fisher score for thyroid diagnosis, and the average accuracy of 97.49% was obtained. In 2012, Li et al. [9] attempted to utilize Extreme Learning Machine (ELM) and Principle Component Analysis (PCA) to assist the task of thyroid diagnosis with the mean accuracy of 97.73%. In 2017, Xia et al. [10] proposed ELM-based approach for thyroid cancer detection and achieved accuracy of 87.72%.

In this paper, we further investigate the effectiveness of the ELM-based approach by solving the thyroid disease diagnosis problem. The kernelized ELM [11] (KELM) learning framework is proposed for the thyroid disease diagnosis task [12]. The KELM with Gaussian kernel nodes doesn't need to know the feature mapping function $h(x)$ of ELM, which has no input weights and hidden biases parameters influence, and it can achieve a good generalization performance in most classification and regression cases.

The parameters in designing KELM are penalty parameter C and gamma γ of Gaussian function. They play a significant role in model design. Regarding the parameter setting, feature selection or feature extraction before building the classification tasks can improve the efficiency and effectiveness of classification accuracy. A feature extraction method, Local Fisher Discriminant Analysis (LFDA) is often examined. LFDA is an extension of Fisher Discriminant Analysis (FDA) which localizes the evaluation of the within-class scatter.

Therefore, in order to improve the efficiency and effectiveness of the classification accuracy for thyroid disease diagnosis, a diagnosis system (LFDA-EKELM) is introduced. The main idea of the proposed system is firstly to employ LFDA to reduce the dimension of the thyroid dataset, then, the obtained reduced feature subset can be served as the input of the designed enhanced-KELM (EKELM) classifier for training an optimal predictor model whose parameters are adaptively adjusted by improved ABC algorithm. Finally, the obtained most discriminative feature subset and the optimal parameters are used for the KELM predictor model to perform the thyroid disease diagnosis task. The objective of the proposed system is to exploit the maximum generalization capability of the KELM based method in diagnosing the thyroid disease problem. The adaptive improved ABC algorithm is proposed to further accelerate and balance the local and global search in ABC, which will lead to a better solution with quick converge rate and less running time. In the optimization stage, we take into account the classification accuracy and number of hidden nodes simultaneously in designing the objective function to exploit the maximum generalization capability of KELM with more compact structure of networks.

The rest of the paper is organized as follows. Section 2 gives brief background knowledge on LFDA and KELM, the improved ABC algorithm is also proposed briefly in this section. The implementation details of the LFDA-EKELM diagnosis system are described in Sect. 3. Section 4 presents the experimental design. Section 5 shows the experimental results and discussion of the proposed method. Conclusions and future work are summarized in Sect. 6.

2 Proposed Method

2.1 Local Fisher Discriminant Analysis

Local fisher discriminant analysis (LFDA) is a relatively new linear supervised dimensionality reduction method for pattern classification, which seeks to maximize between-class separability and preserve within-class local structure at the same time. And LFDA can be practically used for dimensionality reduction into any dimensional spaces, it evaluates the levels of the between-class scatter and the within-class scatter in a local manner. LFDA works well even when within-class multimodality or outliers exist, which has shown its practical usefulness and high scalability in classification tasks through extensive simulation studies in [13].

Let $\tilde{S}^{(w)}$ and $\tilde{S}^{(b)}$ be the local within-class scatter matrix and the local between-class scatter matrix, which are given as follows

$$\tilde{S}^{(w)} = \frac{1}{2} \sum_{i,j=1}^{n} \tilde{W}_{i,j}^{(w)} \left(x_i - x_j \right) \left(x_i - x_j \right)^T \tag{1}$$

$$\tilde{S}^{(b)} = \frac{1}{2} \sum_{i,j=1}^{n} \tilde{W}_{i,j}^{(b)} (x_i - x_j)(x_i - x_j)^T \tag{2}$$

where

$$\tilde{W}_{i,j}^{(w)} \equiv \begin{cases} A_{i,j}/n_l & \text{if } y_i = y_j, \\ 0 & \text{if } y_i \neq y_j \end{cases} \tag{3}$$

$$\tilde{W}_{i,j}^{(b)} \equiv \begin{cases} A_{i,j}(1/n - 1/n_l) & \text{if } y_i = y_j, \\ 1/n & \text{if } y_i \neq y_j \end{cases} \tag{4}$$

Where n_l denotes the number of label samples in class y_i. $A_{i,j}$ is an affinity value between x_i and x_j based on the local scaling heuristic, it is defined as follows:

$$A_{i,j} = \exp\left(-\frac{\|x_i - x_j\|^2}{\sigma_i \sigma_j}\right) \tag{5}$$

The parameter σ_i represents the local scaling around x_i defined by $\sigma_i = \|x_i - x_i^{(k)}\|$, here $x_i^{(k)}$ is the k-th nearest neighbor of x_i. According to the affinity $A_{i,j}$, LFDA algorithm weights the values for the sample pairs in the same class. The LFDA transformation matrix T_{LFDA} is defined as:

$$T_{LFDA} \equiv \underset{T \in R^{d \times r}}{\arg\max} \left[tr\left(\left(T^T \tilde{S}^{(w)} T\right)^{-1} T^T \tilde{S}^{(b)} T \right) \right] \tag{6}$$

That is, to seek a transformation T such that nearby data pairs in the same class are made close and the data pairs in different classes can be separated from each other.

2.2   Kernelized Extreme Learning Machine

The ELM algorithm is originally developed for training single hidden-layer feed-forward neural networks (SLFNs), and then extended to the "generalized" SLFNs. The output function of ELM is defined as follows:

$$f_L(x) = \sum_{i=1}^{L} \beta_i h_i(x) = \text{h}(x)\beta \tag{7}$$

where $\beta = [\beta_1, \beta_2, \ldots, \beta_L]^T$ is the output weight connecting hidden nodes and the output nodes. $H = \{h_{ij}\}$ ($i = 1, \ldots, N$ and $j = 1, \ldots, L$) is called the hidden layer output matrix of the neural network. $h(x)$ actually maps the data from the d-dimensional input space to the L-dimensional hidden-layer feature space H.

The determination of the output weights is computed by means of the least-squares method:

$$\beta' = H^+T \qquad (8)$$

where H^+ is the Moore-Penrose generalized inverse of the hidden layer output matrix H.

To calculate the Moore-Penrose generalized inverse of matrix [14], the orthogonal projection method is adopted: $H^+ = H^T(HH^T)^{-1}$. Finally, the output function is formulized as

$$f(x) = h\beta = h(x)H^T(I/C + HH^T)^{-1}T \qquad (9)$$

When the feature mapping $h(x)$ is unknown to users, a kernel matrix for the ELM is adopted according to the following equation:

$$\Omega_{ELM} = HH^T : \Omega_{ELMi,j} = h(x_i) \cdot h(x_j) = K(x_i, x_j) \qquad (10)$$

So that the output function of KELM classifier can be expressed as follows

$$\begin{aligned}
f(x) = h\beta &= h(x)H^T(I/C + HH^T)^{-1}T \\
&= \begin{bmatrix} K(x, x_1) \\ \vdots \\ K(x, x_N) \end{bmatrix}^T (I/C + \Omega_{ELM})^{-1}T
\end{aligned} \qquad (11)$$

2.3 Improved Artificial Bee Colony

ABC was inspired by the intelligent foraging behavior of honey bees, which was developed for real-parameter optimization [15]. The honey bees consist of three groups: employed bees, onlookers and scout bees. The employed bees search the food source position and store in their memory, and then they pass food information to onlookers, onlookers select the candidate food source from the old ones provided by employed bees.

However, there is still insufficiency in ABC regarding its solution search, which is good at exploration but poor at exploitation. To address this problem, inspired by the differential evolution, we propose an improved method for solution update of employer bees. In our method, the bees search only around the best feasible solution found so far to improve the exploitation. Thus the following update strategy can be applied to enhance exploitation, make converge more quickly:

$$v_{i,j} = x_{r1,j} + F * (x_{best,j} - x_{r1,j}) + F * (x_{r2,j} - x_{r3,j}) \qquad (12)$$

where $v_{i,j}$ is the new candidate solution, x_{r1}, x_{r2}, x_{r3} are selected randomly from the current population, the indices $r1$, $r2$, $r3$ are mutually exclusive integers selected from {1, 2, ..., SN}. SN represents the size of population. F is referred to amplification factor, it is typically a real value in the interval of [−1, 1] that controls the rate at which the population evolves. This strategy relying on the best solution found so far converges rapidly, moreover, two-difference-vectors-based strategy could lead to a better perturbation than one-difference-vector-based strategy. Although the new strategy increases the local research ability, the solution could be easily entrapped in a local optimum. In order to resolve this issue, we introduce a new adjustment mechanism whenever the solution stagnates in the local optimum, the equation is shown as follows:

$$v_{i,j} = x_{i,j} + F * \omega * x_{i,j} \tag{13}$$

where $v_{i,j}$ is a new feasible solution, it is modified from the current position, $\omega = \omega_{min} + \dfrac{MCN - Cycle}{MCN} * (\omega_{max} - \omega_{min})$, the values of ω_{max} and ω_{min} represent the maximum and minimum percentage of the position adjustment respectively. MCN is the maximum cycle number of search process. The solution in the first iteration could be far from the optimal solution and in later iterations, it will converge closely to the optimal solution at fast speed. To enhance the global convergence, the onlooker phase and scout phase will be replaced by an unified search mechanism phase. Equation (13) will be computed with a given probability P to avoid premature convergence, to balance the exploration of the solution search and the exploitation of the adjusted solution search.

3   The Proposed LFDA-EKELM Diagnosis System

In this section, we describe the proposed LFDA-EKELM system for thyroid disease diagnosis. The proposed approach includes two stages. In the first stage, feature extraction is conducted by employing LFDA to eliminate the redundant features and further enhance the classification performance. In the second stage, KELM model is trained on the training datasets via 10-fold CV to get the optimal parameter pair (C, γ), and then the obtained enhanced KELM model is used to perform the classification tasks. In order to achieve this goal, the improved ABC approach is proposed to deal with the parameter optimization. The appropriate feature subset got through LFDA is served as the input into the enhanced KELM (EKELM) model for classification. For EKELM, traditional method always sets the number of hidden nodes large enough, but we hope to get more compact structure of networks with smaller the number of hidden nodes. Therefore, LFDA-EKELM takes into account two fitness values, one is the classification accuracy and the other is the number of hidden nodes. The architecture of proposed system is shown in Fig. 1.

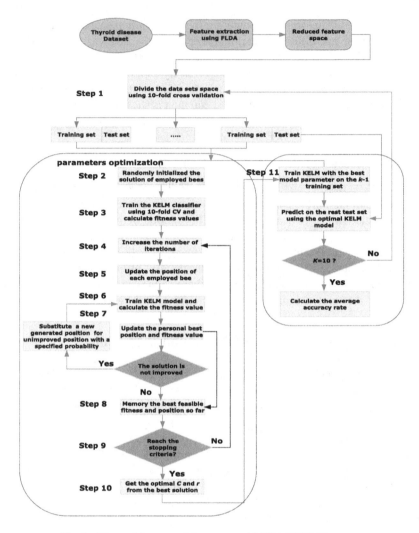

Fig. 1. The architecture of the proposed LFDA-EKELM system

The detailed pseudo-code for the classification procedure is as follows:

Begin
  For j =1 to k
      Training set = k-1 subsets   /*k-fold CV, where k=10*/
      Testing set = rest subset
         Train EKELM model on the training set using the feature subset got from
         feature extraction procedure to find parameter pair (C, γ).
         Test it on the test set and assigns the accuracy to $p(j)$, where p is a vector
         whose element is the corresponding accuracy achieved by each fold.
    End For   •
         Compute the mean value of vector p and store the mean accuracy and opti-
         mal parameter pair.
         Get the optimal parameter C and γ value whose corresponding mean CV
         accuracy is the highest.
         For j =1 to k
            Training set =k-1 subsets
            Testing set = rest subset
            Train the EKELM model on the training set using the obtained
            optimal parameter pair (C, γ)
            Test it on the rest set and save the mean accuracy.
         End For
         Return the average classification accuracy rates of EKELM.
End

3.1   The Feature Extraction and Feature Reduction Phase

Many studies have shown that feature extraction plays an important role in classification, especially for medical applications [16]. Feature extraction seeks to find one reduced representation set of features containing the most relevant information of the original data through transforming the input data into the set of reduced features. LFDA is applied for the thyroid dataset. It is used to eliminate the irrelevant or useless features, so that the dimension of the feature vector is reduced to a lower dimension. It not only improves the computation speed through dimension reduction but also preserves the high discriminate attributes, which increases the accuracy of the resulting model.

3.2   The Classification Phase

KELM model performs the classification tasks using the new feature obtained by LFDA. At first, there is a procedure to conduct the related parameters of KELM model. The regularization parameter C and parameter γ of the kernel function have an important impact on the performance of KELM. Thus we design an improved ABC optimization method to provide the parameters, and then validate the classification performance via the 10-fold CV analysis with these parameters. For each choice of the parameter, we test the average classification accuracy obtained by KELM, finally the one with the highest average accuracy is selected as the optimal parameter. Second, the KELM classifier is utilized to calculate the classification accuracy with the optimal parameter obtained using the reduced feature set, and the average accuracy is calculated as the final results.

The detail of these steps are given as follows:

Step 1: Pre-process the datasets. Separate the transformed dataset provided by LFDA using 10-fold CV method. Each subset consists of nine training set and one testing set;
Step 2: Initialize the individuals of the population with random numbers. Meanwhile, the IABC parameters include the size of the population, the lower and the upper bounds of the population, the number of iterations, etc.;
Step 3: Train KELM classifier with the initialized parameters in Step 2;

We aim to achieve a high classification result with compact structure of networks. Therefore, we take into account both of them in designing the linearly objective function. Here the fitness value is calculated as follows:

$$\begin{cases} f_1 = \text{ACC} \\ f_2 = 1 - L/N \\ f = a * f_1 + (1 - a) * f_2 \end{cases} \tag{14}$$

where ACC represents the classification accuracy rate obtained by the KELM classifier via 10-fold CV, N is the total number of datasets, L is the number of hidden nodes we used. The final objective function f is the weighted summation of the two sub-objective functions. Here, a indicates the weight for the KELM classification accuracy, and $1-a$ is the weight for the selected number of hidden nodes. The weight value can be adjusted to a proper value according to our preliminary experiments. It worth to note that the number of hidden nodes firstly is set up as $Lmin$ (the lower of nodes value). Then the number of hidden nodes is increased from $Lmin$ to $Lmax$ (the upper of nodes value) in interval of 1, and repeat the procedure to get average accuracies. When the average accuracy reaches at a predefined threshold, the corresponding number of hidden nodes is considered as the best value. After the fitness value is calculated, the global optimal fitness value and global personal position are saved;

Step 4: Increase the number of iterations: $iter = iter + 1$;
Step 5: Update the position of employed bee using Eq. (12) in each solution;
Step 6: Train KELM classifier with the result obtained in Step 5 and calculate the fitness value of each solution using Eq. (14);
Step 7: Update the personal optimal position and fitness value by comparing the current fitness value with the previous one. If the current fitness is worse than the previous one, substitute a new solution according to Eq. (13) for the previous one with a specified probability P to avoid getting stuck in a local optimum, and go to Step 6. Otherwise, go to Step 8.
Step 8: Update global optimal fitness value and global optimal position by comparing the fitness with optimal fitness from the whole solutions;
Step 9: If the stopping criteria is satisfied, then go to Step 10. Otherwise, go to Step 4. The termination criterion is that the iteration number achieves the maximum number of iterations;

Step 10:Get the optimal parameter value C and γ from the best solution;
Step 11: Classify the test dataset by KELM with the optimal value C and γ got from
Step 10, similarly, classify the test dataset using the trained KELM with 10 fold CV.
The average accuracy is achieved as a final performance measure.

4 Experimental Design

4.1 Data Description

In this section, we conduct experiments on the thyroid disease dataset provided by the
UCI machine learning repository. This dataset is usually utilized in many other classification systems, we carry out experiments on this dataset as compared other baseline
methods for thyroid disease diagnosis tasks. The dataset comprises of 215 patients with
5 continuous attributes. The overall features along with the description are listed in
Table 1, these individuals are classified into 3 categories based on the diagnosis result
including 150 cases for euthyroidism (normal), 35 cases of hyperthyroidism (hyper) and
30 cases of hypothyroidism (hypo).

Table 1. The detail of the 5 attributes of the thyroid disease dataset.

Attribute	Description	Mean	Std
F_1	T3-resin uptake test (A percentage)	109.595	13.145
F_2	Total serum thyroxin as measured by the isotopic displacement method	9.805	4.697
F_3	Total serum triiodothyronine as measured by radioimmuno assay	2.050	1.420
F_4	Basal thyroid-stimulating hormone (TSH) as measured by radioimmuno assay	2.880	6.118
F_5	Maximal absolute difference of TSH value after injection of 200 mg thyrotropin-releasing hormone compared to the basal value	4.199	8.071

Scaling is a necessary process to prevent the feature values in greater numeric ranges
from dominating those in smaller numeric ranges, and to reduce the numerical difficulties in the calculation. Therefore, datasets need to be normalized by scaling them into
the interval of $[-1,1]$. In this study, k-fold CV is used to evaluate classification results.
The value of k is set as 5. Then the average result over all five trials is calculated. The
advantage of this approach is that all the testing sets are independent. In addition, the
reliability of classification results can be improved.

4.2 Experimental Setup

The proposed LFDA-EKELM model was carried out on the platform of MATLAB 7.0.
Kernel function adopted was Gaussian function. Regarding SVM, LIBSVM implementation was used.

The detailed parameters setting for LFDA-EKELM was given as follows. The number of the iterations and population size were set to 100 and 20, respectively. The value of weight parameter a was equal to 0.75. The probability P value was set to be 0.7. According to our preliminary experiment, the value of w_{max} and w_{min} were set to 1 and 0.2 respectively. For Grid-SVM, the range of the related parameters C and γ were varied between $C = \{2^{-5}, 2^{-3}, \dots, 2^{15}\}$ and $\gamma = \{2^{-15}, 2^{-13}, \dots, 2^{1}\}$, and the grid search technique was employed using 10-fold CV to find out the optimal parameter values of RBF kernel function.

5   Experimental Results and Discussions

We conduct the LFDA-EKELM system with different number of hidden nodes range from 1 to 50. Table 2 provides the results of validation performance in terms of ACC obtained by LFDA-EKELM in the form of average accuracy, stand deviation (STD) and the used value of hidden nodes. Note that if the same best results are obtained with different number of hidden nodes, the smaller hidden nodes number value will be chosen because we hope to get the best performance of models with more compact structure of network. The best validation accuracy can be achieved with the number of hidden nodes are 27, 16, 23, 3 and 14 for different EKELM models corresponding to the reduced dimensionality are equal to 1, 2, 3, 4 and 5 respectively. For convenience, these models are sequentially named Model 1, Model 2, Model 3, Model 4 and Model 5 respectively. Therefore, these values of hidden nodes are chosen to create the training model for the classifiers based on different reduced dimensionality in subsequent analysis respectively.

Table 2. Results of classification of LFDA-EKELM with different reduced dimensions.

LFDA-EKELM	Performance metric	Mean	SD	Number of Hidden nodes
Model 1 Reduced dimension = 1	ACC (%)	97.21	1.04	27
Model 2 Reduced dimension = 2	ACC (%)	95.81	2.02	16
Model 3 Reduced dimension = 3	ACC (%)	96.28	1.27	23
Model 4 Reduced dimension = 4	ACC (%)	98.16	1.21	3
Model 5 Reduced dimension = 5	ACC (%)	98.18	0.95	14

From Table 2 we can see that the validation performance of classifiers with different reduced dimensionality. Among them, the best result can be achieved by Model 5 with respect to ACC. The best result is the highest ACC of 98.18% when the number of hidden nodes is equal to 14. The results of other four models achieved are smaller than Model 5. Although the performance of Model 4 is slightly smaller than that of Model 5, it is interesting to see that the standard deviation by Model 5 is smaller for the acquired performance.

The results of classification accuracy over 5 realizations of 10-fold CV on five models are shown in Fig. 2. It can be observed that Model 5 is slightly higher than that of Model 4 on the average, and obtains better results than others, and has a smaller standard deviation, which indicates Model 5 has excellent consistency and stability.

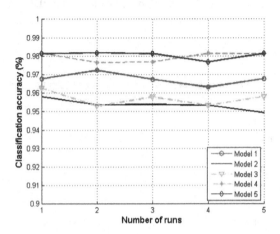

Fig. 2. The classification performance comparison among the five models over 5 runs

Table 3 shows the classification confusion matrix of the best LFDA-EKELM model running one time when the reduced dimension is equal to 5. The confusion matrix sums the 10 subsets in 10-fold CV. It can be seen from the table, LFDA-EKELM correctly classifies the whole 150 normal cases in the provided dataset. For the hyperthyroidism cases, three cases are misclassified as the normal ones, for the hypothyroidism, classifies only one case of hypothyroidism as the normal one.

Table 3. Classification confusion matrix for 10 subsets in one of 10-fold CV

Actual	Predicted		
	Normal	Hyperthyroidism	Hypothyroidism
Normal	150	0	0
Hyperthyroidism	3	32	0
Hypothyroidism	1	0	29

In order to see whether the IABC method indeed enhance the performance of the KELM classifier, we conduct EKELM model on the original feature space, it means that all features are served as the inputs into the EKELM model, as described earlier, EKELM aims at improving the performance KELM by automatically dealing with the parameter optimization. Figure 3 presents the evolution process in EKELM, and the evolution of the best and average fitness values for Model 5 in one run 10-fold CV. Note that the best fitness and average fitness are obtained based on the global best positions and the average positions by the employed bees in each generation respectively. It can be seen that the fitness curves gradually varied from iteration 1 to 100, and the improvements increased slowly after iteration 5, eventually stopped at the iteration 100 where it reached the maximum iteration number. In the beginning of the evolution, the fitness increased quickly, and after certain number of generations, it began to increase slowly. Afterwards, the fitness kept stability and had no significant improvements after iteration 32 until the stopping criterion was satisfied. The phenomenon shows that the model can converge rapidly toward the global optimum, and adjust the solutions efficiently.

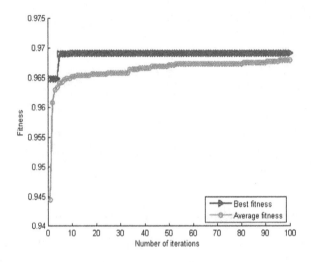

Fig. 3. The average and best fitness in the training stage for one run 10-fold CV

We also present the results of the EKELM model and make a comparison with other ones reported in the literature. Table 4 shows classification results of EKELM in 5 realizations of 10-fold including average classification accuracy in each realization of 10-fold CV, and total average accuracy and standard deviation. In general, as can be seen from the table, EKELM has achieved an average classification accuracy of 97.48%, though does not significantly outperforms PSO-SVM, it is still higher than KELM, SVM and ELM, and has smaller standard deviation when compared with others.

Table 4. Classification comparison of EKELM with PSO-SVM, SVM, KELM and ELM

5 runs of 10-fold CV	EKELM	PSO-SVM	SVM	KELM	ELM
#1 run	97.71	97.23	96.23	95.81	93.94
#2 run	97.19	97.71	94.87	96.74	92.56
#3 run	96.73	96.30	94.87	95.35	94.42
#4 run	98.12	97.21	96.30	97.21	90.70
#5 run	97.64	97.19	96.75	95.81	92.09
Mean ± SD	97.48 ± 0.41	97.13 ± 0.51	95.81 ± 0.88	96.18 ± 0.63	92.74 ± 1.15

Table 5 gives all the comparison results in terms of average accuracy and standard deviation over 5 realizations of 10-fold CV. The results show that LFDA-EKELM has outperformed all others methods in terms of the classification accuracy. The best result is 98.18% and the mean classification result is 98.06%.

Table 5. Comparison of method with FS-PSO-SVM, PCA-SVM, PCA-ELM

5 runs of 10-fold CV	LFDA-EKELM	FS-PSO-SVM	PCA-SVM	PCA-ELM
#1 run	98.16	98.59	96.32	98.1
#2 run	98.18	98.14	96.3	97.16
#3 run	98.14	97.23	95.82	98.1
#4 run	97.68	96.3	96.3	97.64
#5 run	98.12	97.19	97.25	97.64
Mean ± SD	98.06 ± 0.17	97.49 ± 0.9	96.4 ± 0.52	97.73 ± 0.39

Table 6. Classification accuracies achieved with our method and other methods.

Study	Method	Accuracy (%)
[1]	MLP	36.74 (test data)
	LVQ	81.86 (test data)
	RBF	72.09 (test data)
	PPFNN	78.14 (test data)
[2]	MLP with BP	86.33 (average 3-fold)
	MLP with fast BP	89.90 (average 3-fold)
	RBF	79.08
	CSFNN	91.14
[3]	LDA	81.34 (test data)
	C4.5-1	93.26 (test data)
	C4.5-2	92.81 (test data)
	C4.5-3	92.94 (test data)
	DIMLP	94.86 (test data)
	SIM	96.86 (test data)
[4]	AIRS	81.00 (average 3-fold CV)
	AIRS + Fuzzy weighted pre-processing	85.00 (average 3-fold CV)
[5]	ESTDD	95.33 (10-fold CV)
[6]	MLNN with LM	93.19 (10-fold CV)
	PNN	94.81 (10-fold CV)
	LVQ	90.05 (10-fold CV)
[7]	GDA-WSVM	91.86 (test data)
[8]	FS-PSO-SVM	97.49 (10-fold CV)
[9]	PCA-ELM	97.73 (10-fold CV)
[10]	Simple ELM-based	87.72 (10-fold CV)
This study	LFDA-EKELM	**98.06** (10-fold CV)
		98.18 (10-fold CV)

For comparison purpose, Table 6 lists the classification accuracies of our proposed method and baseline methods. As shown in Table 6, our developed LFDA-EKELM system can achieve better classification accuracy than that of all available methods proposed in previous studies.

Through these analysis, obviously, the LFDA-EKELM model is an effective system compared with other methods from above comparative empirical study. Therefore, we can see clearly that LFDA-EKELM is a much more appropriate tool for thyroid disease diagnosis problem in comparison with baseline methods. Consequently, it shows that the proposed system can be very helpful in assisting the physicians to make accuracy diagnosis and will show great potential in the area of clinical thyroid disease diagnosis.

6   Conclusions and Future Work

In this paper, we developed a novel system LFDA-EKELM for assisting the diagnosis of thyroid disease. The main novelty of this system lies in employing the KELM classifier together with the feature reduction technique to perform the diagnosis tasks for thyroid disease. The proposed improved ABC method conducted the KELM classifier whose important parameters C and γ were adaptively specified. In order to remove the irrelevant information in the thyroid data, the local fisher discriminative analysis was used for feature reduction before conducting the EKELM classifier. The experimental results shown that the proposed system performed significantly well in distinguishing the patients with hyperthyroidism, hypothyroidism and normal cases. It was observed that LFDA-EKELM can achieve the mean classification accuracy of 98.06% using 10-fold cross validation. In addition, our developed system outperformed the existing methods proposed in the literature. Therefore, our developed diagnosis system can serve as a promising tool in medical decision-making for thyroid disease diagnosis. Further work will evaluate the proposed method in larger datasets, and the regression problems will be also studied.

Acknowledgements. This research is supported by scientific research project of school under Grant Nos. QN201716, Shenzhen scientific planning project under Grant Nos. ybzz17011.

References

1. Serpen, G., Jiang, H., Allred, L.G.: Performance analysis of probabilistic potential function neural network classifier. In: Proceedings of Artificial Neural Networks in Engineering Conference, St. Louis, MO, vol. 7, pp. 471–476. Citeseer (1997)
2. Ozyilmaz, L., Yildirim, T.: Diagnosis of thyroid disease using artificial neural network methods. In: Processings of ICONIP 2002 9th International Conference on Neural Information Processing, Orchid Country Club, Singapore, vol. 4, pp. 2033–2036. IEEE (2002)
3. Pasi, L.: Similarity classifier applied to medical data sets. In: International Conference on Soft Computing. Helsinki, Finland & Gulf of Finland & Tallinn, Estonia (2004)

4. Polat, K., Şahan, S., Güneş, S.: A novel hybrid method based on artificial immune recognition system (AIRS) with fuzzy weighted pre-processing for thyroid disease diagnosis. Expert Syst. Appl. **32**, 1141–1147 (2007)
5. Keleş, A.: ESTDD: expert system for thyroid diseases diagnosis. Expert Syst. Appl. **34**, 242–246 (2008)
6. Temurtas, F.: A comparative study on thyroid disease diagnosis using neural networks. Expert Syst. Appl. **36**, 944–949 (2009)
7. Dogantekin, E., Dogantekin, A., Avci, D.: An expert system based on Generalized Discriminant Analysis and Wavelet Support Vector Machine for diagnosis of thyroid diseases. Expert Syst. Appl. **38**, 146–150 (2011)
8. Chen, H.L., Yang, B., Wang, G., et al.: A three-stage expert system based on support vector machines for thyroid disease diagnosis. J. Med. Syst., 1–11 (2012)
9. Li, L.N., Ouyang, J.H., Chen, H.L., et al.: A computer aided diagnosis system for thyroid disease using extreme learning machine. J. Med. Syst., 1–11 (2012)
10. Xia, J., Chen, H., Li, Q., et al.: Ultrasound-based differentiation of malignant and benign thyroid nodules: an extreme learning machine approach. Comput. Methods Programs Biomed. **147**, 37–49 (2017)
11. Wong, C.M., Vong, C.M., Wong, P.K.: Kernel-based multiplayer extreme learning machine for representation learning. IEEE Trans. Neural Netw. Learn. Syst. **29**(3), 757–762 (2018)
12. Wang, J., Mi, H., Wu, Y.: Thyroid cancer gene detection algorithm based on feature selection ELM. AER-Adv. Eng. Res. **73**, 1408–1414 (2016)
13. Jia, J.R., Ruan, Q.Q., Jin, Y.: Geometric preserving local fisher discriminant analysis for person re-identification. Neurocomputing **205**, 92–105 (2016)
14. Zhao, Y.P., Huerta, R.: Improvements on parsimonious extreme learning machine using recursive orthogonal least squares. Neurocomputing **191**, 82–94 (2016)
15. Youwei, W., Lizhou, F., Jianming, Z.: Novel artificial bee colony based feature selection method for filtering redundant information. Appl. Intell. **48**(4), 868–885 (2018)
16. Ghaddar, B., NaoumSawaya, J.: High dimensional data classification and feature selection using support vector machine. Eur. Oper. Res. **265**(3), 993–1004 (2018)

Supporting Social Information Discovery from Big Uncertain Social Key-Value Data via Graph-Like Metaphors

Calvin S. H. Hoi[1], Carson K. Leung[1]($\boxtimes$)(iD), Kimberly Tran[1],
Alfredo Cuzzocrea[2,3], Mario Bochicchio[4], and Marco Simonetti[2]

[1] University of Manitoba, Manitoba, MB, Canada
kleung@cs.umanitoba.ca
[2] University of Trieste, Trieste, TS, Italy
[3] ICAR-CNR, Rende, CS, Italy
[4] University of Salento, Lecce, LE, Italy

Abstract. In the current era of big data, huge volumes of a wide variety of valuable data of different veracity (e.g., uncertain data) can be easily collected and generated from a broad range of data sources (e.g., social networking sites) at a high velocity in various real-life applications. Many traditional data management and analytic approaches may not be suitable for handling the big data due to their well-known 5V's characteristics. In this paper, we present a cognitive-based system for social network analysis. Our system supports information discovery of interesting social patterns from big uncertain social networks—which are represented in the form of key-value pairs—capturing the perceived likelihood of the linkages among the social entities in the network.

Keywords: Cognitive computing · Data mining
Knowledge discovery · Big data · Social network · Uncertain data
Key-value store

1 Introduction and Related Work

Nowadays, a wide variety of valuable data of different veracity (e.g., precise, imprecise or uncertain data) can be easily collected and generated from a broad range of data sources at a high velocity in various real-life applications (e.g., bioinformatics, sensor and stream systems, smart worlds, Web, social networks [19, 20, 27–29, 32, 35]). Moreover, volumes of these *big data* [31] are also beyond the ability of commonly-used software to manage, query, process, and analyze within a tolerable elapsed time. Characteristics of these big data can generally be described by the following well-known 5V's:

1. *variety*, which focuses on differences in types, contents, or formats of data (e.g., key-value pairs, graphs);

J. Xiao et al. (Eds.): ICCC 2018, LNCS 10971, pp. 102–116, 2018.
https://doi.org/10.1007/978-3-319-94307-7_8

2. *value*, which focuses on the usefulness of data (e.g., information and knowledge that can be discovered from the big data);
3. *veracity*, which focuses on the quality of data (e.g., precise data, uncertain and imprecise data);
4. *velocity*, which focuses on the speed at which data are collected or generated (e.g., dynamic streaming data); and
5. *volume*, which focuses on the quantity of data (e.g., huge volumes of data).

Embedded in the big data [15,16]—such as banking records, biological data, business transactions, documents, financial charts, Internet of things (IoT), medical images, surveillance videos, texts, web logs, as well as streams of advertisements, marketing, natural and life science, social media, and telecommunication data [2,4,6,14,24,30,40]—are rich sets of useful information and knowledge. Due to the aforementioned 5V's characteristics, many traditional data management and analytic approaches may not be suitable for handling the big data. New forms of techniques are needed for managing, querying, processing, and analyzing big data so as to enable enhanced decision making, insight, process optimization, knowledge discovery and data mining. This drives and motivates research and practices in big data analytics, big data management, and data science. To a further extent, all these research and practices aim toward realizing on-demand services such as infrastructure-as-a-service (IaaS), platform-as-a-service (PaaS), "*sensing intelligence-as-a-service*" (*SIaaS*), and software-as-a-service (SaaS) [18].

To realize SIaaS, effective management of big data in distributed environments supports a wide range of data science activities including analytics, cybersecurity, knowledge discovery and data mining. Many recent applications and systems use cluster, cloud, or grid computing [7,33,36] to manage big data. Once the big data are managed, they can then be analyzed (e.g., inspected, cleaned, transformed, and modelled) and mined by data science techniques. Generally, *data science* aims to develop systematic or quantitative data mining and analytic algorithm [22] for mining and analyzing big data. *Big data analytics* [25,26,37,39], in particular, incorporates various techniques from a broad range of fields, which include cloud computing, knowledge discovery and data mining, machine learning, mathematics, as well as statistics. With the 5V's characteristics (e.g., data volume) of big data, it is natural to handle the big data in a distributed computing environment such as a cloud environment because it represents a "natural" context for big data by providing high performance, reliability, availability, transparency, abstraction, and/or virtualization.

Rich sources of big data include social networks—which are generally made of social entities (e.g., individuals, corporations, collective social units, or organizations) that are linked by some specific types of interdependencies (e.g., friendship, kinship, common interest, beliefs, or financial exchange). In these networks, a social entity is connected to another entity as his friend, next-of-kin, collaborator, co-author, classmate, co-worker, team member, and/or business partner. *Social network analysis* applies big data mining and analytics techniques to social networks so as to (i) computationally facilitate social studies and human-social dynamics in these big data networks, as well as (ii) design and use information and communication technologies for dealing with social context.

Over the past decade, several data science solutions and data mining algorithms [1,34] have been proposed for social network analysis. However, many [41] of them aim to detect communities by using *clustering* techniques. In contrast, we focus on applying *association rule or frequent pattern mining* techniques to analyze and mine big social network data for interdependencies or connections among social entities in a big social network. Moreover, previous works [5,23] focused on mining *precise* social network where the linkages among social entities are known. However, there are many real-life situations in which these linkages are *uncertain*. For example, due to privacy setting, exact linkage information may not be available. As an example, due to name ambiguity (say, multiple social entities having the same name) or limited identity information (say, only know the common names or nicknames of social entities, but do not know their registered names used on the social networking sites). From the *cognitive viewpoint*, we capture the *perceived likelihood* of the linkages (say, user A is 60% likely to be a friend of user B but only 30% likely to be a friend of user C) in these real-life situations. In other words, we mine imprecise and uncertain social data from big social networks. Hence, our *key contribution* of the paper includes our cognitive-based system for social network analysis. Our system supports information discovery of interesting social patterns from big uncertain social networks that are represented in the form of key-value pairs.

The remainder of this paper is organized as follows. The next section provides some background materials. Section 3 presents our cognitive-based system for mining and analyzing big uncertain social network data represented as key-value pairs. Experimental results are shown in Sect. 4; conclusions, ongoing and future work are given in Sect. 5.

2   Background

Nowadays, various social networking sites or services (e.g., Facebook, Google+, LinkedIn, Snapchat, Twitter, and Weibo [21,38]) are commonly in use. These varieties of sites and services easily generate huge volumes of valuable data of different veracity at a high velocity. For instance, a Twitter user can read the tweets of other users by "following" them. Relationships between social entities are mostly defined by following (or subscribing) each other. Each user (social entity) can have multiple followers, and can follow multiple users at the same time. The *follow/subscribe relationship* is *directional*, implying that a Twitter user A may follow another user B but user B may not necessarily follow back.

As another instance, a Facebook user C can create a personal profile, join common-interest user groups, and subscribe or follow public postings of some other Facebook users without the need of adding them as friends via the functionality of "follow". So, for any user C, if many of his friends followed some individual users or groups of users, then user C might also be interested in following the same individual users or groups of users. Furthermore, the "like" button allows users to express their appreciation of content such as status updates, comments, photos, and advertisements. Again, this follow/like relationship is *directional*, implying that a Facebook user C may follow another user D but user D may not necessarily follow back or like C's postings.

In addition to the aforementioned directional follow/subscribe relationship, a Facebook user C can also add other Facebook users as friends, and exchange messages between them. These Facebook users are linked to some other Facebook users via their *mutual friendship*, which is *undirectional* or *bidirectional*. If a Facebook user C is a friend of another Facebook user E, then user E is also a friend of user C. Note that both directional and undirectional data can be found in Facebook data.

Similarly, a LinkedIn user can create a professional profile, establish connections to other LinkedIn users, and exchange messages. In addition, he can also join common-interest user groups and tag his *undirectional* connections (e.g., first-degree, second-degree, and third-degree connections) according to some overlapping categories (e.g., colleagues, classmates, business partners, friends).

Note that, from *cognitive point of view*, social network may not be always precise. They could be imprecise and uncertain [3]. For instance, due to the privacy setting of some social entities, analysts may suspect but cannot guarantee that user F is likely to follow user G. Such suspicion can be expressed in terms of existential probability value in the range of $(0, 1]$. As another instance, due to the ambiguity in name, analysts may suspect but cannot guarantee that user F is likely to follow user G and/or user G' (who has the same or similar name as G). Let us consider a solid example in which a user F know a friend by nick name or common name (say, Gabby), which may not be his official name. Hence, mining from these imprecise and uncertain social can be challenging.

The number of users in these social networking sites has kept growing rapidly (e.g., 2.2 billion monthly active Facebook users[1], more than 562 million registered LinkedIn users[2], and 330 million monthly active Twitter users[3] as of the first quarter of 2018. These big numbers of users in social networks create an even more massive number of linkages (e.g., connections, friendships, follow/subscribe relationships) among users. Hence, having a cognitive-based system for mining and analyzing big social networks for the discovery of some interesting knowledge (e.g., popular users) about these users is desirable. To elaborate, discovery of popular users helps an individual user new to the network to make connection or follow the same popular users. Moreover, many businesses have used social network media to either (i) reach the right audience and turn them into new customers or (ii) build a closer relationship with existing customers. Hence, discovery of customers who follow or subscribe to products or services provided by a business helps the business identify its targeted or preferred customers.

---

[1] https://newsroom.fb.com/company-info/.

[2] https://about.linkedin.com/.

[3] https://about.twitter.com/en_us/company.html.

3 Our Cognitive-Based Social Network Analysis System for Mining Uncertain Social Data

In this section, we present our cognitive-based system for social network analysis on big uncertain social data, which are represented in the form of *key-value pairs*. Such a representation is natural for, and supports, data science (in particular, big data mining and analytics) for the discovery of interesting patterns from big social networks.

3.1 Social Network Analysis on Key-Value Data Capturing Uncertain Follow/Subscribe Relationships

In social networking sites like Twitter and Google+, social entities (users) are linked by the *follow/subscribe (i.e., "following") relationships* such that a user A (i.e., *follower*) follows another user B (i.e., *followee*). Moreover, recall from Sect. 2 that, in addition to the usual "add friend" feature, Facebook also provides users with the "follow" feature. Hence, social entities in Facebook can also be linked by the follow/subscribe relationships too. Note that these follow/subscribe relationships are directional. As explained earlier, social data in these social networking sites may be imprecise and uncertain. Consider Scenario 1.

Scenario 1. For an illustrative purpose, let us consider a small portion of a big uncertain social network. Here, there are $|K| = 12$ users (Anna, Bart, Carl, Dale, Ella, Fitz, Gail, Hugo, Iris, John, Kate, and Luke). Each user is following some others as described below:

- Anna is 90% likely to follow Bart.
- Bart is following Anna and Carl.
- Carl is following Anna and Iris.
- Dale is following Anna, Bart, Carl and Ella.
- Ella is following Anna, Bart, Carl and Dale.
- Fitz is 70% likely to follow Ella and Gail.
- Gail is 60% likely to follow Fitz.
- Hugo is 80% likely to follow Gail.
- Iris is 50% likely to follow Luke.
- John is 90% likely to follow Iris.
- Kate is *not* following anyone.
- Luke is following Carl, Iris and Kate.

We capture these directional relationships (e.g., follow/subscribe relationships) embedded in big uncertain social network data for Scenario 1, and represent them by using *key-value pairs*, where each key captures a follower and the corresponding value captures a list of all his followees—each associated with an *existential probability value* indicating the likelihood that the follower follows that followee. See Table 1.

With this key-value representation of the big uncertain social network data about given $|K|$ social entities in Scenario 1, there are potentially $|K| \cdot (|K| - 1)$

Table 1. Key-value store for directional big uncertain social network data capturing follow/subscribe relationships in Scenario 1

Key (follower)	Value (followees)
Anna	{Bart:0.9}
Bart	{Anna:1.0, Carl:1.0}
Carl	{Anna:1.0, Iris:1.0}
Dale	{Anna:1.0, Bart:1.0, Carl:1.0, Ella:1.0}
Ella	{Anna:1.0, Bart:1.0, Carl:1.0, Dale:1.0}
Fitz	{Ella:0.7, Gail:0.7}
Gail	{Fitz:0.6}
Hugo	{Gail:0.8}
Iris	{Luke:0.5}
John	{Iris:0.9}
Luke	{Carl:1.0, Iris:1.0, Kate:1.0}

follow/subscribe relationships in theory. However, in practice, the number of follow/subscribe relationships is usually lower than its maximum $|K| \cdot (|K| - 1)$ unless for the extreme case where everyone is following each other in a social network. For Scenario 1, there are only 22 follow/subscribe relationships (cf. possibly 132 relationships for $|K|=12$ users), including (Anna, Bart):0.9, (Bart, Anna):1.0, (Bart, Carl):1.0, (Carl, Anna):1.0, (Carl, Iris):1.0, (Dale, Anna):1.0, (Dale, Bart):1.0, (Dale, Carl):1.0, (Dale, Ella):1.0, (Ella, Anna):1.0, (Ella, Bart):1.0, (Ella, Carl):1.0, (Ella, Dale):1.0, (Fitz, Ella):0.7, (Fitz, Gail):0.7, (Gail, Fitz):0.6, (Hugo, Gail):0.8, (Iris, Luke):0.5, (John, Iris):0.9, (Luke, Carl):1.0, (Luke, Iris):1.0, and (Luke, Kate):1.0 for Anna, Bart, Carl, Dale, Ella, Fitz, Gail, Hugo, Iris, John, Kate, and Luke. With this representation of big uncertain social network data on follow/subscribe relationships, our key-value based big uncertain social network analysis system supports the answering of the following questions.

Question 1. Who are the most active followers?
The most active followers can be revealed by finding the key (representing a follower k_i) having the highest number of elements in its corresponding value (representing all followees of k_i). Let $v(k_i)$ give the list of followees being followed by follower k_i. Then, $\#followees(k_i) = |v(k_i)|$. Hence,

$$\text{the most active follower} = \text{argmax}_{k_i \in K} |v(k_i)|.$$

Due to the uncertainty in data, the probability of such $k_i \in K$ be the most active follower can be computed by the following:

$$\Pr(k_i \text{ is the most active follower}) = \prod_j \{p_{ij} \mid v_{ij}:p_{ij} \in v(k_i)\}, \qquad (1)$$

where p_{ij} is an existential probability associated with a followee v_{ij} of follower k_i.

Example 1. For Scenario 1, *both Dale* (who is following Anna, Bart, Carl and Ella) *and Ella* (who is following Anna, Bart, Carl and Dale) *are the two most active followers* who are likely to follow four followees each. This answer is supported by the four values associated with the key "Dale" and "Ella", i.e., *#followees*(Dale) = 4 and *#followees*(Ella) = 4 indicating that Dale and Ella are likely to follow four followees each. With additional information that Pr(Dale is the most active follower) = 1.0 and Pr(Ella is the most active follower) = 1.0, we are certain to say that Dale and Ella are each following four followees.   □

Question 2. Who are the most popular followees?
The most popular followees can be found by first calling the map function to swap key and value. The resulting (value, key)-pairs return (followee, follower) information. Then, call the reduce function to sort and group pairs having the same followee. Let $k(v_j)$ give the list of followers who all follow followee v_j. Then, $\#followers(v_j) = |k(v_j)|$. Hence,

$$\text{the most popular followee} = \text{argmax}_{v_j \in V} |k(v_j)|.$$

In other words, with $followers(v_j) = \{k_i \mid v_j:\_ \in v(k_i)\}$,

$$\text{the most popular followee} = \text{argmax}_{v_j \in V} |followers(v_j)|.$$

Due to the uncertainty in data, the probability of such $v_j \in V$ be the most popular followee can be computed by the following:

$$\Pr(v_j \text{ is the most popular followee}) = \prod_i \{p_{ij} \mid v_j:p_{ij} \in v(k_i)\}, \qquad (2)$$

where p_{ij} is an existential probability associated with a followee v_{ij} of follower k_i.

Example 2. For Scenario 1, *both Anna* (who is followed by Bart, Carl, Dale and Ella) *and Carl* (who is followed by Bart, Dale, Ella and Luke) *are the two most popular followees* who are likely to be followed by four followers each. This answer is supported by the four keys associated with the value "Anna" and "Carl", i.e., *#followers*(Anna) = 4 and *#followers*(Carl) = 4 indicating that Anna and Carl are each likely to be followed by four followers. With additional information that Pr(Anna is the most popular followee) = 1.0 and Pr(Carl is the most popular followee) = 1.0, we are certain to say Anna and Carl are so popular that they are each followed by four followers.   □

3.2 Social Network Analysis on Key-Value Data Capturing Uncertain Mutual Friendships

In social networking sites like Facebook and LinkedIn, social entities (users) are usually linked by the *mutual friendships* such that a user A is a friend (or first-degree connection) of another user B meaning that user B is also a friend of user A. Unlike those directional follow/subscribe relationships described in Sect. 3.1, the mutual friendships are undirectional or bidirectional. Again, social data in these social networking sites may be imprecise and uncertain. Consider Scenario 2.

Table 2. Key-value store for bidirectional big uncertain social network data capturing mutal friendships in Scenario 2

Key (user)	Value (mutual friends)
Anna	{Bart:0.9, Carl:1.0, Dale:1.0, Ella:1.0}
Bart	{Anna:1.0, Carl:1.0, Dale:1.0, Ella:1.0}
Carl	{Anna:1.0, Bart:1.0, Dale:1.0, Ella:1.0, Iris:1.0, Luke:1.0}
Dale	{Anna:1.0, Bart:1.0, Carl:1.0, Ella:1.0}
Ella	{Anna:1.0, Bart:1.0, Carl:1.0, Dale:1.0, Fitz:1.0}
Fitz	{Ella:1.0, Gail:1.0}
Gail	{Fitz:1.0, Hugo:0.9}
Hugo	{Gail:0.9}
Iris	{Carl:1.0, Luke:1.0, John:0.6}
John	{Iris:0.6}
Kate	{Luke:0.8}
Luke	{Carl:1.0, Iris:1.0, Kate:0.8}

Scenario 2. For an illustrative purpose, let us reconsider the same $|K| = 12$ users (Anna, Bart, Carl, Dale, Ella, Fitz, Gail, Hugo, Iris, John, Kate, and Luke) as in Scenario 1. However, each user is a friend of some others in an uncertain social network as described below:

- Anna is a friend of Bart, Carl, Dale and Ella.
- Bart is a friend of Anna, Carl, Dale and Ella.
- Carl is a friend of Anna, Bart, Dale, Ella, Iris and Luke.
- Dale is a friend of Anna, Bart, Carl and Ella.
- Ella is a friend of Anna, Bart, Carl, Dale and Fitz.
- Fitz is a friend of Ella and Gail.
- Gail is a friend of Fitz and 90% likely to be a friend of Hugo.
- Hugo is 90% likely to be a friend of Gail.
- Iris is a friend of Carl and Luke, and 60% likely to be a friend of John.
- John is 60% likely to be a friend of Iris.
- Kate is 80% likely to be a friend of Luke.
- Luke is a friend of Carl and Iris, and 80% likely to be a friend of Kate.

We capture these undirectional (or bidirectional) relationships (e.g., mutual friendships) embedded in big uncertain social network data for Scenario 1 and represent them by using key-value pairs, where each key captures a social entity and the corresponding value captures a list of all his friends—each associated with an existential probability value indicating the likelihood of their mutual friendships. See Table 2.

With this key-value representation of the big uncertain social network data about given $|K|$ social entities in Scenario 2, there are potentially $\frac{|K| \cdot (|K|-1)}{2}$

mutual friendships in theory. However, in practice, the number of mutual friend-ships is usually lower than its maximum unless for the extreme case where every-one is a friend of another in a social network. For Scenario 2, there are only 18 mutual friendships (cf. possibly 72 mutual friendships for $|K|=12$ users). An observant reader may notice that the mutual friendships are symmetric in nature. If user v_j is a friend of user k, then user k is also a friend of user v_j. This explains why there are a total of $2 \times 18 = 36$ list elements (friends) in the 12 lists of mutual friends, one for each of the $K = 12$ users. With this representation of big uncertain social network data on mutual friendships, our key-value pairs based big uncertain social network analysis system supports the answering of the following questions.

Question 3. Who is the most popular user?
Similar to Question 1 of finding the most active followers, the most popular user can be revealed by finding the key (representing a user k_i) having the highest number of elements in its corresponding value (representing all friends, i.e., first-degree connections, of k_i). Let $v(k_i)$ give the list of friends of user k_i. Then, $\#friends(k_i) = |v(k_i)|$. Hence,

$$\text{the most popular user} = \text{argmax}_{k_i \in K} \ |v(k_i)|.$$

Due to the uncertainty in data, the probability of such $k_i \in K$ be the most popular user can be computed by the following:

$$\Pr(k_i \text{ is the most popular user}) = \prod_j \{p_{ij} \mid v_{ij}{:}p_{ij} \in v(k_i)\}, \qquad (3)$$

where p_{ij} is an existential probability associated with a friend v_{ij} of user k_i.

Example 3. For Scenario 2, *Carl* (who is a friend of Anna, Bart, Dale, Ella, Iris and Luke) *is the most popular user* who is likely to have six friends. This answer is supported by the six friends of Carl, i.e., $\#friends(\text{Carl}) = 6$ indicating that Carl is likely to have six friends. With additional information that $\Pr(\text{Carl is the most popular user}) = 1.0$, we are certain to say Carl is so popular that he has six friends. $\qquad \square$

Question 4. Who have the highest number of friends-of-friends (or second-degree connections)?
This question can be answered by first finding all second-degree connections of k and then picking those with the highest numbers of second-degree connections. Let $shortestPath(k_i, v_{ij})$ return (pairs in) the shortest path between nodes k and v, which can be computed by using algorithms like Dijkstra's algorithm [8]. The length of such a path reveals the minimum degree of separation between user k_i and user v_{ij}. Let $v(k_i)$ give the list of friends of user k_i. Then,

$$\text{user with the highest } \#\text{friends-of-friends}$$
$$= \text{argmax}_{k_i \in K} \ |\{u'' \mid u' \in v(k_i) \wedge u'' \in v(u') \wedge |shortestPath(k_i, u'')| = 2\}| \, .$$

Due to the uncertainty in data, the probability of such $k_i \in K$ having the highest number of friends-of-friends can be computed by the following:

$$\Pr(k_i \text{ is the user having the highest } \#\text{friends-of-friends})$$
$$= \prod_{(k_i, u'')} \prod_{p_{ij}} \{p_{ij} \mid (\_, \_):p_i \in shortestPath(k_i, u'')\}. \tag{4}$$

In other words, the probability can computed by multiplying the existence probabilities of the shortest path from user k_i to each friend-of-friend u'', and then multiplying the products of every (user k_i, user u'')-pairs.

Example 4. For Scenario 2, *Fitz, Iris and Luke all likely to have the highest number of friends-of-friends (or second-degree connections).* This answer is supported by the likelihood of Fitz, Iris or Luke having five second-degree connections. Specifically,

- $|shortestPath(\text{Fitz}, v)| = 2$ for each $v \in$ {Anna, Bart, Carl, Dale, Hugo} because Anna is a friend of Ella, who happens to be a friend of Fitz. Similarly, Bart, Carl and Dale are friends of Ella, who happens to be a friend of Fitz. So, Pr(Fitz is a friend-of-friends of v) = 1.0 for $v \in$ {Anna, Bart, Carl, Dale}, which means we are certain that Fitz is a friend-of-friends with Anna, Bart, Carl, and Dale. However, Hugo is 90% likely to be a friend of Gail, who happens to be another friend of Fitz. In other words, Pr(Fitz is a friend-of-friends of Hugo) = 0.9, meaning that Fitz is only 90% likely (but not 100% certain) to be a friend-of-friends of Hugo.
- Similarly, $|shortestPath(\text{Iris}, v)| = 2$ for each $v \in$ {Anna, Bart, Dale, Ella, Kate}. On the one hand, Anna, Bart, Dale and Ella are friends of Carl, who happens to be a friend of Iris. So, Pr(Iris is a friend-of-friends of v) = 1.0 for $v \in$ {Anna, Bart, Dale, Ella}, which means we are certain that Iris is a friend-of-friends with Anna, Bart, Dale, and Ella. On the other hand, Kate is 80% likely to be a friend of Luke, who happens to be a friend of Iris. So, Pr(Iris is a friend-of-friends of Kate) = 0.8, which means Iris is 80% likely (but not 100% certain) to be a friend-of-friends with Kate.
- $|shortestPath(\text{Luke}, v)| = 2$ for each $v \in$ {Anna, Bart, Dale, Ella, John}. On the one hand, Anna, Bart, Dale and Ella are friends of Carl, who happens to be a friend of Luke. So, Pr(Luke is a friend-of-friends of v) = 1.0 for $v \in$ {Anna, Bart, Dale, Ella}, which means we are certain that Luke is a friend-of-friends with Anna, Bart, Dale, and Ella. However, John is 60% likely to be a friend of Iris, who happens to be a friend of Luke. So, Pr(Luke is a friend-of-friends of John) = 0.6, which means Luke is 60% likely (but not 100% certain) to be a friend-of-friends with John.

Among the three users (namely, Fitz, Iris and Luke) who have the highest number of friends-of-friends, Fitz is perceived to be more likely (with 90% probability) to have five friends-of-friends. Iris is less likely (with 80% probability) to have five friends-of-friends, and Luke has the least likelihood (with 60% probability) to have five friends-of-friends.   □

Question 5. Who have the highest number of kth-degree connections?
This question can be answered by first finding all k^{th}-degree connections of user u and then picking those with the highest numbers of kth-degree connections. Note that this question can be considered as an extension or generalization to Questions 3 and 4. Conversely, Questions 3 and 4 can be considered as special cases of the current question where $k = 1$ and $k = 2$, respectively.

Example 5. For brevity, we just provide the answers (without showing the steps) for $k = 1$, 2, 3, 4, and 5 in Scenario 2 as follows. Although Examples 3 and 4 have already found the answers for $k = 1$ and 2, let us include those answers here for completeness.

- For $k = 1$, the highest number of first-degree connections is six. It is certain that Carl has these six friends (Anna, Bart, Dale, Ella, Iris and Luke).
- For $k = 2$, the highest number of second-degree connections is five. Fitz is perceived to have 90% likelihood of having five friends-of-friends (Anna, Bart, Carl, Dale and Hugo), Iris is perceived to have 80% likelihood of also having five but slightly different groups of friends-of-friends (Anna, Bart, Dale, Ella and Kate), and Luke is perceived to have 60% likelihood of having that number of friends-of-friends (Anna, Bart, Dale, Ella and John).
- For $k = 3$, the highest number of third-degree connections is also five. Kate is perceived to have $(0.8)^5 \times 0.6 \approx 20\%$ likelihood of having five third-degree connections (Anna, Bart, Dale, Ella and John), but John is perceived to have $0.8 \times (0.6)^5 \approx 6\%$ likelihood of having five third-degree connections (Anna, Bart, Dale, Ella but Kate).
- For $k = 4$, the highest number of fourth-degree connections is four. Hugo is perceived to have 90% likelihood of having four fourth-degree connections (Anna, Bart, Carl and Dale).
- For $k = 5$, the highest number of fifth-degree connections is two. Hugo is perceived to have 90% likelihood of having two fifth-degree connections (Iris and Luke), whereas Gail is perceived to have $0.8 \times 0.6 = 48\%$ likelihood of having the same number of fifth-degree connections (John and Kate).
- For $k = 6$, the highest number of sixth-degree connections is two. Hugo is perceived to have $(0.9)^2 \times (0.6)^2 \approx 29\%$ likelihood of having two sixth-degree connections (John and Kate). It is also interesting but surprising to observed that all users are connected within six degree, which is consistent with the theory of the *six degrees of separation*.   □

Question 6. Who are the most isolated users?
The most isolated users can be found by first computing all k^{th}-degree connections of every user and then picking those with the highest k.

Example 6. For Scenario 2, *Kate, John and Hugo are perceived to have, respectively, $0.9 \times 0.8 = 72\%$, $0.9 \times 0.6 = 54\%$ and $(0.9)^2 \times (0.6)^2 \approx 29\%$ likelihood of being the three most isolated users.* Each of them has some sixth-degree connections (the highest degrees of connections for Scenario 2).   □

4   Experimental Results

To evaluate the performance of our cognitive-based system by using the following two real-life social network datasets:

1. The Stanford Network Analysis Project (SNAP)[4] ego-Twitter dataset, which contains 81,306 social entities and 1,768,149 directional follow/subscribe relationships among these social entities; and
2. the SNAP ego-Facebook dataset, which contains 4,039 social entities and 88,234 undirectional mutual friendships among these social entities.

All experiments were run using either

1. a single machine with an Intel Core i7 4-core processor (1.73 GHz) and 8 GB of main memory running a 64-bit Windows 7 operating system, or
2. the Amazon Elastic Compute Cloud (EC2) cluster[5]—specifically, 11 High-Memory Extra Large (m2.xlarge) computing nodes.

We implemented our cognitive-based system—which mines and analyzes big uncertain social network data—in the Java programming language. The stock version of Apache Hadoop 2.9.0 was used. With it, the big social network data are divided into several partitions and assigned to different processors. Each processor executes the map and reduce functions. Once the data are properly partitioned and assigned to each processor, the processor handles the assigned data without reliance on the results from other processors.

The results shown in Fig. 1 are based on the average of multiple runs. Runtime includes CPU and I/Os. In particular, Fig. 1 shows that the use of our cognitive-based system running on the cloud cluster to conduct social network analysis on big graph data led to a speedup of above 6 times when compared with that running on a single machine for the SNAP ego-Twitter dataset when answering Questions 1 and 2. Figure 1 also shows that the use of our cognitive-based system running on the cloud cluster to conduct social network analysis on big graph data

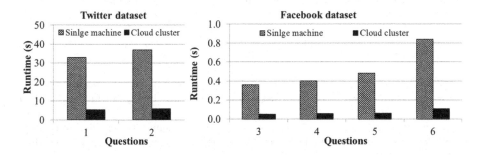

Fig. 1. Experimental results on SNAP (a) ego-Twitter and (b) ego-Facebook datasets

---

[4] http://snap.stanford.edu/data/.

[5] http://aws.amazon.com/ec2/.

led to a speedup of around 7 to 8 times when compared with that running on a single machine for the SNAP ego-Facebook dataset when answering Questions 3, 4, 5 and 6.

Higher speedup is expected when using more processors. Moreover, our system is also shown to be scalable with respect to the number of social entities in the big uncertain social network.

5   Conclusions and Future Work

Huge volumes of a wide variety of valuable data of different veracities (e.g., uncertain data) can be easily collected and generated from a broad range of data sources (e.g., social network) at a high velocity. In the current era of big data, many traditional data management and analytic approaches may not be suitable for handling the big data due to their well-known 5V's characteristics. In this paper, we presented a cognitive-based system for social network analysis so as to support big data mining of interesting patterns from big uncertain social networks—which are represented as key-value pairs—capturing the perceived likelihood of the linkages among the social entities. In particular, our system conducts social network analysis on (i) data capturing directional follow/subscribe (i.e., "following") relationships (e.g., in Twitter) and (ii) data capturing undirectional mutual friendships (e.g., in LinkedIn, Facebook). Experimental results show effectiveness of our cognitive-based system for supporting social information discovery from big uncertain social key-value data via social graph-like metaphors.

As ongoing work, we are conducting more experiments, including an in-depth study on the quality of our system in supporting data science, big data management, big data analytics, knowledge discovery and data mining. Future work is mainly oriented towards extending our system as to make it compliant with novel characteristics of big data, such as *advanced data management methods* (e.g., [9,13,17]) and *privacy preservation techniques* (e.g., [10–12]).

Acknowledgment. This project is partially supported by Natural Sciences and Engineering Research Council of Canada (NSERC) and the University of Manitoba.

References

1. Abu-Salih, B., Wongthongtham, P., Zhu, D., Alqrainy, S.: An approach for time-aware domain-based analysis of users' trustworthiness in big social data. IJBD (now STBD) **2**(1), 41–56 (2015)
2. Braun, P., Cameron, J.J., Cuzzocrea, A., Jiang, F., Leung, C.K.: Effectively and efficiently mining frequent patterns from dense graph streams on disk. Procedia Comput. Sci. **35**, 338–347 (2014)
3. Braun, P., Cuzzocrea, A., Jiang, F., Leung, C.K.-S., Pazdor, A.G.M.: MapReduce-based complex big data analytics over uncertain and imprecise social networks. In: Bellatreche, L., Chakravarthy, S. (eds.) DaWaK 2017. LNCS, vol. 10440, pp. 130–145. Springer, Cham (2017)

4. Braun, P., Cuzzocrea, A., Leung, C.K., Pazdor, A.G.M., Tanbeer, S.K.: Mining frequent patterns from IoT devices with fog computing. In: HPCS 2017, pp. 691–698 (2017)
5. Braun, P., Cuzzocrea, A., Leung, C.K., Pazdor, A., Tran, K.: Knowledge discovery from social graph data. Procedia Comput. Sci. **96**, 682–691 (2016)
6. Chen, I., Guo, J., Tsai, J.J.P.: Trust as a service for SOA-based IoT systems. STIOT **1**(1), 43–52 (2017)
7. Chen, J., Yang, Y.: Grid and workflows. In: Encyclopedia of Database Systems, 2nd edn. (2016). https://doi.org/10.1007/978-1-4899-7993-3_1472-2
8. Cormen, T.H., Leiserson, C.E., Rivest, R.L., Stein, C.: Introduction to Algorithms, 3rd edn. MIT Press, Cambridge (2009)
9. Cuzzocrea, A.: Accuracy control in compressed multidimensional data cubes for quality of answer-based OLAP tools. In: SSDBM 2006, pp. 301–310 (2006)
10. Cuzzocrea, A.: Privacy and security of big data: current challenges and future research perspectives. In: PSBD 2014, pp. 45–47 (2014)
11. Cuzzocrea, A., Bertino, E.: A secure multiparty computation privacy preserving OLAP framework over distributed XML data. In: ACM SAC 2010, pp. 1666–1673 (2010)
12. Cuzzocrea, A., Bertino, E.: Privacy preserving OLAP over distributed XML data: a theoretically-sound secure-multiparty-computation approach. JCSS **77**(6), 965–987 (2011)
13. Cuzzocrea, A., Furfaro, F., Saccà, D.: Enabling OLAP in mobile environments via intelligent data cube compression techniques. JISS **33**(2), 95–143 (2009)
14. Cuzzocrea, A., Han, Z., Jiang, F., Leung, C.K., Zhang, H.: Edge-based mining of frequent subgraphs from graph streams. Procedia Comput. Sci. **60**, 573–582 (2015)
15. Cuzzocrea, A., Lee, W., Leung, C.K.: High-recall information retrieval from linked big data. In: IEEE COMPSAC 2015, vol. 2, pp. 712–717 (2015)
16. Cuzzocrea, A., Leung, C.K.: Upper bounds to expected support for frequent itemset mining of uncertain big data. In: ACM SAC 2015, pp. 919–921 (2015)
17. Cuzzocrea, A., Matrangolo, U.: Analytical synopses for approximate query answering in OLAP environments. In: Galindo, F., Takizawa, M., Traunmüller, R. (eds.) DEXA 2004. LNCS, vol. 3180, pp. 359–370. Springer, Heidelberg (2004)
18. Han, Z., Leung, C.K.: FIMaaS: scalable frequent pattern mining-as-a-service on cloud for non-expert miners. In: BigDAS 2015, pp. 84–91 (2015)
19. Jiang, F., Leung, C.K., Liu, D.: Efficiency improvements in social network communication via MapReduce. In: IEEE DSDIS 2015, pp. 161–168 (2015)
20. Kawagoe, K., Leung, C.K.: Similarities of frequent following patterns and social entities. Procedia Comput. Sci. **60**, 642–651 (2015)
21. Lahoti, P., Garimella, K., Gionis, A.: Joint non-negative matrix factorization for learning ideological leaning on Twitter. In: ACM WSDM 2018, pp. 351–359 (2018)
22. Leung, C.K.: Big data mining applications and services. In: BigDAS 2015, pp. 1–8 (2015)
23. Leung, C.K., Braun, P., Enkhee, M., Pazdor, A.G.M., Sarumi, O.A., Tran, K.: Knowledge discovery from big social key-value data. In: IEEE CIT 2016, pp. 484–491 (2016)
24. Leung, C.K., Cuzzocrea, A.: Frequent subgraph mining from streams of uncertain data. In: C3S2E 2015, pp. 18–27 (2015)
25. Leung, C.K.-S., Hayduk, Y.: Mining frequent patterns from uncertain data with mapreduce for big data analytics. In: Meng, W., Feng, L., Bressan, S., Winiwarter, W., Song, W. (eds.) DASFAA 2013, Part I. LNCS, vol. 7825, pp. 440–455. Springer, Heidelberg (2013)

26. Leung, C.K.-S., Jiang, F.: Big data analytics of social networks for the discovery of "Following" patterns. In: Madria, S., Hara, T. (eds.) DaWaK 2015. LNCS, vol. 9263, pp. 123–135. Springer, Cham (2015). https://doi.org/10.1007/978-3-319-22729-0_10

27. Leung, C.K., Jiang, F., Pazdor, A.G.M., Peddle, A.M.: Parallel social network mining for interesting 'following' patterns. Concurrency Comput. Pract. Exp. **28**(15), 3994–4012 (2016)

28. Leung, C.K., Tanbeer, S.K., Cuzzocrea, A., Braun, P., MacKinnon, R.K.: Interactive mining of diverse social entities. Int. J. Knowl. Based Intell. Eng. Syst. **20**(2), 97–111 (2016)

29. Li, Y.: Socially enhanced account benchmarking in application management service (AMS). IJSC (now STSC) **3**(1), 1–13 (2015)

30. MacKinnon, R.K., Leung, C.K.: Stock price prediction in undirected graphs using a structural support vector machine. In: IEEE/WIC/ACM WI-IAT 2015, vol. 1, pp. 548–555 (2015)

31. Madden, S.: From databases to big data. IEEE Internet Comput. **16**(3), 4–6 (2012)

32. McAuley, J., Leskovec, J.: Discovering social circles in ego networks. ACM TKDD **8**(1), article 4 (2014)

33. Peterson, B., Baumgartner, G., Wang, Q.: A decentralized scheduling framework for many-task scientific computing in a hybrid cloud. STCC **5**(1), 1–13 (2017)

34. Petri, I., Punceva, M., Rana, O.F., Theodorakopoulos, G., Rezgui, Y.: A broker based consumption mechanism for social clouds. IJCC (now STCC) **2**(1), 45–57 (2014)

35. Rahman, Q.M., Fariha, A., Mandal, A., Ahmed, C.F., Leung, C.K.: A sliding window-based algorithm for detecting leaders from social network action streams. In: IEEE/WIC/ACM WI-IAT 2015, vol. 1, pp. 133–136 (2015)

36. Salah, K.: A queuing model to achieve proper elasticity for cloud cluster jobs. IJCC (now STCC) **1**(1), 53–64 (2013)

37. Singh, S., Liu, Y., Ding, W., Li, Z.: Empirical evaluation of big data analytics using design of experiment: case studies on telecommunication data. STBD **3**(2), 1–20 (2016)

38. Taber, L., Whittaker, S.: Personality depends on the medium: differences in self-perception on Snapchat, Facebook and offline. In: ACM CHI 2018, paper no. 607 (2018)

39. Wallace, B., Knoefel, F., Goubran, R., Porter, M.M., Smith, A., Marshall, S.: Features that distinguish drivers: big data analytics of naturalistic driving data. STBD **4**(1), 20–32 (2017)

40. Zeng, J., Min, J.: A systematic framework for designing IoT-enabled systems. STIOT **1**(1), 23–31 (2017)

41. Zhang, J., Jin, S., Yu, P.S.: Mutual community detection across multiple partially aligned social networks. STBD **3**(2), 47–69 (2016)

Application and Industry Track: Mobile Services

Development Status and Trends of Wearable Smart Devices on Wrists

Yunyao Li[1], Jing He[1,2(✉)], Guangyan Huang[3], and Zhijun Xie[4]

[1] Nanjing University of Finance and Economics, Nanjing, China
480245@qq.com
[2] Swinburne University of Technology, Melbourne, Australia
[3] Deakin University, Geelong, VIC, Australia
[4] Ningbo University, Ningbo, China

Abstract. The emergence of wearable smart devices enables people to understand their health level in more details and efficiently process information. According to the physical form of the wearable smart device, this paper classifies the wearable smart devices into four categories and conducts the survey regarding the development of related technologies through in-depth investigations. Furthermore, this paper analyzes the development status and limitations of wearable smart devices and provides the basis for the prospect of wearable smart devices.

Keywords: Wearable smart devices · Smartwatch · Health monitoring

1 Introduction

With the development of society and science and technology, people are no longer satisfied with the single function for jewelry worn on wrists such as watches, bracelets. Therefore, people have tried to integrate these jewelry and smart computing devices, therefore there is the development of wrist-mounted smart devices today. The wearable smart devices (the wearable smart devices mentioned in this article specifically refer to the devices worn on the wrist) contains a very wide range. It is not a single jewelry product, and it incorporates software, sensor detection, data analysis, communication and other special features. As related technologies continue to mature, wearable smart devices have a very broad application prospect in life, medical care and so on.

This paper makes the following contributions. Firstly, we review existing wearable smart devices and classify the wearable smart devices into four categories based on their physical forms. These categories include smart bracelet, smart chain bracelet, smart wristbands and smartwatch. Secondly, we investigate the key technologies involved in wearable smart devices, and explain the development status and role of these technologies in wearable smart devices. Finally, we study and analyze the characteristics and limitations of current products in the market, then make a prospect for the development trend of wearable smart devices.

© Springer International Publishing AG, part of Springer Nature 2018
J. Xiao et al. (Eds.): ICCC 2018, LNCS 10971, pp. 119–129, 2018.
https://doi.org/10.1007/978-3-319-94307-7_9

2   Status and Classification Wearable Smart Device

2.1   Definition

There is currently no single unified concept definition for what is a wearable smart device. Some researchers at the MIT (Massachusetts Institute of Technology) Media Lab believe that computer technology combines multimedia and wireless input or output devices, which do not highlight foreign body sensation such as jewelry, glasses, and clothes, to connect functions of personal area networks, detect a specific situation or become a personal smart assistant, which in turn becomes a tool for users to process messages in a march [1]. It is generally believed that the wearable smart devices are a general name of those devices which are daily wearable devices designed and developed intelligently by using wearable technology. Wearable smart devices have a long history of development and can be traced back to the era of portable calculators. Integrating calculator functions into electronic watches make it easy for people to perform simple digital operations anytime and anywhere.

Based on the above definitions, we believe that wearable smart devices should have been measured by the following attributes: (1) wearable form; (2) independent computing capability; (3) user's experience; (4) perceived ability; (5) Dedicated functions.

2.2   Classification

Smart devices worn on wrist are often classified by physical form (i.e. wearable form), mainly divided into the following categories:

(1) Smart bracelet. The bracelet is an accessory in the history of human development. It has become a fashion element in modern society. Integrating Sensor sensing function chip on the bracelet, adding computing capabilities and Bluetooth-based communication capabilities and realizing data presentation functions through built-in small displays (earlier bracelets were not equipped with screens) have formed smart bracelets currently used mainly in the health field. Smart bracelet is one of the most popular wearable smart devices. For example, Xiaomi Bracelet 2 of China Xiaomi company, Sona Smart Bracelet of United States CAEDEN Co., and American RINGLY's Aries series bracelet.

(2) Smart chain bracelet. The chain bracelet is very similar to the bracelet and it is also the jewelry worn on the wrist. However, chain bracelets are chain-shaped, mostly made of metal products such as gold and silver. At present, only a few companies are doing intelligent work on the chain bracelet, such as Jewelbots company's Pendant Chain Bracelet and Intelligent Happy Bracelet of China Xin Mai intelligent technology company.

(3) Smart wristbands. Wristbands are widely used in medical industry and industry. It is mainly used for identification of inpatients and protecting against static electricity in an industrial production environment. Therefore, the intelligence of wristbands is mainly intellectualized in medical treatment. For example, an intelligent wristband that can detect the epileptic seizures of users, invented by Empatica.

(4) Smartwatch. Smartwatch is one of the most popular wearable smart devices at present. Unlike traditional watches, it integrates computing chips and intelligent operating systems inside the watch, and realizes the presentation and interaction of the content through the watch's display screen, the indicator light, or the vibrations. Smartwatch can be divided into an adult smartwatch, smartwatch for the elderly and smartwatch for children based on their different service objects. At present, Apple, Samsung, Motorola, LG, HUAWEI and other companies have various products in the field of smartwatch.

2.3 Application Field

The symbol of human intelligence extension is the advent of the age of wearable smart devices. Based on these devices, people can better understand the information of external and self, and can be more efficient in processing information with the help of computers, networks and even other people, and can achieve more seamless communication. There are two major applications, namely self-quantification and in vitro evolution.

In the field of self-quantification, it is further divided into two application areas. One is outdoor sports and the other is health care. The users in the former application can use the smartwatch to realize the monitoring, analysis and service of sleep, sports or outdoor data such as heart rate, step frequency, atmospheric pressure, depth of diving, altitude and so on. The latter is mainly concerned with the detection and treatment of medical signs such as blood pressure and heart rate through specialized programs provided by medical portable device manufacturers. For example, in [2], a GPS smartwatch is used to measure patients' mean maximum walking ability measured in their daily life, and [3] uses Apple smartwatch to assist in improving the daily physical activity for chronic obstructive pulmonary disease.

In the field of in vitro evolution, this kind of wearable smart devices can help users to improve the ability of information perception and processing. This application field is extremely wide. From leisure entertainment, information communication to industry applications, users can achieve enhancement or innovation of their own skills through a variety of wearable smart devices with diversified sensing, processing, connection and display functions [4]. For example, use a smartwatch to listen to music, check the incoming call reminder displayed on the watch screen, use a watch to quickly reply to SMS, check the weather information, use a watch for map navigation, traffic and shopping payment, and use a watch to connect with a smart home to control other smart devices in the home (such as opening the door, turn on the lamp of the living room and other operations).

3   Technology Supporting Wearable Smart Devices

The emergence of wearable smart devices is due to the disciplinary development and integration of many fields. The core technologies to support the development of smart devices include chip technology, smart operating system, MEMS technology, interaction design and battery-related technology. As shown in Table 1, several smart device products are selected in this paper, and lists some relevant technical parameters.

Table 1. Parameter comparison of some smart devices.

Product	Chip	Smart operating system	Interactive form	Battery capacity/mAh
Apple Watch S3	Apple W2, Dual-core	WatchOS4	Screen, voice	279
Samsung Gear S3 Frontier	Exynos7270 Dual-core ARMCortex-A53	TizenOS2.3.1	Screen, mechanical turntable, voice	360
Moto 360 Sport	Qualcomm 400	Android Wear	Screen, voice	300
HUAWEI WATCH 2 Pro	Qualcomm 2100 4-core processor	Android Wear 2.0	Screen, voice	420
HUAWEI bracelet B3	MCU	Nothing	Screen	91
XiaoMi bracelet 2	MCU	Nothing	Screen	70

3.1 Chip Technology

Chip is the core of the computing equipment, and the intelligence of smart device comes from the computing power of the device. The chip is therefore at the core position of the smart device. Due to the physical size limitation of the wearable smart devices, the capacity of battery carried by devices is very limited. In order to adapt to this situation, devices typically use chips based on the simple instruction set to reduce power consumption. Currently, the chips based on complex instruction set are at a disadvantage in the field of low power consumption [5]. For example, in a relatively single PC era of demand, Intel has become an industry-leading dominance, while Table 1 shows that the diversified wearable smart device product form and the large difference in demand for the chip make Intel's competition at a disadvantage.

The chip of wearable smart device, here, refers not only to the CPU, but also includes digital signal processing (DSP), Micro Controller Unit (MCU) System-on-a-Chip (SoC). For example, accelerometer and gyroscope belong to the category of DSP. Simple CPU, DSP MCU or SoC can't represent the quality of a smart device. Its measurement factor should be the degree of integration of chips and softwares. For example, [6] introduced a SoC, in which by combining frequency and power modes switching with extra reverse body-biasing, the system power consumption is drastically reduced by 2x and 61x in, respectively, sleep and deep sleep modes. [7] presents an ultra-low-power bracelet, which combines low-power design and energy efficient algorithms, with several sensors that is able to run multi-layer neural networks learning algorithms to process data efficiently, and proves that neural networks applications can fit within the mW power and memory envelope of a commercial ARM Cortex M4F microcontroller.

3.2   Smart Operating System

The smart operating system is an indispensable part of expandability and customization of wearable smart devices. With the increasing functions of smart devices, the development difficulty and maintenance cost will increase when developers use traditional microcontrollers to develop applications. Using an operating system-to-application development model will be an unquestionable choice. For a smart device, due to the existence of the smart operating system, the third-party developers can develop the applications that are suitable for corresponding devices. Therefore, it can enrich the functions of the equipment to the maximum extent.

At present, the major smart operation systems are Watch OS, Android Wear, Pebble, Tizen and Ticwear. As shown in Table 1, Watch OS, Android Wear and Tizen are frequently used. Android Wear can be used by many manufacturers, while Watch OS and Tizen can only be used on Apple and Samsung smart devices, respectively. On May 19, 2016, Google released the latest smart device operating system (mainly used on smart watches) Android Wear 2, and the latest operating system will no longer rely on a mobile phone for running. Furthermore, it adds Google Assistant, mobile payment and other functions to smart devices. Apple released a new Apple smart watch operation system Watch OS 4 at the 2017 Apple WWDC Developers Conference. The new version of the system has enriched the fitness function and added interfaces supporting sports devices.

3.3   MEMS Technology

Thanks to the development of sensors, wearable smart devices can collect many indicator information on human body and environmental that humans cannot get. Most of the smart devices use micro-electro-mechanical systems (MEMS) technology. MEMS-based components (sensors and actuators) began to enter the wearable market about 10 years ago. In the pedometers, the accelerometer replaced the mechanical spring for the first time. Due to the development of MEMS technology, today it is possible to integrate various sensors into the very limited space of wearable smart devices. For example, inertial sensors such as accelerometers, gyroscopes and magnetometers, environmental sensors such as pressure, humidity and UV index and human body sensors such as heart rate, body temperature, amount of sweating. Therefore, some people think that the future wearable smart devices must be the integration of complex sensors.

3.4   Interaction Design

The quality of interaction design is related to the user's operating experience to a large extent. At present, the main interactive forms of smart devices are a screen, voice, and somatosensory. The screens of wearable smart devices are relatively small, so it also increases the difficulty of text input. In response to this issue, [8] proposes a new text input method for smartwatches, which utilizes motion sensor data and machine learning approaches to detect letters written in the air by a user, and its experimental results are close to 71% accuracy in letter recognition. For another example, users can say "Ok

Google" to the Moto 360 watch, then they can ask questions or send tasks to the voice assistant. When the arm is lifted, the watch's screen will automatically light up.

3.5 Battery-Related Technology

To some extent, the capacity of battery restricts the practical application of smart devices. Smart devices generally maintain frequent calculations and network communication. At present, the smart devices with perfect functions maintain the frequency of charging once a day. This puts forward higher requirements on battery technology, power supply management and fast charging technology. [9] describes a kind of nano generator used to collect human motion energy, and the energy collected can continuously supply power for commercial smart watches. At present, graphene battery has the characteristics of fast charging, high energy storage and low cost, so it will hopefully promote the development of wearable smart devices in the future.

4 Development of Smart Devices Market

At present, Apple, Google, HUAWEI, Samsung and other companies have corresponding smart devices. Their products have their own characteristics, respectively, and their functions are also uneven. As shown in Table 2, several products and their corresponding functions are listed.

Table 2. Related product functions.

Product	Information reminder	Health monitoring	Connecting smart home	NFC payment	Map navigation	Independent call
Apple Watch S3	✓	✓	✓	✓	✓	✓
Samsung Gear S3 Frontier	✓	✓	✓	✓	✓	✓
Moto 360 Sport	✓	✓	✗	✓	✓	✗
HUAWEI WATCH 2 Pro	✓	✓	✗	✓	✓	✓
LG Watch Sport	✓	✓	✗	✓	✓	✗
CAEDEN Sona bracelet	✗	✓	✗	✗	✗	✗
XiaoMi bracelet 2	✓	✓	✗	✗	✗	✗

Apple Watch S3 will recommend new sports goals for users every Monday based on last week's activity data. When the user receives a notification, Taptic Engine will prompt him immediately by Tap. At the same time, Apple Watch can send Sketch, Tap and heart rate to other Apple Watch users through Digital Touch. The UBER is built into the watch, and the watch can unlock the room door directly. As a boarding card, Passbook can watch videos and images remotely. Support payment, map navigation and other functions. It allows developers to develop medical applications, such as real-time monitoring of blood pressure and heart rate.

Samsung Gear S3 Frontier can be positioned by Find My Watch function on Samsung mobile phones. Email, SMS, and other messages can be quickly previewed. The WatchON application on the phone can be controlled by the SmartRemote, a smart remote control application, to remotely control the TV. The camera mounted on the GALAXY Gear's strap has a 1.9 megapixel BSI sensor and auto-focus lens, which can take low resolution video or 720p video for 10 s, and just do this by twisting your wrists. Support Samsung S Voice for voice command. Through the device users can adjust the alarm clock, make a call and complete other functions. In China, Baidu voice assistant is supported to implement the call of corresponding functions.

Moto 360 Sport supports real-time monitoring of exercise heart rate. With built-in GPS positioning, it can accurately record movement distance, time and calories consumption independently from mobile phones. Music can be synchronized to Moto 360 Sport through WearADay application, and play music independently from the mobile phone. Support voice control and checking instant messaging quickly.

HUAWEI WATCH 2 Pro supports independent calls and playing music. Voice control is supported and subway, bus and shopping payments can be made via NFC.

LG Watch Sport is equipped with Google's latest Android Wear 2 system, supporting map, Google Now service. LG Watch Sport has three entity buttons, and the functions of the three buttons are fast launch Google Fit, Google Assistant and Android Pay, respectively. Twisting the middle crown can also slide the list, which is similar to the crown function of Apple Watch.

The CAEDEN Sona bracelet is more focused on stress testing. Sona APP has five modes for users to choose. Officials say that these modes are based on the natural heart rate model of the human body to carry out different exercise plans for different users' characteristics to help users to relieve psychological and physiological stress.

Being relative to Xiaomi's previous generation product, XiaoMi bracelet 2 not only supports pedometer, sleep monitoring, sedentary reminder, heart rate monitoring (real-time monitoring), incoming call reminder, screen unlocking (Android system), vibration alarm and other functions, but also add the screen display function. The payment function is only supported in Chinese Alipay free secret payments, and did not work independently from the mobile phone.

From the Table 2, we have found that health monitoring is the standard for smart devices. Payment, navigation, independent call and other advanced functions are only equipped in smartwatch products. Smart bracelet and smart chain bracelet are difficult to support such applications. In order to make more efficient use of the data collected and enrich the functions of the product, the mainstream manufacturers all have developed sports tracking, sleep quality monitoring and other functions according to the data collected by heart rate sensor, altimeters, GPS and accelerometers sensor. Such as step counter, calorie consumption, running or riding speed, running or riding mileage, climbing height, swimming time, sleep depth and so on. These allow users to freely and reasonably plan exercise time, amount of exercise and adjust the quality of sleep.

5   Limitations of Smart Devices

5.1   Self-quantification Limitations

There are many indicators that can reflect people's health level. In addition to heart rate indicator, body temperature, blood pressure, blood glucose, blood oxygen saturation, etc. are also our common health indicators. Blood pressure is an important indicator of cardiovascular and cerebrovascular diseases, and blood glucose is an important indicator of diabetes. The indicator of single heart rate does not fully and reasonably reflect a person's health status. Therefore, this paper, aiming at the standard function (health inspection) of smartwatch, investigates the related products in the market, and lists the data items that can reflect the health conditions detected by the latest products of the top companies in the global smartwatch market, as shown in Table 3.

Table 3. Health indicators that can be detected by some products.

Product	Heart rate	Blood oxygen saturation	Body temperature	Blood pressure	Blood glucose
Apple Watch S3	✓	✗	✗	✗	✗
Samsung Gear S3 Frontier	✓	✗	✗	✗	✗
Moto 360 Sport	✓	✗	✗	✗	✗
HUAWEI WATCH 2 Pro	✓	✗	✗	✗	✗
XiaoMi bracelet 2	✓	✗	✗	✗	✗

The survey found that wearable smart devices have significant limitations in health monitoring function. At present, the wearable smart devices on the market can only accurately collect the heart rate data in the health indicators. A very small number of manufacturers use certain indirect methods to estimate blood pressure, and the accuracy need yet to be verified. For example, Netgen SmartWatch S18 provides heart rate and blood pressure monitoring function. According to Amazon's user feedback, blood pressure detection is very inaccurate, and the error rate reaches 5%. For body temperature, the temperature of the skin can only be detected. In order to detect blood glucose at present, all accurate detection methods must puncture the skin to obtain a small amount of blood as a sample for further testing, and there is no recognized nondestructive testing technology. Users will not accept the method that allow the smart devices to automatically puncture the skin to detect blood glucose.

As shown in Table 3, smartwatches of several famous brands can only detect heart rate data. Heart rate variability (HRV) is an important indicator of mental stress level. Some products, such as CAEDEN Sona bracelet, detect heart rate as well as detect heart rate variability, and then detect the stress level of users. A smartwatch-based system is proposed in [10] to collect biological signal data such as heart rate, current skin response (GSR) and skin temperature (ST), and then analyze and detect mental stress. At present, the mental stress can be analyzed according to heart rate and blood oxygen saturation. However, the detection of blood oxygen saturation is mainly from the finger, earlobe and other non-wrist areas. For example, Samsung S7 smart phone is equipped with corresponding sensors for detecting heart rate and blood oxygen saturation. The corresponding data can be displayed on the App side and the stress level can be analyzed. FitOn smartwatch provides blood oxygen saturation detection function. According to a report on the disassembly of Apple Watch S3, Apple Watch S3 hardware supports blood oxygen detection, but Apple Corp didn't activate this function.

In a word, the health monitoring function of wearable smart devices is not perfect enough yet, and the detection items are single. For important blood glucose, blood pressure and other health indicators, there is no corresponding technology in smart devices which specifically refer to the devices worn on the wrist at present, which can achieve goals with small errors. For all current wearable smart devices, the detected data is only displayed to the user, and the detected data is not fully utilized to predict the change of the user's health indicators to alert users. For example, learning the changes in the heart rate of the user, and then predicting when the heart rate will increase or decrease, can be a great help in wise medical.

5.2   In Vitro Evolution Limitations

Smart devices have been able to complete the function of mobile phone independently from mobile phone, such as listening to music, checking incoming calls, making phone calls, quickly answering SMS, checking weather information, map navigation, traffic and shopping payment, etc. However, these are not just needs, and have strong substitutability. At present, the public free WiFi coverage is not wide. Once the smartwatch is disconnected from the network, a considerable part of its functions will not be available. Moreover, as can be seen from Table 2, there are very few devices that can connect smart homes. Connecting smart homes is an important scene in the era of Internet of Things. However, for other devices in other scenes, the number of connectable devices is almost zero. In addition, products of different brands cannot be connected to each other at present.

6   Prospects

Future wearable smart devices will be able to detect more health indicators on self-quantification, such as body temperature, blood pressure and blood glucose. A Samsung's patent has proposed a new method to measure blood pressure. It is similar to the light sensor method used in heart rate sensor. It irradiates the light to the target area of a user and receive the scattered light from the target area. According to the intensity of the scattered light received, the value of the user's blood pressure is determined [11]. A patent from Apple shows that it is possible to measure the pulse transit time (PTT) and use the PTT to calculate the blood pressure value. Using the acceleration sensor to detect the starting time of the left ventricular blood pressure pulse, using the photoelectric sensor and the pulse pressure sensor to detect the arrival time of the pulse, calculate the PTT from the left ventricle to the wrist, and the blood pressure value is calculated based on the PTT [12]. As technology advances, non-invasive blood glucose measurement methods will certainly replace invasive methods, and corresponding methods should be integrated into smart devices. Wearable smart devices in the future can integrate multiple health indicators to reflect users' health level. It also contributes to the detection of blood pressure and blood glucose to prevent cardiovascular and cerebrovascular diseases and diabetes, respectively. What's more, it can detect in vitro health data. For example, [13] uses a smartwatch to track accelerometer and gyroscope data of users and then uses supervised machine learning algorithms to classify eating behaviors from not eat behaviors. In addition, it should also have the ability to predict the user's future health indicators. For example, by studying user's heart rate data, it is possible to predict the development of the user's future heart rate. At present, the Robot and VR laboratory at Nanjing University of Finance and Economics is doing the related work. The prototype of a smart watch was developed in April, 2018.

With the development of Internet of Things, the connection attributes of wearable smart devices will become stronger, and the corresponding functions can be used in various scenarios. For example, users can use a smartwatch to pass corporate access control, open the door of users' home, control the TV at home, and exchange contacts quickly with customers. For another example, [14] introduced the feasibility of smartwatches in IoT devices communication. [15] proposes a wearable smartwatch with user customized gestures used to control a web browser on a smart TV running the Tizen Operating System.

In general, the development prospect of wearable smart devices is broad.

Acknowledgements. This work is supported by National Natural Science Foundation of Innovative Research Groups Science Foundation of China (51221004), ARC DECRA and ARC Discovery projects (DE130100911, DP130101327), the NSFC funding (61332013), the International Science and Technology Cooperation Projects (No. 2016D10008, 2013DFG12810, 2013C24027), the Municipal Natural Science Foundation of Ningbo (No.2015A610119), the Guangzhou Science and Technology Project under Grants (2016201604030034), the Major Projects of Natural Science Research in Jiangsu Higher Education Institutions (No. 14KJA520001), Jiangsu Production and Research Project (No. BY2015010-05), the Natural Science Foundation of Zhejiang Province (No. Y16F020002), the Ningbo Natural Science Fund (No. 2015A610119), International Science & Technology Cooperation Projects of Ningbo (No. 2016D10008) and the project of research and development of intelligent resource allocation and sharing platform for marine electronic information industry (No. 2017GY116).

References

1. Interaction Paradigm. https://zh.wikipedia.org/w/index.php?title=%E4%BA%A4%E4%BA %92%E8%8C%83%E5%BC%8F&oldid=10425617. Accessed 10 Mar 2018
2. Dallacosta, G., Radaelli, M., Maida, S., et al.: Smart watch, smarter EDSS: improving disability assessment in multiple sclerosis clinical practice. J. Neurol. Sci. **383**, 166 (2017)
3. Hataji, O., Nishii, Y., Ito, K., et al.: Smart watch-based coaching with tiotropium and olodaterol ameliorates physical activity in patients with chronic obstructive pulmonary disease. Exp. Ther. Med. **14**(5), 4061–4064 (2017)
4. Wearable Smart Devices. https://baike.baidu.com/item/%E7%A9%BF%E6%88%B4%E5%BC %8F%E6%99%BA%E8%83%BD%E8%AE%BE%E5%A4%87/1886368. Accessed 2 Apr 2018

5. Feng, S.: Wearable devices development status and trend. Inf. Commun. Technol. **3**, 52–57 (2014). (in Chinese)
6. Lallement, G., Abouzeid, F., Cochet, M., Daveau, J.M., Roche, P., Autran, J.L.: A 2.7 pJ/ cycle 16 MHz, 0.7 μW deep sleep power ARM Cortex-M0+ core SoC in 28 nm FD-SOI. IEEE J. Solid-State Circ. (2018)
7. Magno, M., Pritz, M., Mayer, P., Benini, L.: DeepEmote: towards multi-layer neural networks in a low power wearable multi-sensors bracelet. In: IEEE International Workshop on Advances in Sensors and Interfaces, pp. 32–37. IEEE (2017)
8. Moazen, D., Sajjadi, S.A., Nahapetian, A.: AirDraw: leveraging smart watch motion sensors for mobile human computer interactions. In: IEEE Consumer Communications & Networking Conference, pp. 442–446. IEEE (2016)
9. Lai, Y., Deng, J., Zhang, S.L., et al.: Single-thread-based wearable and highly stretchable triboelectric nanogenerators and their applications in cloth-based self-powered human-interactive and biomedical sensing. Adv. Funct. Mater. **27** (2016)
10. Ciabattoni, L., Ferracuti, F., Longhi, S., et al.: Real-time mental stress detection based on smartwatch. In: IEEE International Conference on Consumer Electronics, pp. 110–111. IEEE (2017)
11. Maxim, A.B.B., Mikhail, B.B.P., Andrey, V.B.K., Jo, J.J., Demetrius, A.B.J.C., Sergei, A.B.Y., Samsung Electronics Co., Ltd.: Method of measuring blood pressure and apparatus therefor. WO patent WO2018030665A1, 15 February 2018
12. Narasimhan, R., Kimoto, R.C., Sullivan, T.J., Whitehurst, T.K., Young, D.P., Zeng, Z., Klaassen, E., Apple Inc.: Wrist worn accelerometer for pulse transit time (PTT) measurements of blood pressure. US patent US20170281024A1, 5 October 2017
13. Using Machine Learning on Wearable Smart Watch Devices to Track Nutritional Intake. https://alzulas.com/Pages/PDFs/SmartWatch-2.pdf
14. MCU-Bluetooth design: making smartwatch talk to IoT devices. https://archive.eetindia.co.in/ www.eetindia.co.in/ART_8800704241_1800013_NT_9fb4d9a1.HTM. Accessed 29 Apr 2018
15. Seetharamu, V.K., Bose, J., Sunkara, S., Tigga, N.: TV remote control via wearable smart watch device. In: India Conference, pp. 1–6. IEEE (2015)

Localized Mandarin Speech Synthesis Services for Enterprise Scenarios

Yishuang Ning[1,2,3](✉), Huan Chen[2,3], Chunxiao Xing[1], and Liang-Jie Zhang[2,3]

[1] Research Institute of Web Information, Tsinghua University, Beijing, China
ningyishuang@126.com
[2] National Engineering Research Center for Supporting Software of Enterprise Internet Services, Hong Kong, China
[3] Kingdee Research, Kingdee International Software Group Company Limited, Shenzhen, China

Abstract. Speech interaction systems have been gaining popularity in recent years. For these systems, the performance of speech synthesis has become a key factor to determine quality of service (QoS) and user experience in real-world speech interaction systems. How to improve the efficiency of speech synthesis has become a hot topic and represents one of the main streams in specific scenarios of human-computer interactions. In this paper, we propose a low-latency hidden Markov model (HMM)-based localized Mandarin speech synthesis architecture which uses a shared global variance for all the Gaussian mixture models (GMMs). Through this strategy, the memory consumption for loading the acoustic model has been reduced greatly. We also encapsulate the speech synthesis as a service using epoll mechanism so that the synthesis engine can be initialized by preloading the text analysis model and acoustic model, and can be invoked by multiple processes simultaneously, thus further improving the efficiency of speech synthesis. Experimental results demonstrate that our proposed method can significantly reduce the time latency while maintaining voice quality of synthesized speeches.

Keywords: Localized Mandarin speech synthesis
Hidden Markov model · Low latency

1 Introduction

Speech is an intuitive and direct way for both human beings communication and machinery user interface [1]. With the rapid development of speech techniques, speech has become the most natural way for linking customers and the entrance for the next generation human-computer interactions in enterprise scenarios. Speech synthesis, also known as text-to-speech (TTS) seeks generating speech waveforms from a given text [2]. As a new way of speech output for intelligent devices, it plays a significant role in people's daily life. In recent years, the performance of speech synthesis has become one of the key factors of determining

© Springer International Publishing AG, part of Springer Nature 2018
J. Xiao et al. (Eds.): ICCC 2018, LNCS 10971, pp. 130–143, 2018.
https://doi.org/10.1007/978-3-319-94307-7_10

quality of service (QoS) and user experience as well. Many application scenarios such as chatbots or smart speakers utilize the online speech synthesis application programming interfaces (APIs) to connect with their businesses. Although it can receive fast response when the network quality is fine, it may become difficult to work normally or even fail to work when the network quality is poor or there is no network connection in the current workplaces, thus degrading users' satisfaction greatly.

In the long tradition of researches dealing with speech synthesis, people have proposed numerous approaches including speech waveform concatenation and parameterized synthesis models [3,4]. The former mainly focuses on concatenating the pre-recorded speech units (like diphones or triphones) to synthesize fluent speeches [5]. Although this method can achieve high speech quality, it requires a large memory to store the speech units. Therefore, it is not suitable for low-resource platforms [6–8]. To address this problem, [7] proposed a small-unit concatenation system. In this method, less than a few thousand speech units have been used, thus requiring lower memory usage. However, it suffers from the problems of pitch, phase and spectral discontinuities, leading to lower speech quality. The latter dedicates to fulfilling the speech synthesis task with the statistical parametric speech synthesis (SPSS) framework [8,9]. With the rapid development of deep learning techniques, SPSS based on artificial neural networks (ANNs) has become popular in the TTS research and application areas in recent years. As a variation of recurrent neural networks (RNNs), long short-term memory (LSTM)-RNNs [10,11] not only offer an efficient and distributed representation of complex dependencies between linguistic and acoustic features, but also provide an elegant way to model speech-like sequential data given its capability in leveraging long short-term contextual dependencies [12]. For example, [12] proposed a streaming speech synthesis model using unidirectional LSTM-RNNs with a recurrent output layer. Though it enabled low-latency speech synthesis in some applications, it was still slower than hidden Markov model (HMM)-based SPSS [10].

The objective of this work is to implement a light-weight speech synthesis system that can be used on a low-resource (low memory and low computational resources) [7] platforms. To achieve this objective, it requires the synthesis method to be optimized and providing speech synthesis capability with low time latency. In this paper, we propose an HMM-based localized speech synthesis service framework that is suitable for deployment on mobile or embedded devices. Firstly, to guarantee high speech quality and naturalness, we use a large scale of speech corpus with a single speaker to train an HMM-based acoustic model. To reduce the memory cost occupied by the model, we conduct one optimization which uses a shared variance for all the Gaussian mixture models (GMMs) while the traditional methods use one variance for each GMM. After the optimization, it costs much lower memory for storing the acoustic model. Secondly, we employ an Epoll based Socket Server/Client mechanism [13] to pre-load the text analysis model and acoustic model to initialize the synthesis engine.

The rest of the paper is structured as follows. Section 2 presents the proposed framework for speech synthesis as a service in our work. Section 3 carries out an extensive of experiments to evaluate the performance of the proposed method. Section 4 summarizes the paper and gives a brief introduction to our future work.

2   Methodology

2.1   Overall Architecture

As can be seen from Fig. 1, the overall architecture of our proposed localized Mandarin speech synthesis service can be divided into server part and client part. In the server part, speech synthesis engine will be first initialized by loading the text analysis model and the acoustic model. Then the socket will be initialized by the epoll mechanism and start a listener thread. After the connection being constructed between the server and the client, the client will send the input text to the server with epoll. And the server will generate the pronunciation and prosodic features from the input text with the text analysis module. Leveraging the parameter generation module, the acoustic parameters will be generated from the initialized engine. Finally, the speech waveform will be synthesized from the speech synthesis module. If there is no active events, the socket will be closed from epoll.

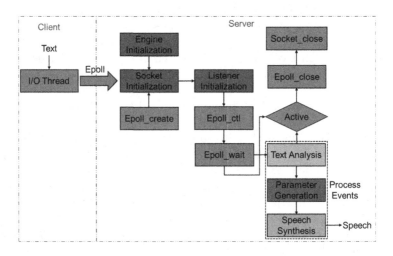

Fig. 1. Overall architecture of our proposed localized Mandarin speech synthesis service.

2.2   Text Analysis

The text analysis module implements the conversion from the natural text to pronunciation and the generation of prosody. It usually includes the following modules: document structure generation, text normalization, word segmentation and prosodic structure generation, grapheme-to-phoneme conversion and prosody prediction. The processing flow is shown is Fig. 2.

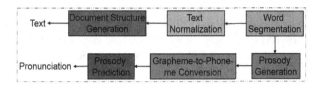

Fig. 2. Flowchart of the text analysis module.

Document Structure Generation. Since the basic data structure in our Mandarin speech synthesis system is SSML document which is an XML-based binary tree, the input text is firstly processed by the document structure generation module so as to provide a mechanism to access the elements of the SSML tree. Figure 3 shows an example of the document structure for our proposed Mandarin TTS engine.

```
<?xml version="1.0" encoding="UTF-16" ?>
<speak version="1.1" xml:lang="zh-cmn">
  <p>
    <s>金蝶软件中国有限公司始创于
      <say-as interpret-as="number" format="year"> 1 9 9 3 </say-as>年
      <say-as interpret-as="punctuation" format="s">。</say-as>
    </s>
  </p>
</speak>
```

Fig. 3. Document structure for our proposed Mandarin TTS engine.

Text Normalization. In real-world interaction scenarios, the input text generally contains homographs, numbers and abbreviations that ultimately require to expand into a phonetic representation. To address this problem, the text normalization module is used to convert all written form (orthographic form) of non-Chinese characters (e.g. symbols, punctuations, digit numbers, and English characters, etc.) into Chinese characters as is shown in Fig. 4.

```
<?xml version="1.0" encoding="UTF-16" ?>
<speak version="1.1" xml:lang="zh-cmn">
  <p>
    <s>金蝶软件中国有限公司始创于
      <w role="m">一九九三</w>年
      <break />
    </s>
  </p>
</speak>
```

Fig. 4. Sample output of the text normalization module.

Word Segmentation. The functionality of the word segmentation module is in two folds: (1) segment the input sentence into lexicon words according to pronunciation lexicon; (2) generate the part-of-speech (POS) information for each word. For Mandarin language, the word boundary information is very important for determining the meaning and pronunciation of a word in the sentence, since there is no boundary between different words. In this paper, the word segmentation is processed by an automatic procedure based on statistical learning. Figure 5 gives a sample output of the word segmentation module.

```
<?xml version="1.0" encoding="UTF-16" ?>
<speak version="1.1" xml:lang="zh-cmn">
  <p>
    <s>
      <w role="n">金蝶</w>
      <w role="n">软件</w>
      <w role="ns">中国</w>
      <w role="n">有限公司</w>
      <w role="v">始创</w>
      <w role="p">于</w>
      <w role="m">一九九三</w>
      <w role="q">年</w>
      <break />
    </s>
  </p>
</speak>
```

Fig. 5. Sample output of the word segmentation module.

Prosodic Structure Generation. During speaking, the speakers always tend to insert appropriate breaks between different words or phrases. To make the synthesized speeches much more natural and intelligent, the prosodic structure generation module is always adopted to generate the prosodic word boundary

```
<?xml version="1.0" encoding="UTF-16" ?>
<speak version="1.1" xml:lang="zh-cmn">
  <p>
    <s>
      <w role="n">金蝶</w>
      <w role="n">软件</w>
      <w role="ns">中国</w>
      <break strength="weak" />
      <w role="n">有限公司</w>
      <break strength="medium" />
      <w role="v">始创</w>
      <w role="p">于</w>
      <break strength="weak" />
      <w role="m">一九九三</w>
      <w role="q">年</w>
    </s>
  </p>
</speak>
```

Fig. 6. Result of the prosody generation module. Two levels of breaks including weak break and medium break have been inserted into different words.

and phrase boundary, as is shown in Fig. 6. We use statistical rules such as mono-syllable word and C4.5 or maximum entropy model to achieve these objectives, respectively.

Grapheme-to-phoneme Conversion. The grapheme-to-phoneme module is to generate the pronunciation for each lexicon word so that the speech synthesizer can enquire how to read out that word. The input of this module is the document with word segmentation and POS information, and outputs the phoneme information for each word. Figure 7 shows an example of the grapheme-to-phoneme module where a new node "<phoneme>" has been generated.

```
<?xml version="1.0" encoding="UTF-16" ?>
<speak version="1.1" xml:lang="zh-cmn">
  <p>
    <s>
      <w role="n">
        <phoneme alphabet="x-pinyin" ph="jin1-die2">金蝶</phoneme>
      </w>
      <w role="n">
        <phoneme alphabet="x-pinyin" ph="ruan3-jian4">软件</phoneme>
      </w>
```

Fig. 7. Sample output of the grapheme-to-phoneme module.

Prosody Prediction. In natural speech, the prosody of the word often changes to express the intention, the attitude and emotion of a speaker. Therefore, the prosody prediction module plays a significant role for enhancing the expressivity of the synthesized speech. It is generally implemented by adding "<prosody>" element in the sentence.

2.3 HMM-Based Mandarin Speech Synthesis

In the speech synthesis module, we utilize the HMM-based speech synthesis framework which typically uses an HMM as its generative model [5]. Similar with the unit selection approach, both the phoneme sequences and context of the linguistic specification are represented as HMMs. In this paper, we first give the framework of HMM-based speech synthesis which has been introduced in many research literatures [14]. Then we present the training procedure to make people further familiar with the whole framework.

Framework. The HMM-based speech synthesis can be divided into training phase and synthesis phase as shown in Fig. 8.

In the training phase, acoustic features including fundamental frequency (F0) and spectral parameters are first extracted from the speech waveforms in the

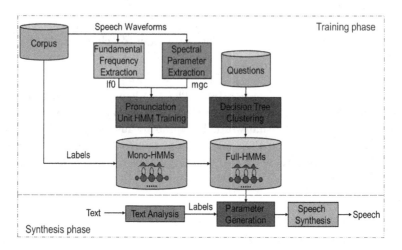

Fig. 8. HMM-based Mandarin speech synthesis framework.

corpus. In this paper, the mel-generalized cepstral (MGC) is used as the spectral parameter. Then, the contextual questions are carefully designed for decision tree clustering and appropriate HMM unit is selected according to the scale of the corpus. To consider all kinds of pronunciation mechanisms of model units, we use consonant and vowel as the phonemes. Finally, the HMMs including F0 and MGC are trained guided by the context-dependent labels obtained in Sect. 3.2 and the designed contextual questions.

In the synthesis stage, a given text is first processed into a sequence of context-dependent labels. Then a sentence-level HMM is constructed by concatenating context-dependent HMMs. The duration of each state of the phonemes is determined to maximize its probability based on its state duration probability distribution. Acoustic parameters are generated by the parameter generation algorithm. Finally, a speech waveform is synthesized directly from the generated acoustic parameters by using a speech synthesizer, such as hts_engine or STRAIGHT. Considering the synthesis efficiency, we use hts_engine in this paper.

Training Procedure. The training process of HMM-based speech synthesis includes the following steps: define an HMM prototype, initial training and parameter re-estimation of monophone HMMs, parallel embedded re-estimation of the monophone HMM parameters, generation of the context-dependent HMMs, context decision tree clustering and re-estimation of the clustered HMM parameters. This paper gives the detailed introduction in the following subsections.

Define an HMM Prototype. Before training, we need to define an appropriate HMM prototype, such as the form and topology of the HMM, the state transition parameters and the output probability parameters. The observation vector of the HMM is typically divided into several independent data streams, with its own weight for each stream. And each state definition should show the required number of streams and mixture components in each stream.

Initial Training and Parameter Re-estimation of Monophone HMMs. After setting up an appropriate prototype, an HMM can be initialized firstly by reading in all the training data and monophone labels. Then the initial parameters are computed repeatedly using Viterbi alignment [15] to segment the training observations. The piece-wise K-means clustering algorithm [16] is also used to cluster the vectors within each state. Finally, the Baum-Welch algorithm [17] is used to re-estimate the parameters. This involves finding the probability of being in each state at each time frame using the Forward-Backward algorithm [18].

Parallel Embedded Re-estimation of the Monophone HMM Parameters. This process typically operates in two distinct stages. In the first stage, each input data file contains the processed training data and the accumulators for state occupation, state transition, means and variances are updated. In the second stage, the accumulators are used to calculate new estimates for the HMM parameters. Since the training set is large, we split it into separate chunks that are processed in parallel multiple processors, thus speeding up the training process.

Generation of the Context-dependent HMMs. The purpose of this step is to generate parameters with a full-context HMM model, including the state transition probability matrix of each phoneme, the weight, mean and variance of each stream of the HMMs. Theoretically, when the labeled training data is sufficient, the more parameters of the model, the higher the accuracy is. However, in real-world scenarios, the labeled data is often not only very limited, but also unbalanced. If a large number of parameters are used for training, it will be impossible to train the model sufficiently, thus making the prediction of the parameters influenced a lot. To address this problem, the context decision tree clustering algorithm is used to share some parameters, so that one or more HMM models can share the same parameter set.

Context Decision Tree Clustering. When the same words are located in different contexts, their acoustic characteristics are different. Similarly, there are differences for the same words in different contexts. In the decision tree clustering process, the decision tree will cluster the training data with close acoustic features according to the context characteristics [19]. The acoustic features of the nodes with similar contextual information in the decision tree are close to each other. For example, the acoustic features of the data in the leaf nodes are similar to their sibling nodes and parent nodes. Therefore, it is reasonable to predict feature parameters from their sibling nodes and parent nodes. Based on this perspective, [20] proposes the context model.

(1) Contextual Information for Clustering. In addition to the phoneme information, a lot of contextual information has also been used for clustering which has been shown in Table 1.

(2) Context Decision Tree Clustering. In HMM-based speech synthesis training framework, it provides an effective decision tree based clustering mechanism which offers a solution to the unseen context problem.

Actually, a decision tree is a binary tree in which a yes/no phonetic question is attached to each node. Initially all states in a given phoneme list are placed at the root node of a tree. The pool of states is successively split and this continues until the states have trickled down to leaf nodes. The question at each node is chosen to locally maximize the log likelihood of the training data given the final set of the state tyings. Each question takes the form "Is the left or right context in the question set?". For example, "Is the right context a vowel?". Then the general decision tree is constructed by the minimum description length (MDL) criterion [14] to minimize the difference of the original model and the model after being split.

Re-estimation of the Clustered HMM Parameters. We use full contextual labels to re-estimate the parameters of the HMMs.

Finally, the trained model and decision trees are saved in the format of the hts_engine synthesizer.

Synthesis Procedure. During the synthesis phase, full contextual labels are provided to the HMM model to predict the acoustic feature parameters of the speech. Finally, the corresponding speech is synthesized by the Vocoder in the official hts_engine.

2.4   Speech Synthesis as a Service with Epoll

Epoll Mechanism. Epoll is a mechanism for processing service-oriented concurrency problems. Different from the select mechanism, epoll applies for a simple file system in the kernel of the Linux system first, and then creates an epoll object which has an independent event poll struct for storing newly-added events. All the events are regarded as the nodes of a red black tree. The events which are added repeatedly will be recognised by the tree efficiently. Besides, epoll maintains a bidirectional linked list for storing the occurred events. If the list is not empty, epoll will copy the occurred event to the user mode and return the event number to the user.

Speech Synthesis as a Service with Epoll. The epoll-based speech synthesis service is divided into two parts: the server part and the client part. The server part will first create a speech synthesis connection descriptor that will be used in epoll calls later. Then it will add the descriptor to the epoll and wait for incoming connections from the client. The server will also preload the text analysis model and speech synthesis model to initialize a speech synthesizer. The client part will initiate a connection request to the server. When a new connection arrives, the server will send accepted connection socket to the client. After the connection being created, the client wilsl send the text to be synthesized to the server.

Finally, the server will generate the full labels through the text analysis module and synthesize speech with the speech synthesis module.

Table 1. Contextual information for clustering.

Contextual level	Content
Phoneme	The phoneme before the previous phoneme
	The previous phoneme
	The current phoneme
	The next phoneme
	The phoneme after the next phoneme
	Forward position of the current phoneme in the current syllable
	Backward position of the current phoneme in the current syllable
Syllable	The tone of the previous syllable
	The number of the phonemes in the previous syllable
	The tone of the current syllable
	The number of the phonemes in the current syllable
	Forward position of the current syllable in the current word
	Backward position of the current syllable in the current word
	Forward position of the current syllable in the current phrase
	Backward position of the current syllable in the current phrase
	Forward position of the current syllable in the breath group
	Backward position of the current syllable in the breath group
	The boundary type before the current syllable
	The boundary type after the current syllable
	The consonant of the current syllable
	The tone of the next syllable
	The number of the phonemes in the next syllable
Word	The number of the syllables in the current word
	Forward position of the current word in the current phrase
	Backward position of the current word in the current phrase
	Forward position of the current word in the breath group
	Backward position of the current word in the breath group
Phrase	The number of the syllables in the current phrase
	The number of the words in the current phrase
	Forward position of the current phrase in the breath group
	Backward position of the current phrase in the breath group
Breath group	The number of the words in the current breath group
	The number of the phrases in the current breath group
	The type of the current breath group

3   Experiments

3.1   Experimental Setup

Corpus. To synthesize natural speech, a set of text prompts are carefully designed and the corresponding speech utterances are recorded for modeling. Specifically, 5003 text prompts are designed to consider all kinds of pronunciation mechanisms of phonemes. And the context characteristics of the phonemes are also covered by the text prompts as many as possible. A female professional speaker was invited to record the speech utterances in a sound proof studio. All the speech data was saved as waveform files (16 bit stereo, sampled at 48 kHz). The speech data were downsampled to 16 kHz, then 25-dimensional MGC parameters and log F0 values were extracted every 5 ms. 5-state left-to-right HMMs were used to train the acoustic model. From the 5003 text prompts, 30 prompts are randomly selected as the test set for experimentation, while all the others are used to train an HMM with the context-related question set described above.

System Configuration. To assess the effectiveness of the proposed method, we test our system on an embedded Raspberry Pi system with 1.2 GHz CPU and 1 GBytes memory. Compared with a server which has high processing capability, it is very resource-limited.

Comparison Method. We designed two HMM-based models to compare the performance with our proposed method: (1) an HMM model with respective mean and variance for each GMM (resp-GMM); (2) an HMM model with shared variance for all the GMMs (shared-HMM); (3) our proposed method which is implemented with epoll mechanism with the same configuration as (2) (proposed).

In all the experiments, we evaluate the average synthesis time which is defined as the time to get the entire audio.

3.2   Experimental Results

Real-Time Performance with Different Models. Table 2 shows the performance of synthesis efficiency using different comparison methods. From the results, we can see that tying the variance of all the GMMs can significantly reduce the average synthesis time. Besides, when the epoll mechanism is used, it has achieved the highest time performance, thus demonstrating the effectiveness of our proposed method.

Real-Time Performance with Different Prosody Level. To evaluate the performance with different prosodic level, we conduct a series of experiments, including word, prosodic phrase, sentence and paragraph. Experimental results are shown in Table 3. It can be learned from the table that for all prosodic levels,

Table 2. Real-time performance with different models.

Models	Average synthesis time (s)
Resp-HMM	5.2
Shared-HMM	3.6
Proposed	**1.5**

Table 3. Real-time performance with different prosody level. Average latency and total time in seconds to synthesize a word, prosodic phrase, sentence and paragraph.

Prosody level	Average synthesis time (s)	
	Shared-HMM	Proposed
Word	2.3	**0.8**
Prosodic phrase	3.1	**1.6**
Sentence	5.3	**2.3**
Paragraph	9.8	**7.8**

the epoll-based method is superior to the one without epoll, which indicates the usability and reasonability of our proposed method for using on low resource systems.

Subjective Evaluation. To subjectively evaluate the performance of our proposed method, the mean opinion score (MOS) test was conducted using 15 utterances randomly selected from the test set. 10 subjects were invited, and asked to listen to the synthetic speeches and to indicate the voice quality based on a five-point scale: '1' (bad); '2' (poor); '3' (fair); '4' (good); '5' (excellent). The average MOS of different models are shown in Table 4, where the confidence intervals (CI) at confidence level 0.95 ($\alpha = 0.95$) are also given. As can be seen from the table, the MOS of the proposed method is almost the same as other methods, which means the two processing strategies have little influence on the voice quality of the synthesized speeches.

Table 4. Experimental results on the quality of the synthesized speeches, where the confidence intervals (CI) of the mean opinion scores (MOS) are given at the confidence level $\alpha = 0.95$.

Models	MOS	CI
Resp-HMM	3.78	[3.66, 3.90]
Shared-HMM	3.73	[3.63, 3.83]
Proposed	3.68	[3.60, 3.76]

4   Conclusions and Future Work

This paper investigates implementing localized Mandarin speech synthesis as a service on low-resource hardware platforms for enterprise scenarios. To reduce the scale of the model, we use a shared variance for all the GMMs instead of respective variance for each GMM in training phase. Through this strategy, it costs much lower memory to store the acoustic model, thus increasing the loading speed of the model. Besides, we also encapsulate the speech synthesis system as a service with epoll mechanism so that the synthesis engine can be initialized by pre-loading the text analysis model and acoustic model, and can be invoked by multiple processes simultaneously. Experimental results show that our method can significantly improve the efficiency of speech synthesis while hardly influencing the voice quality of synthesized speeches.

Future work will be dedicated to improving the expressiveness of the synthesized speeches and the implementation of localized expressive speech synthesis (e.g. emphasis, or emotion, etc.) for specific application scenarios.

Acknowledgements. This work is partially supported by the technical projects No. c1533411500138 and No. 2017YFB0802700. This work is also supported by NSFC(91646202).

References

1. Na, X., Xie, X., Kuang, J.: Low latency parameter generation for real-time speech synthesis system. In: Proceedings of the IEEE International Conference on Multimedia and Expo (ICME), pp. 1–6 (2014)
2. Zen, H., Tokuda, K., Black, A.: Statistical parametric speech synthesis. Speech Commun. **51**(11), 1039–1064 (2009)
3. Meng, F., Wu, Z., Jia, J., Meng, H., Cai, L.: Synthesizing English emphatic speech for multimodal corrective feedback in computer-aided pronunciation training. Multimedia Tools Appl. **73**(1), 463–489 (2014)
4. Wu, Z., Ning, Y., Zang, X., Jia, J., Meng, F., Meng, H., Cai, L.: Generating emphatic speech with hidden Markov model for expressive speech synthesis. Multimedia Tools Appl. **74**(22), 9909–9925 (2015)
5. Tokuda, K., Nankaku, Y., Toda, T., Zen, H., Yamagishi, J., Oura, K.: Speech synthesis based on hidden Markov models. Proc. IEEE **101**(5), 1234–1252 (2013)
6. Tth, B.: Optimizing HMM speech synthesis for low-resource devices. J. Adv. Comput. Intell. **16**(2), 327–334 (2012)
7. Sheikhzadeh, H., Cornu, E., Brennan, R., Schneider, T.: Real-time speech synthesis on an ultra low-resource, programmable DSP system. In: Proceedings of the IEEE International Conference on Acoustics, Speech, and Signal Processing (ICASSP) (2002)
8. Parlikar, A., Black, A.: Data-driven phrasing for speech synthesis in low-resource languages. In: Proceedings of the IEEE International Conference on Acoustics, Speech and Signal Processing (ICASSP), pp. 4013–4016 (2012)
9. Zen, H., Tokuda, K., Black, A.: Statistical parametric speech synthesis. Speech Commun. **51**(11), 1039–1064 (2009)

10. Zen, H., Agiomyrgiannakis, Y., Egberts, N., Henderson, F., Szczepaniak, P.: Fast, compact, and high quality LSTM-RNN based statistical parametric speech synthesizers for mobile devices. arXiv preprint arXiv:1606.06061 (2016)
11. Fan, Y., Qian, Y., Xie, F. L., Soong, F.: TTS synthesis with bidirectional LSTM based recurrent neural networks. In: Proceedings of the Annual Conference of the International Speech Communication Association (2014)
12. Zen, H., Sak, H.: Unidirectional long short-term memory recurrent neural network with recurrent output layer for low-latency speech synthesis. In: Proceedings of the IEEE International Conference on Acoustics, Speech and Signal Processing (ICASSP), pp. 4470–4474 (2015)
13. Verhaeghe, P., Verslype, K., Lapon, J., Naessens, V., De Decker, B.: A mobile and reliable anonymous ePoll infrastructure. In: Schmidt, A.U., Russello, G., Lioy, A., Prasad, N.R., Lian, S. (eds.) MobiSec 2010. LNICST, vol. 47, pp. 41–52. Springer, Heidelberg (2010). https://doi.org/10.1007/978-3-642-17502-2_4
14. Yamagishi, J.: An introduction to HMM-based speech synthesis. Technical report (2006)
15. Huang, X., Acero, A., Alleva, F., Hwang, M., Jiang, L., Mahajan, M.: Microsoft windows highly intelligent speech recognizer: whisper. In: Proceedings of the IEEE International Conference on Acoustics, Speech and Signal Processing (ICASSP) (1995)
16. Burkardt, J.: K-means clustering. Virginia Tech, Advanced Research Computing, Interdisciplinary Center for Applied Mathematics (2009)
17. Baggenstoss, P.: A modified Baum-Welch algorithm for hidden Markov models with multiple observation spaces. IEEE Trans. Speech Audio Process. **9**(4), 411–416 (2001)
18. Yu, S., Kobayashi, H.: Practical implementation of an efficient forward-backward algorithm for an explicit-duration hidden Markov model. IEEE Trans. Signal Process. **54**(5), 1947–1951 (2006)
19. Ning, Y., Wu, Z., Jia, J., Meng, F., Meng, H., Cai, L.: HMM-based emphatic speech synthesis for corrective feedback in computer-aided pronunciation training. In: Proceedings of the IEEE International Conference on Acoustics, Speech and Signal Processing (ICASSP), pp. 4934–4938 (2015)
20. Meng, F.: Analysis and generation of focus in continuous speech. Ph.D. Thesis, Tsinghua University (2013)

Short Paper Track: Cognitive Modeling

Biologically Inspired Augmented Memory Recall Model for Pattern Recognition

K. Ashwin Viswanathan[(⊠)], Goutam Mylavarapu[(⊠)],
and Johnson P. Thomas[(⊠)]

Department of Computer Science, Oklahoma State University,
Stillwater, OK 74074, USA
{ashwin.kannan,goutam.mylavarapu,johnson.thomas}@okstate.edu

Abstract. The concept of modeling a machine which can adapt to the dynamic changes in environment has fascinated the field of Artificial Intelligence. Machine Learning has made inroads in every possible domain. New techniques are developed which can mimic human like responses and thoughts. Cognitive computing has developed renewed interest in the community with advent of Artificial Neural Nets (ANN). In this paper, we present a biological inspired approach to building a augmented memory recall model which can learn usage access patterns and reconstruct from them when presented with noisy or broken concepts. We use Hopfield Networks in a distributed parallel architecture like Hadoop. We also present a mechanism for augmenting the memory capacity of Hopfield Nets. Our model is tested on a real world dataset by parallelizing the learning process thereby increasing the computing power to recognize patterns.

Keywords: Cognitive computing · Hopfield nets
Biological architecture

1 Introduction

Interest in developing a cognitive system has sparked renewed research interests giving rise to *Deep Learning* [17]. Human brain modeling started as the precursor to modern deep learning systems. Genesis to such models started with the step of developing computation techniques simulating the human brain. Scientific paradigms like *Brain Inspired Cognitive Architecture (BICA)* are endeavors started to that effect. Another aspect of cognitive systems is concerned with interpreting biological process like thinking and logical reasoning. This leads to the duality of brain hemispheres [8]. Modern research has paved way to realizing these structures in terms of computing units. Among various cognitive process exhibited by humans, the most important considered for intelligence is the ability to learn and recall. Human memory is perceived to be auto-associative. It can store learned concepts in memory and recall upon seeing partial or broken patterns. Recent research work in BICA [5–7] consider using Hopfield type of

© Springer International Publishing AG, part of Springer Nature 2018
J. Xiao et al. (Eds.): ICCC 2018, LNCS 10971, pp. 147–154, 2018.
https://doi.org/10.1007/978-3-319-94307-7_11

processors to model the dual hemispherical structure of the brain. Hopfield nets [12] are a form of Recurrent Neural Nets (RNN), the recurrence property stems from the fact that, the neurons or nodes are bi-directional. They also possess content addressable memory [13] which is biologically similar to the human brain in forming associations. This property makes them ideal for use in pattern recognition, image reconstruction and information retrieval [2]. Another aspect of ANN is its ability to parallelize the learning and recall process. For parallelization, we implement our model on a distributed Hadoop MapReduce framework.

Our aim in this paper is to create a parallelized Augmented Memory Recall Model using Hopfield Nets and Hadoop [1]. We showcase a novel way of using Hopfield Networks in recognizing usage access patterns in Web Server logs to detect most frequently accessed paths. This finds its use in detecting anomalous patterns or behaviors aiding in Web security. It can also be used to secure paths which records high activity. We use a real world dataset consisting of Web Server access logs of all HTTP requests made to the NASA[1] Kennedy Space Center WWW server in Florida. Our model works by establishing associations of HTTP requests made on every day. The generated weight matrices for each pattern is then merged thereby augmenting its capacity to predict or recall hybrid varieties of the originally learned concept. The rest of this paper is structured as follows. In Sect. 2 we will look at research done in BICA. In Sect. 3, the proposed system is described by relating it with biological models. Section 4 talks about data and experiments performed to validate our model. Section 5 talks about the results from our experiments. Section 6 concludes this research and talks about future work.

2   Related Work

Our architecture draws upon research conducted in BICA which focuses on creating a computational model inspired by human mind. Within BICA, a principle called the *Dynamic Theory of Information (DTI)* was proposed by [6] which gives a formal description of computationally modeling the components of human mind (i.e.) *memory, thought and emotions*. The concept of *Dynamic Formal Neuron (DFN)* proposed by [5] talks in detail of building a neuron processor using *Hopfield* [12] and *Grossberg* [9,10] processors. The concept of brain hemispherical duality was explored in [7]. This provided a premise to model a framework analogous to the human brain. Further studies by [15] indicate the means to realize cognitive structures. Based on the above research and aligning closely with the works of [5,6], we chose the Hopfield Network to model our architecture. ANN's [11,18] emerged as the foremost computing systems whose functioning resembled the human mind. Principles of self-organization [14] which uncovers semantic relationship in sentences are some of the features present in ANN. Based on the above research works, our model can be applied to identify associations or similarity in datasets. ANN's inherent memory mechanism and parallel processing capacity are used in pattern recognition problems [16]. As

---

[1] http://ita.ee.lbl.gov/html/contrib/NASA-HTTP.html.

Hopfield models provide content addressable or auto-associative memory [12,13], we base our architecture on using Hopfield nets. On the application front, we chose to analyze logs as they provide information which can be formulated into pattern recognizing problems. In the era of Big Data, web servers are increasingly under attack because of huge amount of data logs being generated. They carry important information about usage patterns and are critical for debugging or performing after crash analysis. It becomes paramount to build automated models that can identify key patterns in logs reducing manual effort in processing and drawing conclusions. Deep Learning Nets [19] and Machine Learning techniques [4] are increasingly employed to understand log files better.

3 Augmented Memory Recall Architecture

3.1 Overview of Memory Recall Architecture

Our architecture depicted in Fig. 1 consists of two modules akin to the dual hemispheres of the brain. Using Hadoop's MapReduce framework, we have split the Right Hemisphere as the Mapper. This layer consumes concepts in a parallel manner which is analogous to how the right side of the brain learns. There are sub-modules within this layer which corresponds to lobes of the brain. These consists of Hopfield Networks which process patterns and generates weight matrices. The Reducer is analogous to the Left Hemisphere of the brain. Here the weight matrices are augmented based on similarity of learned concepts. We will describe each of the layers in following sections[2].

3.2 Right Hemisphere: Mapper

Temporal Lobe: In this layer, input patterns are fed to a layer of Hopfield Networks to learn and memorize. The input patterns are represented as a class of vectors $(p_1, p_2, ..., p_n)$. For each of these p_1 to p_n patterns, a learned weight matrix is generated. Hadoop's Mapper parallelizes this process thereby increasing the data processing rate.

Hippocampus: The generated weight matrices w_1 to w_k are stored along with its corresponding patterns in this layer. As in biological brain, this layer acts as the Hippocampus which serves as the storage layer of learned concepts. The following holds true regarding the weight matrix:

- $W_{i,i} = 0 \ \forall i$
- $W_{i,j} = W_{j,i} \ \forall i, j$

---

[2] National Institute on Drug Abuse (1997) Mind Over Matter: The Brain's Response to Drugs, Teacher's Guide.

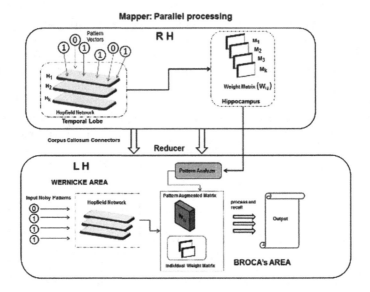

Fig. 1. Brain inspired architecture.

Hopfield nets are trained using the Hebb's rule. Hebbian principle rests on the fact that when an axon of neuron i repeatedly takes part in firing another neuron j, then the strength of connection between i and j increases. This rule is both local and incremental. It is implemented in the following manner, when learning k binary patterns:

$$\Delta w_{i,j} = \alpha x_j * y_i \tag{1}$$

where α represents learning rate. Capacity of this rule is $0.14k$ where k is number of distinct patterns. Gradual decay of memory is experienced over a period of time. Continued exposure to similar patterns results in a stronger memory retention while recalling.

3.3   Left Hemisphere: Reducer

Pattern Analyzer: This module receives the trained weight matrices and its patterns. For each pattern p_1 to p_n, we check the cosine score between them and if it exceeds a threshold metric θ, the corresponding weight matrices are augmented. When there is no similarity, they are appended after finding all patterns and matrices which are augmented. Cosine similarity is given in Eq. 2.

$$\cos(\theta) = \frac{A.B}{\parallel A \parallel B \parallel} \tag{2}$$

Let $f(n)$ be the function denoting cosine similarity. Then, the rule for augmenting is given by

$$W_{ik} := \begin{cases} \sum_{k=1}^{n} w_{ik} & \text{if } f(p_i, p_k) \geq \theta \\ W = (w_{ik}, w_{jk}) & \text{otherwise.} \end{cases} \tag{3}$$

Wernicke Area: The process of recalling is conceptually equivalent to the *Wernicke Area* present on the left side of the brain which is responsible for speech comprehension. In this region, information is processed in a sequential manner [3]. This layer uses *Reducer* to combine the individual chunks of pattern-memory information from the RH and pattern analyzer. Test patterns are queried in this layer consisting of hopfield networks with the augmented weight matrix.

Broca's Area: The output region of the network is similar to the *Brocka's Area* (as shown in Fig. 1) which is responsible for generating patterns of interest by reconstructing from memory.

From the functions of both the RH and LH layers, we see a inherent equivalence between biological neurons and artificial Hopfield nets implemented in our model.

4   Experiments Using Real World Dataset

The dataset we chose to use are web logs collected by NASA Kennedy Space Center WWW server in Florida. Table 1 gives a description of the data. Logs are collected for a period of 30 days (July 1–31). The aim of our experiment using server logs is to get the most frequently accessed resource path on each day. We consider only two levels of folder accesses (i.e.) From Table 1 for */shuttle/resources/orbiters* we drill down only till */shuttle/resources*. For each of $t_1, t_2, ..., t_k$ timestamps, we extract folders visited and generate $p_1, p_2, ...p_k$ patterns. Our model uses Discrete Hopfield Networks and input is represented as binary vectors consisting of 0 and 1. Example of how the folders are represented as binary vectors to Hopfield Network is shown in Fig. 2. Each of these patterns produces learned weight matrices w_{ij} for Hopfield layers $h_1, ..h_k$. For each of these folders visited, we generate a key-value pair of its corresponding patterns-weight matrices $(p_i : w_{ik})$. These pairs are produced parallelly by the Mapper (RH). These key-value pairs are sent to the *Pattern Analyzer* in the Reducer (LH) where each p_i is compared with p_j using cosine similarity whose values ranges from 0 to 1. Then using Eq. 3, weight matrices w_{ik} and w_{jk} are augmented. This results in stronger associations and learning of hybrid patterns. For k trained patterns, let q_i be the querying pattern. Result p_{r_i} represents the path most frequently accessed to reach q_i from p_i.

Table 1. NASA WWW server log data

IP	Tiimestamp	Folder accessed
199.72.81.55	01/Jul/1995:00:00:01	/history/apollo/
unicomp6.unicomp.net	01/Jul/1995:00:00:06	/shuttle/countdown/
ccspar2.cadence.com	03/Jul/1995:04:33:10	/shuttle/resources/orbiters/
199.166.39.14	01/Jul/1995:00:05:21	/cgi-bin/imagemap/countdown?

Table 2. Count of test patterns found in dataset from July 1–3

01/Jul/95	02/Jul/95	03/Jul/95
'apollo': 2153	'apollo': 2482	'apollo': 1925
'missions': 5802	'missions': 5498	'missions': 3854
'technology': 838	'technology': 688	'technology': 515
'imagemap': 859	'imagemap': 772	'imagemap': 345
'resources': 630	'resources': 568	'resources': 354

5   Results

We are presenting the results derived for a period of 7 days. The aim of this experiment is to only observe the recall capacity of Hopfield Networks by augmenting the weight matrix. Following test patterns were used as queries: ('/resources','/missions','/technology','/apollo', '/soils','/imagemap'). Table 2 gives the count of each entry in the test pattern that appears as part of the folders accessed in the dataset. *For example: In day 1 for 'apollo' the pattern '/history/apollo' was trained 2153 times.* The total result predicting the most commonly accessed path is given in Fig. 2. On observing the pattern and frequency of the folder paths in Fig. 2, we see how the Hopfield network creates-

Timestamp	Pattern	Frequent Path	% Frequency	Timestamp	Pattern	Frequent Path	% Frequency
01/Jul/1995	/resources	/shuttle/resources	71%	03/Jul/1995	/resources	/shuttle/resources	71%
	/missions	/shuttle/missions	71%		/missions	/shutle/missions	71%
		/shutle/missions	51%				
	/technology	/shuttle/technology	100%		/technology	/shuttle/technology	71%
	/apollo	/history/apollo	71%		/apollo	/history/apollo	71%
	/soils	None	0%		/soils	None	0%
	/imagemap	/cgi-bin/imagemap	77%		/imagemap	/cgi-bin/imagemap	71%
		/htbin/imagemap	58%			/htbin/imagemap	71%
02/Jul/1995	/resources	/shuttle/resources	71%	04/Jul/1995	/resources	/shuttle/resources	71%
	/missions	/shuttle/missions	71%		/missions	/shutle/missions	71%
		/shutle/missions	71%				
	/technology	/shuttle/technology	100%		/technology	/shuttle/technology	100%
	/apollo	/history/apollo	71%		/apollo	/history/apollo	71%
	/soils	None	0%		/soils	None	0%
	/imagemap	/cgi-bin/imagemap	74%		/imagemap	/cgi-bin/imagemap	41%
		/htbin/imagemap	55%				
Timestamp	**Pattern**	**Frequent Path**	**% Frequency**	**Timestamp**	**Pattern**	**Frequent Path**	**% Frequency**
05/Jul/1995	/resources	/shuttle/resources	71%	06/Jul/1995	/resources	/shuttle/resources	71%
	/missions	/shuttle/missions	47%		/missions	/shuttle/missions	47%
	/technology	/shuttle/technology	51%		/technology	/shuttle/technology	51%
	/apollo	/history/apollo	71%		/apollo	/history/apollo	71%
	/soils	None	0%		/soils	None	0%
	/imagemap	/cgi-bin/imagemap	0%		/imagemap	None	0%
Hopfield Learning	Pattern Example	**Folder**	**Binary Pattern**	**Timestamp**	**Pattern**	**Frequent Path**	**% Frequency**
		/shuttle	000100	07/Jul/1995	/resources	/shuttle/resources	100%
		/missions	001000		/missions	/shuttle/missions	71%
		/apollo	100000		/technology	/shuttle/technology	70%
		/history	010000		/apollo	/history/apollo	51%
		/shuttle/missions	000100001000		/soils	None	0%
		/history/apollo	010000100000		/imagemap	None	0%

Fig. 2. Query prediction result showing the timestamp of folders for each day, patterns trained, predicted patterns and frequency of similarity related to the trained pattern.

break associations like the human brain. Consider the pattern *'/missions'*, in Table 2. On day 1, the Hopfield network has no stored memory and forms associations of all patterns it learns. From Fig. 2, the frequently accessed path to reach *'/missions'* is *'/shuttle/missions' and '/**shutle**/missions'* for day 1. As it keeps acquiring patterns and forms associations, we see a trend where the association becomes weaker if it does not see enough entries to create a stronger memory imprint. In days 5 and 6, the occurrence of *'/missions'* decreases and the layer starts to forget indicated by the lower frequency of similarity value in the result. A similar trend can be observed for *'/imagemap'*. From day 1 to 3, it can be reached via *'/cgi-bin'* and *'/htbin'* which are the most commonly accessed paths. The model partially forgets on day 4 and recollects marginally better on day 5 before forgetting on subsequent days. This is because it does not see sufficient patterns of *'/imagemap'* in the training dataset to be deemed significant and so it forgets from its memory and forms new associations of other patterns instead.

Table 3. Count of test patterns found in dataset from July 4–7

04/Jul/95	05/Jul/95	06/Jul/95	07/Jul/95
'apollo' : 1051	'apollo': 1238	'apollo': 529	'apollo': 400
'missions' : 1717	'missions': 1731	'missions': 991	'missions': 1218
'technology': 285	'technology': 232	'technology': 168	'technology': 172
'imagemap' : 220	'imagemap' : 271	'imagemap': 140	'imagemap': 144
'resources' : 170	'resources' : 237	'resources': 90	'resources': 145

6   Conclusions

In this paper, we have presented a biologically inspired augmented memory recall model. It is powered by MapReduce which allows the framework to compute enormous volume of data. Inspired by BICA, our model contains Hopfield nets which is used to learn and recall information. We have developed a model where the learned weight matrices of Hopfield Networks are augmented based on the similarity of concepts it learns. This makes the associations even stronger. The Mapper (RH) is used to process and learn new concepts and Reducer (LH) is used to predict the output based on learned knowledge from the right. This is akin to the *Temporal lobe (RH)* and *Wernicke-Broca's (LH)* area of the brain. *Reducer* in LH combines the chunks of information received from Mapper (RH) to produce the augmented Hopfield memory network. We have evaluated our model based on experiments using a real world dataset to recall the most frequently accessed folder on web servers. This is to mainly understand the behavior of this model to recall by augmenting weight matrices. This model can be used in anomaly or intrusion detection by narrowing down areas of high activity. Future research would involve comparing with other Machine Learning models and evaluating by computing metrics like F1 Score, precision and recall among others.

References

1. Apache Software Foundation: Hadoop. https://hadoop.apache.org
2. Ayoubi, R.A., Ziade, H., Bayoumi, M.A.: Hopfield associative memory on mesh. In: Proceedings of the 2004 International Symposium on Circuits and Systems, ISCAS 2004, vol. 5, P. V IEEE (2004)
3. Bianki, V.: Parallel and sequential information processing in animals as a function of different hemispheres. Neurosci. Behav. Physiol. **14**(6), 497–501 (1984)
4. Cao, Q., Qiao, Y., Lyu, Z.: Machine learning to detect anomalies in web log analysis. In: 2017 3rd IEEE International Conference on Computer and Communications (ICCC), pp. 519–523, December 2017. https://doi.org/10.1109/CompComm.2017.8322600
5. Chernavskaya, O., Chernavskii, D.: Natural-constructive approach to modeling the cognitive process. Biophysics **61**(1), 155–169 (2016)
6. Chernavskaya, O., Chernavskii, D., Karp, V., Nikitin, A., Shchepetov, D.: An architecture of thinking system within the dynamical theory of information. Biol. Inspired Cogn. Archit. **6**, 147–158 (2013)
7. Chernavskaya, O., Chernavskii, D., Rozhylo, Y.: On the modelling an artificial cognitive system based on the human-brain architecture. In: Advances in Neuroergonomics and Cognitive Engineering, pp. 107–121. Springer (2017)
8. Goldberg, E.: The wisdom paradox: how your mind can grow stronger as your brain grows older. Penguin, New York (2006)
9. Grossberg, S.: Studies of mind and brain: Neural Principles of Learning, Perception, Development. Cognition, and Motor Control (Reidel, Boston, 1982) (1982)
10. Grossberg, S.: The Adaptive Brain I: Cognition, Learning, Reinforcement, and Rhythm, vol. 42. Elsevier, New York City (1987)
11. Gupta, N.: Artificial neural network. Netw. Complex Syst. **3**(1), 24–28 (2013)
12. Hopfield, J.J.: Neural networks and physical systems with emergent collective computational abilities. Proc. Natl. Acad. Sci. **79**(8), 2554–2558 (1982)
13. Hopfield, J.J.: Neurons with graded response have collective computational properties like those of two-state neurons. Proc. Natil. Acad. Sci. **81**(10), 3088–3092 (1984)
14. Kohonen, T.: The self-organizing map. Proc. IEEE **78**(9), 1464–1480 (1990)
15. Laird, J.E.: Extending the soar cognitive architecture. Front. Artif. Intell. Appl. **171**, 224 (2008)
16. Lin, W.G., Wang, S.S.: A new neural model for invariant pattern recognition. Neural Netw. **9**(5), 899–913 (1996)
17. Wang, H., Raj, B., Xing, E.P.: On the origin of deep learning. arXiv preprint arXiv:1702.07800 (2017)
18. Wang, S.C.: Artificial neural network. In: Interdisciplinary Computing in Java Programming, pp. 81–100. Springer, Boston (2003)
19. Yang, T., Agrawal, V.: Log file anomaly detection

Utilizing the Capabilities Offered by Eye-Tracking to Foster Novices' Comprehension of Business Process Models

Michael Zimoch[1]([✉]), Rüdiger Pryss[1], Georg Layher[2], Heiko Neumann[2], Thomas Probst[3], Winfried Schlee[4], and Manfred Reichert[1]

[1] Institute of Databases and Information Systems,
Ulm University, Ulm, Germany
{michael.zimoch,ruediger.pryss,manfred.reichert}@uni-ulm.de
[2] Institute of Neural Information Processing,
Ulm University, Ulm, Germany
{georg.layher,heiko.neumann}@uni-ulm.de
[3] Department for Psychotherapy and Biopsycho Health,
Danube University Krems, Krems an der Donau, Austria
thomas.probst@donau-uni.ac.at
[4] Department of Psychiatry and Psychotherapy,
Regensburg University, Regensburg, Germany
winfried.schlee@googlemail.com

Abstract. Business process models constitute fundamental artifacts for enterprise architectures as well as for the engineering of processes and information systems. However, less experienced stakeholders (i.e., novices) face a wide range of issues when trying to read and comprehend these models. In particular, process model comprehension not only requires knowledge on process modeling notations, but also skills to visually and correctly interpret the models. In this context, many unresolved issues concerning the factors hindering process model comprehension exist and, hence, the identification of these factors becomes crucial. Using eye-tracking as an instrument, this paper presents the results obtained of a study, in which we analyzed eye-movements of novices and experts, while comprehending process models expressed in terms of the Business Process Model and Notation (BPMN) 2.0. Further, recorded eye-movements are visualized as scan paths to analyze the applied comprehension strategies. We learned that experts comprehend process models more effectively than novices. In addition, we observed particular patterns for eye-movements (e.g., back-and-forth saccade jumps) as well as different strategies of novices and experts in comprehending process models.

Keywords: Business process model comprehension · Eye-tracking
Cognition · Eye-Movement Modeling Examples
(Hidden) Markov Model

© Springer International Publishing AG, part of Springer Nature 2018
J. Xiao et al. (Eds.): ICCC 2018, LNCS 10971, pp. 155–163, 2018.
https://doi.org/10.1007/978-3-319-94307-7_12

1   Introduction

Business Process Management (BPM) aims at the creation, improvement, as well as automation of business processes and has become vital for the success of any enterprise [1]. In this context, a *process model* acts as a blueprint comprising tasks, decisions, and actors dedicated to a specific process. Usually, these process models are expressed in terms of textual or graphical artifacts. The latter, in turn, are utilized to advance the understanding of business processes (i.e., *process model comprehension*) for all involved stakeholders [2].

Generally, process models should be created in a way such that process stakeholders do not face any problems in comprehending them. Still, stakeholders are encountering challenges in the comprehension of process models [3], especially the less experienced ones (i.e., *novices*) [4]. In this context, the use of *eye-tracking* might provide valuable insights into the cognitive processes of comprehending process models [5]. Amongst others, assertions about the *cognitive load* can be made and the *process model comprehension strategies* applied can be identified, e.g., by visualizing the corresponding *scan path*. In detail, the *scan path* reflects the chronological order of *fixations* (i.e., gaze over informative areas of interest) and *saccades* (i.e., quick eye-movements between *fixations*) [6].

This paper presents the results we obtained from a process model comprehension study relying on eye-tracking. In detail, *novices* and *experts* in the domain of process modeling had to study three different process models expressed in terms of the *Business Process Model and Notation (BPMN) 2.0* [7], whilst their *fixation* and *saccade patterns* were recorded by an eye-tracker. The objective of the study is to deliberately disclose the approaches applied by novices and experts to comprehend process models. Further, we want to investigate whether or not there are differences in comprehending process models, e.g., in which way the applied comprehension strategies between the participants differ. The study insights can be used to derive comprehension guidance, especially for novices, and be used to augment tools with features fostering process model comprehension. The remainder of the paper is structured as follows: Sect. 2 describes the context and setting of the study. Study results, in turn, are analyzed and discussed in Sect. 3. Related work is discussed in Sect. 4. Finally, a summary and an outlook on future work are given in Sect. 5.

2   Study Context

In general, *comprehension* constitutes a cognitive process that establishes relations between available information on objects and events in the long-term memory, together with information perceived at the moment from the sensory, working, or short term-memory [8]. In this context, *process model comprehension* can be termed as the process for decoding and capturing the information documented in process models [9]. To be more precise, individuals must cope with the complexities involved of parsing the relevant *syntactic*, *semantic*, and *pragmatic information* in a process model. As a consequence, novices are frequently confronted with the challenge to properly read and comprehend process models [10]. To systematically study this challenge, we conducted an eye-tracking study on how to foster the comprehension of process models. For this purpose, we identify the *scan paths* (i.e., chronological order of *fixations* and *saccades*) of both novices and process modeling experts while comprehending process models documented in terms of *BPMN 2.0*. Moreover, it is found in eye-tracking studies that experts comprehending a *stimulus* (e.g., picture) are more likely to reflect a smaller number of *fixations*, *saccades*, and consequently a shorter *scan path length* compared to novices [11]. Therefore, amongst others, the use of eye-tracking enables us to measure the cognitive load as well as to reveal visual stumbling blocks in a process model, which, in turn, might hinder overall comprehension.

2.1   Study Setting

First of all, we want to identify the strategies for reading and comprehending process models and analyze whether or not there are differences between novices and experts. Therefore, we invite novices ($n = 17$) and experts ($n = 19$) from the field of process modeling to participate in the study. This categorization into two samples (i.e., novices and experts) is accomplished by a median split, i.e., based on the time spent on process modeling so far, as provided through a self-reporting. In the study, participants are asked to read and comprehend **three** different BPMN 2.0 process models. These process models cover three different scenarios, i.e., *fitness training*, the *purchase of an item in an auction*, and the *ordering of a pizza*. Further, the process models reflect three different *levels of complexity*, i.e., *easy*, *medium*, and *hard*. In detail, the *easy process model* only comprises a sequence of basic modeling elements of BPMN 2.0. With increasing *level of complexity*, new BPMN elements are introduced, previously not contained in the process models, and the total number of elements is increased. After comprehending a process model, participants need to answer *four true-or-false comprehension questions*, solely referring on the semantics of the process scenario. The questions are used in order to ensure that participants actually study the process models. Moreover, *relative fixations* and *saccade patterns* are recorded with the SMI iView X Hi-Speed system at a sampling rate of 240 Hz. Demographic data and qualitative feedback, in turn, are gathered based on questionnaires. In addition, participants are given the instruction to complete the study as fast as possible but, on the other, as meticulous as possible.

3   Analysis of Eye-Movements

Tables 1 presents *mean* and *standard deviation (SD)* for all values obtained from the two samples, i.e., novices and experts. For each *level of complexity* (i.e., *easy*, *medium*, and *hard*), the process model comprehension *duration (in s)*, the *fixation* and *saccade counts* as well as the length of the *scan path (in px)* are shown. As expected, a clear difference between the single *levels of complexity* is

Table 1. Descriptive results (i.e., both, novices, and experts)

	Factor	Both		Novices		Experts	
		Mean	(SD)	Mean	(SD)	Mean	(SD)
Easy	Duration	35.37	(14.52)	38.53	(16.26)	31.78	(12.29)
	Fixation	121.42	(41.57)	138.76	(39.41)	104.84	(43.39)
	Saccade	120.81	(39.81)	130.47	(36.12)	111.11	(43.84)
	Scan path	24398.44	(9349.76)	26342.18	(7192.88)	22454.89	(11107.53)
Medium	Duration	54.11	(22.05)	63.11	(23.28)	46.05	(16.30)
	Fixation	187.08	(57.98)	209.12	(56.37)	167.47	(57.54)
	Saccade	204.36	(68.50)	220.41	(69.54)	188.32	(68.94)
	Scan path	42181.03	(29357.56)	47364.35	(38368.67)	37543.32	(17865.93)
Hard	Duration	67.14	(29.02)	73.07	(33.04)	62.16	(24.01)
	Fixation	240.94	(79.16)	264.94	(99.88)	216.00	(56.04)
	Saccade	233.69	(83.85)	260.06	(88.90)	207.47	(81.50)
	Scan path	45217.22	(16077.79)	49534.24	(18576.74)	40900.32	(13962.37)

discernible, i.e., an apparent increase in respective factors. Further, juxtaposing the results obtained for novices and experts, novices need more time for process model comprehension. *Fixation* and *saccade counts* reflect a higher number and this results in a longer *scan path* for the comprehension of process models.

Data collected with eye-tracking during the study is analyzed and visualized with SMI BeGaze software, which allows for an extensive analysis of recorded eye-movements. After analyzing of the obtained data, different *scan paths* for comprehending a process model (i.e., *process model comprehension strategies*) are derived for novices and experts respectively. However, both samples show alike comprehension strategies in the *first iteration*, i.e., after having a first glance on the process models. More precisely, beginning from the start element of a process model, both samples visually consider all elements in a process model through an *element-to-element procedure*. After completing the first iteration, strategies of novices and experts respectively differ during the *second iteration*. Thereby, particular eye-movement patterns become apparent, e.g., *back-and-forth saccade jumps* and *targeted search*. Many novices reconsider the process model once more from the start element, but with a stronger emphasis on single elements and *modeling constructs* (e.g., parallelism, decision points before splitting control flows into alternative paths), indicating strong variabilities in *saccade patterns* as well as *fixation times*. Experts, in turn, focus on decisive *modeling constructs* (e.g., decision points) in the process models and, hence, their attention shifts between these elements. As opposed to experts, the *scan paths* of novices reflect higher *fixation* and *saccade counts*. Further, they require a *greater duration* for comprehending a process model (cf. Table 1). Figures 1 and 2 illustrate two identified *scan paths*, one from a novice and one from an expert.

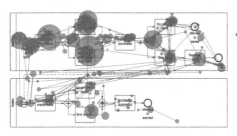 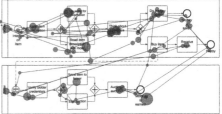

Fig. 1. Scan path of a novice   **Fig. 2.** Scan path of an expert

In Fig. 1, the *scan path* of a novice is shown. It consists of *301 fixations, 254 saccades*, and an overall *comprehension duration of* 98.17 s. On the contrary, the experts' *scan path* (cf. Fig. 2) comprises *100 fixations* and *99 saccades*. In addition, the *comprehension duration is* 27.47 s. Comparing both *scan paths*, it becomes apparent that the novice spent more time studying the elements in the process models, whereas the expert moved quickly over the elements.

3.1 Discussion

An explanation for our study findings might be that process models reflect complex business processes with high information density. Thus, the process of comprehending such models leads to a high cognitive load, especially regarding novices [12]. Process model comprehension not only requires knowledge on process modeling notations, but also the capability to visually interpret these models. Usually, these capabilities evolve over time due to increasing practical experiences [13]. However, existing research revealed that the visual observation capabilities of experts can be efficiently conveyed to novices [14]. To evaluate this, we are currently conducting another exploratory study, in which we explicitly show the novices how experts visually comprehend process models. For this purpose, we are analyzing the *scan paths* of modeling experts more deeply with the goal to derive an *average scan path*. Furthermore, decisive *modeling constructs* (e.g., parallelism) are identified, which are essential regarding the correct comprehension of process models. Consequently, novices can be directed through a process model by selective reading, ensuring a correct process model comprehension.

The material used in the current study is provided in terms of *Eye-Movement Modeling Examples (EMMEs)*, which shall serve as a basis for guiding novices in comprehending process models [15]. *EMMEs* either reflect the *scan paths of experts* or highlight *specific modeling constructs* superimposed onto a process model. In general, the use of *EMMEs* allows us to focus on the various dimensions in a process model. More specifically, any process model contains information related to different dimensions, e.g., *syntactics* or *semantics* [16]. Amongst others, the *syntactic* dimension refers to compliance with modeling rules, whereas *semantics* refer to proper and complete documentation of a scenario in a process

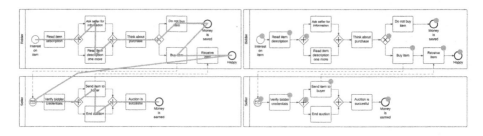

Fig. 3. Path display condition   **Fig. 4.** Dot display condition

model. Therefore, based on the dimension set, the *EMMEs* can reflect different conditions (cf. Figs. 3 and 4). Figure 3 shows the *Path Display Condition*, which visualizes the derived *experts average scan path* in a process model. The *Path Display Condition* traverses the process model with all relevant elements, ensuring a proper comprehension of the process scenario. The *Dot Display Condition* (cf. Fig. 5), in turn, is used for highlighting specific *modeling constructs* as well as their *function* (e.g., process model behavior) with solid dots that can dynamically change their size (i.e., larger or smaller), according to the *fixation counts*. We believe that the process model comprehension of novices can be increased by exploiting modeling experts' eye-movements in a process model.

After applying the *EMMEs*, we will evaluate the performance of novices in respect to process model comprehension with the results obtained from the first study. Moreover, we will perform a third study, the *scan paths* from the third study will be analyzed and interpreted using a *(Hidden) Markov Model (HMM)* to detect potential latent strategies for model comprehension [17]. Besides the observable states (e.g., *back-and-forth saccade jumps*), there are non-observable states of eye-movements, which can be utilized to foster process model comprehension. In this context, we will introduce a taxonomy to identify latent fixations and saccades in eye-tracking data based on a probabilistic *(Hidden) Markov Model*. Finally, Fig. 5 summarizes the *three-stage study*.

4   Related Work

A categorization of empirical works that focus on the influence of both objective and subjective factors on process model comprehension is presented in [18]. This work also involves a discussion of the factors having an impact on model comprehension. A more specific work is presented in [19], which investigates how the characteristics of an individual (e.g., theoretical knowledge) influence the subjective process model comprehensibility, whereas [20] focuses on objective model comprehensibility suggesting guidelines for improving BPMN 2.0 process models. Taking cognitive aspects of process model comprehension into account, [21] shows that cognitive styles as well as theoretical knowledge on process modeling notations are correlated with the performance in comprehending process

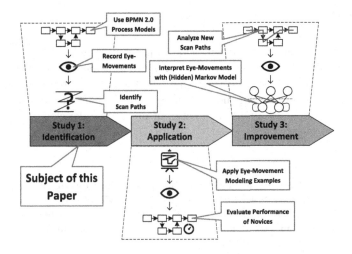

Fig. 5. Three-stage study to foster process model comprehension

models. In turn, a cognitive overload impairs model comprehension as demonstrated in [22]. Using eye-tracking in the context of process model comprehension, [23] shows how the performances of individuals vary confronting them with different comprehension tasks. Furthermore, [23] provides insights into the development of strategies for comprehending process models. The study presented in [24], in turn, demonstrates the positive impact of *EMMEs* on learning processes. Further, the improvement of learning styles with derived latent behavior patterns based of a Decision Tree and a (Hidden) Markov Model is reported in [25].

5   Summary and Outlook

We presented results obtained from a process model comprehension study that uses eye-tracking. In detail, the strategies applied by novices and experts in process model comprehension were identified through the analysis of their *fixation* and *saccade counts*, i.e., *scan paths*. While both samples reveal similar strategies for comprehending a process model in the *first iteration* (i.e., after having a first glance on the process model), the strategies applied between novices and experts vary with time passed. Particularly, experts are comprehending process models in a more efficient manner, i.e., *scan paths* reflect less *fixations* and *saccades*. In general, the presented study is part of a *three-stage study* aiming to foster process model comprehension. In detail, all studies utilize the capabilities offered by eye-tracking. As novices obviously experience difficulties in the visual comprehension of process models, support and guidance should be improved to enable proper process model comprehension. Currently, we use the scan paths gathered from experts as *Eye-Movement Modeling Examples (EMMEs)* in another study to teach and convey the applied strategies for process model comprehension to novices. Finally, in a third study, we will use a *(Hidden) Markov Model (HMM)* to unravel latent strategies for process model comprehension. Based on the three-stage study, the objective is to provide guidance and directives, especially for novices, enabling a better comprehension of process models. Moreover, training in model comprehension can be particularly tailored focusing on difficulties to comprehend modeling constructs. Further, the findings can be used to augment tools with features improving the reading and comprehension of process models by providing visual cues about the syntax of process model elements.

References

1. Lohrmann, M., Reichert, M.: Effective application of process improvement patterns to business processes. Softw. Syst. Model. **15**, 353–375 (2016)
2. Johansson, L.O., Wärja, M., Carlsson, S.: An evaluation of business process model techniques, using moody's quality criterion for a good diagram. In: CEUR Workshop, vol. 963, pp. 54–64 (2012)
3. Mendling, J., Strembeck, M.: Influence factors of understanding business process models. In: Abramowicz, W., Fensel, D. (eds.) BIS 2008. LNBIP, vol. 7, pp. 142–153. Springer, Heidelberg (2008). https://doi.org/10.1007/978-3-540-79396-0_13
4. Figl, K., Laue, R.: Cognitive complexity in business process modeling. In: Mouratidis, H., Rolland, C. (eds.) CAiSE 2011. LNCS, vol. 6741, pp. 452–466. Springer, Heidelberg (2011). https://doi.org/10.1007/978-3-642-21640-4_34
5. Zimoch, M., Pryss, R., Schobel, J., Reichert, M.: Eye tracking experiments on process model comprehension: lessons learned. In: Reinhartz-Berger, I., Gulden, J., Nurcan, S., Guédria, W., Bera, P. (eds.) BPMDS/EMMSAD -2017. LNBIP, vol. 287, pp. 153–168. Springer, Cham (2017). https://doi.org/10.1007/978-3-319-59466-8_10
6. Salvucci, D.D., Goldberg, J.H.: Identifying fixations and saccades in eye-tracking protocols. In: Proceedings of 2000 Symposium on Eye Track Research and Applications, pp. 71–78. ACM (2000)
7. OMG: Business Process Management & Notation 2.0 (2018). www.bpmn.org. Accessed 27 Feb 2018
8. Anderson, J.R.: Cognitive Psychology and Its Implications. WH Freeman/Times Books/Henry Holt & Co., New York (1985)
9. Mendling, J., Reijers, H.A., van der Aalst, W.M.: Seven process modeling guidelines (7PMG). Inf. Softw. Technol. **52**, 127–136 (2010)
10. Becker, J., Rosemann, M., von Uthmann, C.: Guidelines of business process modeling. In: van der Aalst, W., Desel, J., Oberweis, A. (eds.) Business Process Management. LNCS, vol. 1806, pp. 30–49. Springer, Heidelberg (2000). https://doi.org/10.1007/3-540-45594-9_3
11. Raney, G.E., Campbell, S.J., Bovee, J.C.: Using eye movements to evaluate the cognitive processes involved in text comprehension. J. Vis. Exp. **10** (2014)
12. Moody, D.L.: Cognitive load effects on end user understanding of conceptual models: an experimental analysis. In: Benczúr, A., Demetrovics, J., Gottlob, G. (eds.) ADBIS 2004. LNCS, vol. 3255, pp. 129–143. Springer, Heidelberg (2004). https://doi.org/10.1007/978-3-540-30204-9_9
13. Davies, I., et al.: How do practitioners use conceptual modeling in practice? Data Knowl. Eng. **58**, 358–380 (2006)
14. Van Gog, T., et al.: Attention guidance during example study via the model's eye movements. Comput. Hum. Behav. **25**, 785–791 (2009)

15. Jarodzka, H., Balslev, T., Holmqvist, K., Nyström, M., Scheiter, K., Gerjets, P., Eika, B.: Conveying clinical reasoning based on visual observation via eye-movement modelling examples. Instr. Sci. **40**, 813–827 (2012)
16. Krogstie, J., et al.: Process models representing knowledge for action: a revised quality framework. J. Inf. Syst. **15**, 91–102 (2006)
17. Simola, J., Salojärvi, J., Kojo, I.: Using hidden Markov model to uncover processing states from eye movements in information search tasks. Cogn. Syst. Res. **9**, 237–251 (2008)
18. Figl, K.: Comprehension of procedural visual business process models. Bus. Inf. Syst. Eng. **59**, 41–67 (2017)
19. Mendling, J., Recker, J., Reijers, H.A., Leopold, H.: An empirical review of the connection between model viewer characteristics and the comprehension of conceptual process models. Inf. Syst. Front. 1–25 (2018)
20. Corradini, F., et al.: A guidelines framework for understandable BPMN models. Data Knowl. Eng. **113**, 129–154 (2018)
21. Turetken, O., Vanderfeesten, I., Claes, J.: Cognitive style and business process model understanding. In: Metzger, A., Persson, A. (eds.) CAiSE 2017. LNBIP, vol. 286, pp. 72–84. Springer, Cham (2017). https://doi.org/10.1007/978-3-319-60048-2_7
22. Houy, C., Fettke, P., Loos, P.: On the theoretical foundations of research into the understandability of business process models. In: 22nd ECIS (2014)
23. Petrusel, R., Mendling, J., Reijers, H.A.: How visual cognition influences process model comprehension. Decis. Support Syst. **96**, 1–16 (2017)
24. Mason, L., Pluchino, P., Tornatora, M.C.: Using eye-tracking technology as an indirect instruction tool to improve text and picture processing and learning. Br. J. Educ. Technol. **47**, 1083–1095 (2016)
25. Cha, H.J., Kim, Y.S., Park, S.H., Yoon, T.B., Jung, Y.M., Lee, J.-H.: Learning styles diagnosis based on user interface behaviors for the customization of learning interfaces in an intelligent tutoring system. In: Ikeda, M., Ashley, K.D., Chan, T.-W. (eds.) ITS 2006. LNCS, vol. 4053, pp. 513–524. Springer, Heidelberg (2006). https://doi.org/10.1007/11774303_51

Detecting Android Malware Using Bytecode Image

Yuxin Ding[✉], Rui Wu, and Fuxing Xue

Department of Computer Sciences and Technology,
Harbin Institute of Technology Shenzhen Graduate School, Shenzhen, China
yxding@hit.edu.cn, ruiwwww@163.com

Abstract. In recent years, there is a rapid increase in the number of Android based malware. In this paper we propose a malware detection method using byte-code code image. We firstly extract bytecode file from Android APK file, and then convert the bytecode file into an image file. Finally we use convolution neural network (CNN) to classify malware. the proposed method directly convert a bytecode file into an image data, so CNN can automatically learn features of malware, and use the learned features to classify malware. Especially for malware which uses polymorphic techniques to encrypt functional code, the proposed method can detect it without using unpacking tools. The experimental results show it is feasible to detect malware using CNN, especially for detecting encrypted malware.

Keywords: Convolutional neural network · Malware · Android · Binary data

1 Introduction

With the popular of Android based smart devices, smart phone users face more and more security problems [1, 2]. Due to the openness of Android system, android-based mobile devices have been become the attacking target of malware, and more and more attacks are happened on android smartphones.

The traditional detection methods, signature based detection method need experts manually extract malware signature, which is a labor-intensive work. To solve this problem, we study how to use deep learning algorithm, the convolution neural network (CNN) to automatically learn the feature representation of malware, and use the feature representation to recognize malware.

2 Related Works

There are two types of different malware detection methods, one is called dynamic detection method, and the other is static detection method. The dynamic method need to run samples when detecting malware. Different from dynamic method, static method does not need to run samples.

Usually dynamic methods run samples in a sandbox and monitor their behaviors in real time [3]. Because the samples do not run in a real environment, malicious samples cannot cause damages to the real system.

© Springer International Publishing AG, part of Springer Nature 2018
J. Xiao et al. (Eds.): ICCC 2018, LNCS 10971, pp. 164–169, 2018.
https://doi.org/10.1007/978-3-319-94307-7_13

In [4] the program instrumentation technology is applied to monitor malware behaviors [4]. Xu et al. [5] monitored the inter-component communication to detect malware. Chin et al. [6] detect malware by intercepting the intent information and analyzing the inter-application communication. Afonso et al. [7] used the tool strace to monitor API calls, and detected malware by analyzing the frequency of APIs.

Different from dynamic detection method, the static detection methods usually decompile Android application and extracts malware features for malware detection. In [8] the authors extracted sensitive application programming interface (API) and use them to detect malware. In [9] the bytecode features are extracted from Android APK file, and used as data features for malware detection. In [10, 11], the authors extracted application permissions, signatures for malware detection.

The static detection method is a lightweight and efficient detection method. However, malware writers can use polymorphic technique or encryption technology to prevent application from being decompiled and analyzed. Under this situation, static detection methods loss the capability for malware detection. To solve this issue, in this paper we study the malware detection method which does not need to decompile Android applications.

3 Malware Detection Method Based on CNN

3.1 Visualization of Android APK File

Android application is programmed in Java language. The Android SDK tools compile the application, data and resources together, and generate an Android package, an archive file named with an .apk suffix. In this study we use CNN to detect android malware. The input of CNN is a two-dimensional matrix like an image. So we need to represent Android application as an image. We call this procedure as visualization of Android APK file.

We unzip the android APK file and extract classes.dex file which contains the whole bytecode to be interpreted by Dalvik virtual machine. The classes.dex file header records some of the attributes of the DEX file and the relative offset of the data structure of the rest of the data in the file. To avoid analyzing the classes.dex, we see the file as a binary byte stream, and each byte corresponds to a pixel having values from 0 to 255. The binary byte stream is a sequence data, we need to change it into a two-dimensional data. In our work we uniformly cut the whole sequences into m subsequences, where $m = \left\lceil \sqrt{n} \right\rceil + 1$, and n is the length of the whole sequence. The symbol $\left\lceil \sqrt{n} \right\rceil$ defines as the integer part of $\sqrt{n}$. Each subsequence is seen as a row of matrix M, for the subsequence whose length is smaller than m, we add 0 into it. In this way we change a classes.dex into a $m \times m$ matrix. The input data of CNN is fixed size data, however, different classes.dex files have different length. To solve this issue, we scale a matrix to a fixed 512×512 matrix. Figure 1 shows a grayscale image of an Android APK file. We can see different APK files have different image textures. CNN has a strong power to analyze image features, and can automatically extract features from images.

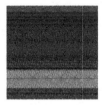

Fig. 1. A grayscale image of an android classes.dex file

3.2 Malware Classification

CNN has widely used to recognize images and classify natural language text, and achieved higher performance [12]. CNN has a deep structure and can learn different levels of data features if sufficient training data is supplied. It can find the hidden patterns of raw data, which cannot be observed by experts.

In our work, each Android application is converted into two-dimensional image, so we can use CNN to recognize malware. CNN includes two types of layers, convolution layer and pooling layer. The convolution layer's parameters consist of a set of kernels. This layer convolutes kernels to inputs to extract features. The pooling layer uses pooling operation to sample the output of the previous convolutional layer to decrease the effect of small position shifting. Pooling is a form of non-linear down-sampling. There are several down-sampling functions, we choose Max-Pooling with 2×2 filters and stride 2. In our study we test different CNN structures, whose convolution-pooling layers vary from one to four. We also set different number of filters for each convolution layer, and the size of each kernel is 11×11. The output layer has two units to represent malicious and benign classes (Fig. 2).

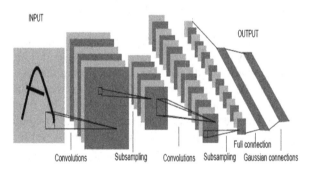

Fig. 2. Structure of CNN

After deciding the structure of CNN, we apply BP algorithm to train CNN. Let $\delta(i+1)$ be the error of the $(l+1)$-st layer and the cost function is $J(W, b; x, y)$. (W, b) are the parameters, and (x, y) are the training data. If the l-th layer is fully connected with the $(l+1)$-st layer, then the error item for the l-th layer is computed as (1).

$$\delta^{(l)} = ((W^{(l)})^T \delta^{(l+1)}) \bullet f'(z^{(l)}) \tag{1}$$

and the gradients are

$$\nabla_{W^{(l)}} J(W, b; x, y) = \delta^{(l+1)} (a^{(l)})^T \tag{2}$$

$$\nabla_{b^{(l)}} J(W, b; x, y) = \delta^{(l+1)} \tag{3}$$

If the l-th layer is a convolutional and down-sampling layer then the error item is computed as (4).

$$\delta_k^{(l)} = upsample((W_k^{(l)})^T \delta_k^{(l+1)}) \bullet f'(z_k^{(l)}) \tag{4}$$

Where k is the filter number and $f'(z_k^{(l)})$ is the derivative of the activation function of neuron. The upsample operation passes the error through the pooling layer by calculating the error w.r.t to each unit incoming to the pooling layer. In max pooling the unit which was chosen as the max receives all the error since very small changes in input would perturb the result only through that unit. The gradient of W and b is compute as (5) and (6).

$$\nabla_{W_k^{(l)}} J(W, b; x, y) = \sum_{i=1}^{m} (a_i^{(l)}) * rot90(\delta_k^{(l+1)}, 2) \tag{5}$$

$$\nabla_{b_k^{(l)}} J(W, b; x, y) = \sum_{a,b} (\delta_k^{(l+1)})_{a,b} \tag{6}$$

Where $a^{(l)}$ is the input of the l-th layer, and $a^{(1)}$ is the input image. The operation $(a_i^{(l)}) * \delta_k^{(l+1)}$ is the "valid" convolution between i-th input in the l-th layer and the error w.r.t. the k-th filter.

After training, we test CNN using testing samples. We convert a sample into a 2-dimentional image, and input it to CNN. CNN produces a two dimensional vector in the output layer and each unit of the output vector represents the probability that the input is malicious or benign. If the probability that a file is malicious is higher than that of the benign, the input data is classified as malware.

4   Experimental Results

We define the following criteria, classification accuracy and the true positive rate (TPR) and false positive rate (FPR) to assess the performance of CNN. The classification accuracy, TPR, and FPR are defined in Eqs. (7), (8) and (9), respectively. In these equations, the true positive value (TR) is the number of malicious samples classified as malicious samples, the true negative value (TN) is the number of benign samples classified as benign samples, the false positive value (FP) is the number of benign samples classified as malicious samples, the false negative value (FN) is the number of malicious samples classified as benign samples.

$$Accuracy = \frac{TP + TN}{TP + FN + TN + FP} \qquad (7)$$

$$TPR = \frac{TP}{TP + FN} \qquad (8)$$

$$FPR = \frac{FP}{TN + FP} \qquad (9)$$

In the experiment, the dataset is from the DREBIN project of University of Gottingen (www.sec.cs.tu-bs.de/~danarp/drebin). We choose 3962 malware samples, which are from 14 families. The benign samples are downloaded from the Anzhi store. We use ten-fold cross validation to evaluate the performance of the classifiers. We evaluate the performance of CNN with different convolution-pooling layers, and the number of convolution-pooling layers varies from one to five. For each convolutional layer, we set six filters, and the size of each kernel is 11 × 11. The experimental result is shown in Table 1.

Table 1. Experimental results of CNN with different layers

No. of convolution layer	Accuracy	TPR	FPR
1	0.9052	0.9055	0.0146
2	0.9415	0.9415	0.0100
3	0.9335	0.9336	0.0091
4	0.9435	0.9436	0.0079
5	0.9375	0.9375	0.0089

From the experimental results, we can see the accuracy of CNN is bigger than 90 percent, and the false positive rate is smaller than 2%. It shows that CNN can find effective features for malware detection. With the increase of convolution-pooling layer, the overall performance of CNN is increased. We get a better experimental results when the number of layers is four. When we still increase the layers, the performance of CNN become stable.

5   Conclusions

This paper propose an Android malware classification method based on bytecode image. We firstly convert Android applications into images, and then use CNN to detect malware. The advantages of the proposed method is as follows: we need not decompile samples, so encrypted malware can be detected. CNN can automatically find the features for malware detection, which can detect a large number of malware efficiently. In this study we only verify the feasibility of the deep learning method for malware detection. Our future work is to further test the performance the proposed method and compare it with more base-line methods.

Acknowledgements. This work was partially supported by Scientific Research Foundation in Shenzhen (Grant No. JCYJ20160525163756635), Guangdong Natural Science Foundation (Grant No. 2016A030313664) and Key Laboratory of Network Oriented Intelligent Computation (Shenzhen).

References

1. Aafer, Y., Du, W., Yin, H.: DroidAPIMiner: mining API-level features for robust malware detection in Android. In: Zia, T., Zomaya, A., Varadharajan, V., Mao, M. (eds.) Security and Privacy in Communication Networks. SecureComm 2013. LNICST, vol 127. Springer, Cham (2013). https://doi.org/10.1007/978-3-319-04283-1_6
2. Enck, W., et al.: On lightweight mobile phone application certification. In: Proceedings of the 16th ACM Conference on Computer and Communications Security, pp. 235–245. ACM (2009)
3. Ding, Y., et al.: Control flow-based opcode behavior analysis for malware detection. Comput. Secur. **44**(7), 65–74 (2014)
4. Chin, E., et al.: Analyzing inter-application communication in Android. In: International Conference on Mobile Systems, Applications, and Services, pp. 239–252. ACM (2011)
5. Xu, R., et al.: Aurasium: practical policy enforcement for Android applications. In: Usenix Conference on Security Symposium, p. 27. USENIX Association (2012)
6. Xu, K., et al.: ICCDetector: ICC-based malware detection on Android. IEEE Trans. Inf. Forensics Secur. **11**(6), 1252–1264 (2016)
7. Afonso, V.M., et al.: Identifying Android malware using dynamically obtained features. J. Comput. Virol. Hacking Tech. **11**(1), 9–17 (2015)
8. Yuxin, D., et al.: A malware detection method based on family behavior graph. Comput. Secur. **73**(1), 73–86 (2018)
9. Chan, P., et al.: Static detection of Android malware by using permissions and API calls. In: International Conference on Machine Learning and Cybernetics, pp. 82–87 (2015)
10. Aung, Z., et al.: Permission-based android malware detection. Int. J. Sci. Technol. Res. **2**(3), 228–234 (2013)
11. Karbab, E.B., et al.: DySign: dynamic fingerprinting for the automatic detection of Android malware. In: International Conference on Malicious and Unwanted Software, pp. 1–8. IEEE (2017)
12. Zhang, X., et al.: Character-level convolutional networks for text classification. In: Advances in Neural Information Processing Systems, pp. 649–657 (2015)

The Study of Learners' Emotional Analysis Based on MOOC

Hongxiao Fei and Hongyuan Li[✉]

School of Software, Central South University, Changsha, China
hxfei@csu.edu.cn, scora@foxmail.com

Abstract. "MOOC" (Massive Open Online Course) is a large-scale open online learning platform. MOOC forum is the learner to learn the mutual place, through the course of the forum interactive text data as the data base, the combination of word2vec and machine learning algorithm to build emotional, and then combined with the learning emotion of this emotion classifier on learners' emotional tendency judgment, thus obtains the MOOC learning environment learning and emotional changes the exchange of learning, which can make up for the learning between the loss of emotion and increase the learning and improve the learning efficiency and learning quality of learners.

Keywords: MOOC · Emotional analysis · Word2vec
Machine learning algorithm

1 Introduction

MOOC is a large-scale open online course. In this learning environment, learners do not need to have school status, they can also freely use curriculum resources, and do not limit [1] to learners, learners' learning background and learning contents. Through these courses, the learners solve the problem of uneven distribution of educational resources in space and solve the problem of inequality in the distribution of educational resources. At the same time, the difference of [2] MOOC courses and face-to-face courses as well as traditional online courses lies in "teaching content needs to be fragmented [3] decomposition according to knowledge, made into a short video each no more than 20 min for learning [4].

Compared with traditional classroom, MOOC online learning environment is dispersed by learners' time and space, and learners are lonely in physical position. Therefore, interaction with other learners and assistants is especially important. The interaction between teachers and students is mainly for learners to answer questions [5]. The interaction between learners is mainly collaborative learning and discussion based learning, which enables learners to exchange learning experience and share learning outcomes, so that knowledge level can be improved by [6]. The two interactions mainly focus on cognitive interaction, ignoring emotional interaction and relative lack of interaction. Emotion is an important feature of human intelligence. It plays an important role in the process of human cognition and decision-making. At the same time, emotion is closely related to learning process and affects the final result of learning [7].

MOOC discussion area is a communication and interaction place provided by [8] MOOC platform for learners and learners. Learners use MOOC forum to interact with all kinds of learning topics [9]. Text is a medium for learners to communicate. These texts contain massive [10] of learners' interaction and information, reflecting the learning state of learners and problems encountered by learners.

Sentiment analysis refers to the use of relevant technology to dig out the text generated by the user exchange in the emotional information, learners learn, change [11] his emotional state with learning activities and dynamic, so the text sentiment analysis that the learner's learning emotional state can understand the learning state and knowledge [12] the level of learning ability, mental state, [13] etc. Therefore the use of interactive data of course forum sentiment analysis can analyze the change that the learning emotion of learners, and provide targeted personalized learning policy adjustment programs for the learners, which adapt to the learner's emotional changes, which can improve the learning efficiency, optimize the learning effect of [14]. Therefore, modeling for learners' learning emotions helps to overcome the shortcomings of online learning for learners, so as to provide learners with more precise learning strategies.

2 Related Work

The main research contents of text emotion analysis are text emotion classification, text opinion mining, word polarity determination, text emotion recognition and so on. Mckewon [15] and others determine the emotional tendencies of these words by identifying the subjective vocabulary in the corpus by using machine learning methods. Li [16] and others judge the semantic tendencies of the whole text by the semantic tendencies of the emotional words in the text. Some scholars use the multi granularity topic model to mine the evaluation object in the product review. Zhang [17], on the basis of the construction of the emotional classification corpus, uses relevant algorithms to study the related issues of emotion recognition.

Word2Vec is an open source tool released by Google Corporation, the open source tool kit is the language model based on deep learning, the role of the toolkit can be text content into real K dimensional space vectors, then the similarity between the space vector clustering of text content, so as to get the word vector [18] model. The use of this method based on word vectors can learn the potential semantic relations between words, thus constructing an emotional dictionary in a certain field.

The role of Word2vec including [19], document mining of new words, first of all, Word2vec will use the words to quantify, then select Dalian emotional vocabulary as the base dictionary, then calculate the similarity between the new words and the base dictionary with polarity words to judge the new words of emotion the polarity, thereby completing the emotional classification of new words at the same time, the paper also presents the use of SVM classifier based on dictionary classification learning, then the classifier is applied to classify new words. The document [20] uses Word2vec to transform words into word vectors, and then calculates the 10 words with the highest degree in the basic lexicon and new words, so as to expand the basic emotional lexicon. Document [21] regards two new words as a new word, then calculates the similarity between the new words and the emotional polarity words in the basic emotional lexicon, so as to complete the classification of the new words' emotional polarity.

The learners' affective analysis is mainly through the analysis of learner interaction course forum text information so that the learning emotion tendency of learners, and will use the Word2vect words into word vector, word vector can be expressed some semantic information at the same time, the analysis method can be combined with contextual information, help more accurate the analysis of learning emotional changes in the learning process. Therefore, this topic proposes using word2vec and machine learning algorithm to analyze the emotion of MOOC forum interaction data and train emotion classifiers, so as to get learners' learning and emotional orientation.

3   Realization of Learner's Emotion Classification Algorithm Based on Word2vec

Use the Word2Vect method to convert word vector of the text, it can be given to the training set of contextual information of text data in the corpus, and then through the words generated by space vector to calculate the distance to determine the degree of similarity between words and words, according to the similarity of words in the new text and emotion in the corpus to determine the new the text contains the sentiment polarity, thus completing the affective polarity judgment, and ultimately through the MOOC data analysis of learner's affective state.

Affective state classification main steps as shown in Fig. 1, mainly divided into the stage of training and classification stage, each stage needs to complete the task, get emotional type classifier from the corpus in the training phase, in the classification stage is the emotion classifier using training phase to the learner's emotional decision.

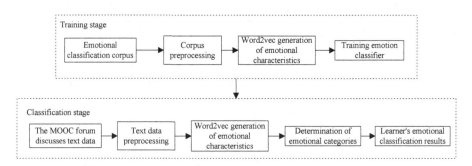

Fig. 1. Flow chart of learner's emotional class determination

The main steps of learners' emotion classification are training emotion classifier, emotional feature selection, emotion semantic representation, emotion classifier training and emotion category judgement.

(1) Training emotion classifier. The basic idea is that Twitter polarity data has been discussed based on annotation, then determine the addition of unlabeled sentiment polarity is positive or negative comments emotional feelings, aims to build a model

from the text data of the comment, which can determine the other reviews customer sentiment. Because the corpus training in the field of corpus selection emotion training classifier, can capture the expression of similar user reviews and some vocabulary, this can improve the Word2Vec training vector when the relation between word accuracy, because the Word2vec is based on the context, the same context appears several times when Word2Vec can capture the association between the two words, so if the use of field data to train the Word2Vec model, it can capture the emotional changes of learners.

(2) The choice of emotional features and the semantic description of the text. Corpus and forum data are natural language text information in the form of expression, so in the further analysis, when the use of certain methods to convert text to the algorithm can be understood in the form of this topic selection of text training using the word2vec model, the comment text into the corresponding word vector, as compared to Word2Vec, only need to we will review this model corresponding to the input text to convert text to word vector corresponding to the use of emotion, classifier trained in sentiment classification, so it can be a label and label free emotion is an emotional comments data sets together and using Word2Vec vector training (training and emotion classifier the model with tag data set).

(3) The learner's emotion classifier is trained and the emotion category is determined. After converting text content into word vector, a classifier is selected to analyze text data of learners, and it is concluded that learners who do not have emotional category labels say that I have emotional inclination. In training phase, training word vector is used as classifier input data to train the classifier and get an emotion classifier. Then, the emotion classifier is used to determine the tendency of learning emotion expressed by each learner's text content. At present, the text classification algorithm is very rich, the more famous including KNN, NB, SVM and so on, these classification methods can be used as the method of emotion classifier.

4   Data Acquisition and Construction of Emotional Corpus

4.1   Data Acquisition

Emotional analysis can be referred to as opinion tendency analysis, opinion and emotion mining, subjective emotional analysis and so on. Text emotional analysis is the process of analysis, data processing and data mining of text with subjective emotions. The MOOC forum is the main place for users to communicate. The form of forum data is shown in Table 1. Therefore, using forum data text analysis can identify learners' learning and emotional orientation.

Table 1. Forum data examples

---

forum data examples

👍 *
  beautiful nymph,i am back,up

👎 * It is too hard for me to learn

👍 *
  Haha,thanks for building this study group! I want to join in.

👎 * I think I will give up learning the project

The data characteristics of the MOOC forum is sparse, and the lack of context features, and some text and not apparent show their emotional state, and the method of analysis of the current emotion does not contain obvious emotional words and semantic features of the text does not contain identity but implicit emotion recognition. Therefore, this paper will combine machine learning algorithm and labeled emotional tag emotional corpus to build emotion classifier, and then combine emotion classifier to predict the sentiment of MOOC forum.

Twitter is a social media platform that has a wide range of influence. The text data represented by twitter represent a trend of public opinion and a manifestation of public sentiment. For example, some researchers have concluded that Twitter has a certain correlation with other public feelings. By collecting and analyzing Twitter users' emotions, we can predict consumer confidence index [22], stock prices and real-time quotes [23]. The MOOC forum does not provide users with the mutual exchange of learning experience places, learning emotion so to interactive text on learners' analysis can draw learners; literature [24, 25] by twitter and other social media to extract emotional information is used to analyze the MOOC learners' learning emotion; literature with emotion category labels [26] Twitter as a corpus of emotional category labels to construct semantic word clusters to determine the learning category. Therefore, this topic will use Twitter, which has been labeled emotional polarity, as a corpus and Word2Vec method to train the emotional classifier.

4.2 Corpus Construction

This topic selects the data of the xuetangX learning platform, and then the data is cleaned, including:

(1) use regular expressions to remove HTML tags.
(2) remove repeated comments.
(3) remove punctuation.
(4) use the English word segmentation tool to decompose the text content into separate word segmentation.
(5) remove the discontinuation words and so on.

(6) Fig. 2 is part of the commentary data for learners. Each data of each learner's forum in this data has corresponding learner's personal basic information, as shown below.

course_i d	userid_ DI	register ed	view ed	explored	cert ifie	final_ cc_cna	LoE_DI	YoB	gend er	grad e	start_ti me_DI	last_eve nt_DI	nevents	ndays_ac t	nplay_vi deo	nchapter s	nforum_ posts	post_text
HarvardX/MHxPC13(	1	1	0	0	Austra	Secondar;	1993	f	0	41263	41438	110	5	1	1	3	HEY GIRLS & BOYS, IT'S TIME
HarvardX/MHxPC13(	1	1	0	0	India	Secondar;	1991	m	0	41345	41421	43	2	6	2	5	Aha! I can find you everywhe;
HarvardX/MHxPC13(	1	1	0	0	German;	Masters	1983	m	0	41114	41229	28	2	1	2	1	beautiful nymph, i am back, up.
HarvardX/MHxPC13(	1	1	0	0	India	Masters	1989	m	0	41114	41233	278	4	107	2	2	Haha, thanks for building this
HarvardX/MHxPC13(	1	1	0	0	India	Bachelor;	1990	m	0	41202	41202	9	1	4	1	7	I think IPython has recently
																		Facebook group about Strong
HarvardX/MHxPC13(	1	1	0	0	German;	Bachelor;	1982	m	0	41114	41205	39	3	4	3	18	A. I. :

Fig. 2. The part of the commentary data of the learner

5 Experimental Results and Analysis

Firstly, learner corpus and text using the word2vec encoding process, this method can be converted into text encoding, the method can be used to reduce the data size to capture the context information at the same time, and contributes to data processing further sentiment classification, in the conversion of word vector in the process, need to set the parameters, only to make the optimal classification performance of classifier, the parameters involved include: num_features, min_word_count, num_workers, context, downsampling, where num_features is the number of dimensions of the word vector (300 ~ 500), context represents the size of the window.

The text corpus data with labels become the feature vector, the data is divided into training set and test set, which is mainly used when the training set training machine learning classification algorithm, the test set is mainly used to test the classification performance of the classifier, the evaluation criteria for the AUC, TPR etc. Then, combined with the classification algorithm, we trained the classifier generated by word2vec. The selected algorithm includes SVM, logistic regression and decision tree. The results of the experiment are as follows:

Figure 3 experimental results showed when contex was 5, SVM algorithm and logistic regression algorithm with the increase of num_features, sentiment classifier AUC decreases; and the decision tree algorithm AUC values increased, but the maximum AUC value for the SVM algorithm AUC, and when contex is 10, the three algorithms in logistic regression algorithm to obtain the maximum value of AUC, but the AUC value is less than 5 contex and num_features 300 AUC value. Therefore, when the text is transformed into a vector of 300 dimensions, and the window size of its context is 5, and SVM is used as its classification algorithm, the classifier performs best. The text is converted into a form Fig. 4 of a vector.

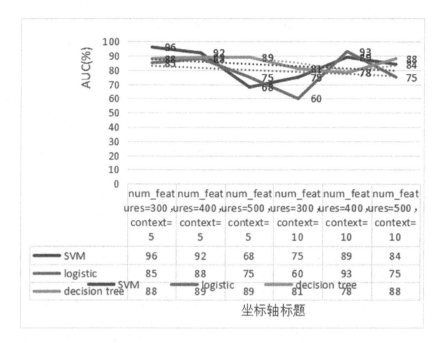

The chart shows AUC(%) on the y-axis (0 to 100) with six parameter configurations:

	num_features=300, context=5	num_features=400, context=5	num_features=500, context=5	num_features=300, context=10	num_features=400, context=10	num_features=500, context=10
SVM	96	92	68	75	89	84
logistic	85	88	75	60	93	75
decision tree	88	89	89	81	78	88

坐标轴标题

Fig. 3. Word2Vec experimental parameters and experimental results

	2	3	4	5	6	7	8	9	...	290	291	292	293	294	295	
61	-0.047549	0.060955	-0.010721	-0.038596	0.081066	-0.012990	-0.011319	...	-0.000985	-0.012707	0.032608	-0.016090	0.039781	0.032727	-(
157	0.055872	-0.019862	-0.037977	-0.035307	-0.027820	0.001561	-0.129409	...	0.008825	0.009351	0.049074	0.014700	0.043716	0.011905	0
356	0.058519	-0.032740	-0.041366	-0.040640	-0.028992	0.003062	-0.137413	...	0.005369	-0.013331	0.059558	0.024479	0.050037	-0.001663	0
958	0.074397	-0.052212	-0.057439	-0.031738	-0.056832	-0.000745	-0.113041	...	0.010415	0.004558	0.043055	0.021555	0.039725	0.004048	0
765	0.091571	-0.036604	-0.050196	-0.046816	-0.042025	-0.003283	-0.122668	...	0.010910	0.001553	0.053563	0.023637	0.045796	-0.002470	0
731	0.086973	-0.036270	-0.048417	-0.044380	-0.044170	-0.005037	-0.119343	...	0.012488	0.003973	0.051991	0.021783	0.046017	-0.001836	0
714	0.065881	-0.037331	-0.048628	-0.027499	-0.053144	-0.001303	-0.110252	...	0.011511	-0.002993	0.057591	0.029693	0.054491	0.004466	0
985	0.061200	-0.031626	-0.037466	-0.025803	-0.048408	0.000529	-0.115414	...	0.012342	0.002719	0.056549	0.025309	0.052291	0.007249	0

Fig. 4. Text vector of word2vec transformation

Then the word2vec generated text Forum on learners' word vector model training, emotion classification learners use the emotion classifier, as shown in Fig. 5 results to complete the classification, the sentiment classification label emotional classification classify the learners, emotional classification 1 represents the learning emotion is positive contrary to the emotion, negative emotion, the emotional tendency of learners learning.

course_id	userid_DI	registered	viewed	explored	certified	final_c c_remov _DI	LoE_DI	YoB	gender	grade	start_time _DI	last_event _DI	nevents	ndays_act	nplay_vide o	nchapters	nforum_po sts	post_text	Emotional classification
HarvardX/MHxPC13C	1	1	0	0		Austra	Secondary	1993	f	0	41263	41438	110	5	1	1	3	HEY GIRLS & BOYS, IT'	-1
HarvardX/MHxPC13C	1	1	0	0		India	Secondary	1991	m	0	41345	41421	43	2	6	2	5	Aha! 1 can find you e	1
HarvardX/MHxPC13C	1	1	0	0		German	Masters	1983	m	0	41114	41229	28	2	1	2	1	beautiful nymph, i am	1
HarvardX/MHxPC13C	1	1	0	0		India	Masters	1989	m	0	41114	41233	278	4	107	2	2	Haha, thanks for build	1
HarvardX/MHxPC13C	1	1	0	0		India	Bachelors	1990	m	0	41202	41202	9	1	4	1	7	I think IPython has r Facebook group about	1
HarvardX/MHxPC13C	1	1	0	0		German	Bachelor	1982	m	0	41114	41205	39	3	4	3	18	Strong A.I.:	-1
HarvardX/MHxPC13C	1	1	0	0		India	Secondary	1991	f	0.1	41114	41224	2489	13	386	5	0	Wow, is this still an	-1

Fig. 5. The learner's emotional model data

6   Conclusion

This paper classifies the learners' learning emotions on the basis of the forum text data of the learners to communicate. The data in the MOOC forum are characterized by sparse features and lack of context, and some of them. Text can not clearly show its emotional state, and the current method of sentiment analysis can not accurately identify texts that contain no obvious emotional words and semantic features but contain implicit emotions. This paper will use the word2vec text into word vector, and then combined with the machine learning algorithm and converted into word vector labeled emotion label emotion corpus as the feature to construct the emotion classifier, the emotion classifier of judgment emotional tendency of the data on the MOOC forum.

This topic has made some theoretical research achievements in the analysis and research of learners' learning emotion. But the human emotion is a complex problem of the subjective, the only emotion of learners of two classification of polar, and not of human good complex emotions are well described, so in the next step of the work with the psychology of emotion theoretical basis. From a variety of ways to better describe the emotional characteristics of learners, which can be a more comprehensive description of the learner's emotional changes.

References

1. Christensen, G., Steinmetz, A., Alcorn, B., et al.: The MOOC phenomenon: who takes massive open online courses and why? Social Science Electronic Publishing (2016)
2. 游晓明, 方志军, 姚兴华. MOOC + 翻转课堂混合教学模式下应用型高校教学改革与实践. 软件导刊·教育技术 **16**(1), 7–9 (2017)
3. Rieber, L.P.: Participation patterns in a massive open online course (MOOC) about statistics. Br. J. Educ. Technol. **48**(6), 1295–1304 (2017)
4. 张慧毅, 徐荣贞, 孙杰,等. 基于 MOOC 教学平台的教学模式建构研究. 中国教育信息化 **2**, 32–34 (2017)
5. Sunar, A., Su, W., Abdullah, N., et al.: How learners' interactions sustain engagement: a MOOC case study. IEEE Trans. Learn. Technol. **PP**(99), 475–487 (2017)
6. Brouns, F., Teixeira, A., Morgado, L., et al.: Designing massive open online learning processes: the sMOOC pedagogical framework. In: Open Education: from OERs to MOOCs. Springer, Heidelberg (2017). https://doi.org/10.1007/978-3-662-52925-6_16
7. Liu, Z., Zhang, W., Sun, J., et al.: Emotion and associated topic detection for course comments in a MOOC platform. In: International Conference on Educational Innovation Through Technology. IEEE (2017)

8. 秦蓬若, 傅钢善. MOOC 课程讨论区中的社会性交互研究——以中国大学 MOOC 平台《现代教育技术》课程为例. 中国教育信息化 **5**, 20–24 (2017)

9. Bergner, Y., Kerr, D., Pritchard, D.E.: Methodological challenges in the analysis of MOOC data for exploring the relationship between discussion forum views and learning outcomes. In: International Conference on Field Programmable Logic and Applications. IEEE, pp. 1–4 (2015)

10. Wong, J.S., Pursel, B., Divinsky, A., et al.: Analyzing MOOC discussion forum messages to identify cognitive learning information exchanges. In: Asis&t Meeting: Information Science with Impact: Research in and for the Community. American Society for Information Science, p. 23 (2015)

11. Dillon, J., Bosch, N., Chetlur, M., et al.: Student emotion, co-occurrence, and dropout in a MOOC context. In: EDM, pp. 353–357 (2016)

12. Tao, H.: The ethical risks and controlling of the participation of university library in MOOC construction. Library Work & Study (2017)

13. 马相春, 钟绍春, 徐姐. 大数据视角下个性化自适应学习系统支撑模型及实现机制研究. 中国电化教育 **4,** 97–102 (2017)

14. Wise, A.F., Cui, Y., Vytasek, J.: Bringing order to chaos in MOOC discussion forums with content-related thread identification. In: International Conference on Learning Analytics & Knowledge, pp. 188–197. ACM (2016)

15. Dupré, D., Mckeown, G.: Dynamic analysis of automatic emotion recognition using generalized additive mixed models. In: Aisb Convention (2017)

16. 李晓磊. 面向评论的文本倾向性分析中关键问题的研究. 北京化工大学 (2016)

17. 张向阳, 那日萨. 基于复杂网络的情感分类特征选择. 计算机应用研究 **4**, 1000–1003 (2017)

18. 曹杰, 冯雨晖, 宿晓坤,等. 基于深度学习模型 Word2Vec 的短文本语义相似性判别方法和系统, CN 106844346 A[P] (2017)

19. 隋浩. 基于 Word2Vec 的微博情感新词识别与倾向判断研究. 广西大学 (2016)

20. 陆峰. 基于 word2vec 扩充情感词典的商品评论倾向分析. 电脑知识与技术 **13**(5), 143–145 (2017)

21. 付丽娜, 肖和, 姬东鸿. 基于 OC-SVM 的新情感词识别. 计算机应用研究 **7,** 1946–1948 (2015)

22. O'Connor, B., Balasubramanyan, R., Routledge, B.R., Smith, N.A.: From tweets to polls: Linking text sentiment to public opinion time series. ICWSM **11,** 122–129 (2010)

23. Bollen, J., Mao, H., Zeng, X.: Twitter mood predicts the stock market. J. Comput. Sci. **2**(1), 1–8 (2011)

24. Abeywardena, I.S.: Public opinion on OER and MOOC: a sentiment analysis of twitter data. In: International Conference on Open and Flexible Education (2014)

25. Costello, E., Nair, B., Brown, M., et al.: Social media #MOOC mentions: lessons for MOOC research from analysis of twitter data. In: Show Me the Learning Proceedings Ascilite (2016)

26. Wen, M., Yang, D., Rosé, C.P.: Sentiment analysis in MOOC discussion forums: what does it tell us? In: Educational Data Mining (2014)

Source Detection Method Based on Propagation Probability

Yuxin Ding[(✉)], Longfei Wang, Rui Wu, and Fuxing Xue

Department of Computer Sciences and Technology,
Harbin Institute of Technology Shenzhen Graduate School, Shenzhen, China
yxding@hit.edu.cn, zhus_hitsz@hotmail.com

Abstract. In this paper, we study how to locate network information sources given the propagation subgraph of information. We introduce the propagation probability into the complex network, which is used to describe the information transmission capability of the network nodes. The aim of the proposed model is to decrease the source locating error caused by the imbalance of information diffusion. We simulate the propagation of information in different types of complex networks. Experiments show that the propagation probability model can effectively improve the location accuracy.

Keywords: Information source · Social network · Infection subgraph

1 Introduction

On line social network has become an important channel for people to obtain and propagate information. Information propagation has been one of the focuses in social network research. The studies in this field can be divided into two categories. One is studying the diffusion process of information in social network [1–3]. In this paper, we study the reverse of the diffusion problem: given a snapshot of the information propagation process at time t, can we detect which node is the source of the diffusion?

Many researchers develop novel algorithms to detect information source. Based on the solution of dynamics of message-passing equations, Lokhov et al. [5] proposed an efficient probabilistic algorithm for detecting information source. Zhu and Ying [6] developed a sample-path-based approach where the estimator of the information source is chosen to be the root node associated with the sample path that most likely leads to the observed snapshot.

Shah and Zaman [4] proposed the source centrality model for source detection. They assigned each node a likelihood, also named as the source centrality, and then defined the maximum likelihood estimator (MAP) for locating information source based on source centrality. Dong et al. [7] introduced the source centrality model to characterize the correct detection probability of the source estimator upon observing n infected nodes. The MAP estimator maximizes the average correct detection probability. Chang et al. [8] also proposed a MAP estimator to detect information source for general graphs based on the source centrality model. The above mentioned works assume that only a single

© Springer International Publishing AG, part of Springer Nature 2018
J. Xiao et al. (Eds.): ICCC 2018, LNCS 10971, pp. 179–186, 2018.
https://doi.org/10.1007/978-3-319-94307-7_15

snapshot observation is made in the detection. Papers [9–11] propose to use multiple observations to improve the source location accuracy.

In this field, one of the most widely used detection model is the source centrality model [9]. The model assumes that information is spread among the network nodes with equal probability, but in a real network, especially the social network, the social relationship between users determines the probability that information is transmitted. To improve the source location accuracy, we use the propagation probability to describe the relationship between nodes, and propose the source detection model based on propagation probability.

2 Information Source Detection Model Based on Propagation Probability

2.1 Problem Description and the Source Centrality Model

We assume that an information has spread in a network $G(V, E)$, V is the set of nodes and E is the set of edges. We get to observe G at some point, finding a snapshot of N infected nodes with the information. The information propagation subgraph is represented as $G_N(V, E)$, which is a subgraph of $G(V, E)$. The actual information source is denoted as v^*, we assume that each node is equally likely to be the source, so the problem of the information source detection can be transformed into the problem of estimating the maximum a posteriori probability of v^* [4], which is shown as (1).

$$v^* = \arg\max_{v \in G_N} P(G_N | v^* = v) \tag{1}$$

However, it is difficult to estimate $P(G_N | v^* = v)$. To solve this issue, the final infection network G_N can be seen as a permutation sequence, which is subject to the ordering constraints set by the structure of G_N. As shown in Fig. 1, if node v_1 is the source, node v_2 will be the next infected node. So $\{1, 2, 4\}$ is a permitted permutation, whereas $\{1, 4, 2\}$ is not. Therefore, the probability $P(G_N | v^* = v)$ can be calculated by summing all the probability of permitted permutations. Let $R(v, G_N)$ denote the number of all possible permitted permutations that produce G_N with v as the source. The problem of information source detection becomes the problem of calculating the maximum number of restriction sequences, as shown in Eq. (2). $R(v, G_N)$ is called the source centrality of node v [4].

$$\hat{v} = P(G_N | \hat{v} = v) \propto \arg\max_{v \in G_N} R(v, G_N) \tag{2}$$

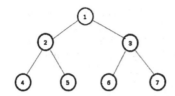

Fig. 1. A sample of an infection graph

2.2 Research Motivation

The source centrality model assumes that the probability that information is transmitted between nodes is equal. However, this assumption is not satisfied in a real network, especially in a social network. In social network information diffusion depends on the relationship between nodes (or users), the closer the relationship between nodes, the easier it is to transfer information in a network. The relationship between the nodes determines the propagation path of information in a network.

In general, the complex network can be regarded as a combination of linear networks. We take the linear network as an example to analyze the problem of the source centrality model. Figure 2 shows a linear network G_L. The number on the edge represents the relationship between nodes. We use the propagation probability to describe the relationship between nodes. The propagation probability describes the probability that information is transmitted between the nodes. Usually, the closer the relationship between nodes, the larger the propagation probability is.

Fig. 2. Information spreading on a linear graph

In Fig. 2 the relationships between nodes v_5, v_6, v_7, v_8 and v_9 are close, on the contrary, there are not close connections among nodes v_1, v_2 and v_3. If we choose v_9 as the source, the number of permitted permutations of v_9 is $R(v_9, G_L)$. In the same way if we choose v_1 as the source, the number of permitted permutations of node v_1 is $R(v_1, G_L)$. Because the propagation probability between v_9 and its neighbors is big, node v_9 has a greater chance to transmit information to its neighbors, and thus is more likely to generate the infection network in Fig. 2. In contrast, node v_1 has a small chance to transfer information to its neighbors, therefore, it is unlikely for v_1 to generate $R(v_1, G_L)$ permitted permissions. So v_9 is more likely to be a source than v_1. However, according to the source centrality model, $R(v_1, G_L)$ and $R(v_9, G_L)$ have the same value, so v_1 and v_9 have the same probability to be a source. We can see the result of the source centrality model contradicts the above analysis. From this instance, we can see that the source centrality model does not take into account the information propagation capacity between nodes, thus can not accurately evaluate whether a node may be a source.

2.3   Detection Model Based on Propagation Probability

To solve the above issue, we introduce propagation probability into the source centrality model. The propagation probability is used to define the probability that information will be transmitted between two nodes.

Definition 1: Suppose there is a propagation path from node v_i to node v_j, the probability distance PD from v_i to node v_j is defined as formula (3).

$$PD(v_i, v_j) = \prod_{p,q \in Path(v_i, v_j)} \rho_{p,q} \tag{3}$$

In (3), p and q are adjacent nodes on the path from v_i to v_j, and $\rho_{p,q}$ is the propagation probability between nodes p and q. if there are M paths from v_i to v_j, the probability distance PD from v_i to v_j is the maximum probability distance in M paths. We can see the greater the probability distance between two nodes, the shorter the distance between the two nodes is. For the convenience of understanding, we define the distance between two nodes as follows Eq. (4).

$$D(v_i, v_j) = 1 - log(PD(v_i, v_j)) \tag{4}$$

In (4), we use the logarithm function to avoid the value of $PD(v_i, v_j)$ being too small, and adding 1 ensures that the distance between two nodes is greater than zero and the minimum distance is 1 hop.

Let $T_{v_j}^v$ denote the number of nodes in the subtree rooted at node v_j, with node v as the source. For example in Fig. 1, $T_2^1 = 3$. Assuming that the source v has k neighbors, $(v_1, v_2, \ldots v_k)$, each of these neighbors is the root of a subtree with $T_{v_j}^v$ nodes, and each node in the subtrees can receive the information after its respective root has the information.

A permitted permutation consists of N nodes, the first node is the source node v, then from the remaining $N - 1$ nodes, we choose $T_{v_1}^v$ nodes for the subtree rooted at v_1. These nodes can be ordered in $R(v_1, T_{v_1}^v)$ different ways. We continue this way recursively to obtain the number of permitted permutations of G_N, which is shown as formula (5), and iterated by formula (5) to obtain formula (6).

$$R(v, G_N) = \binom{N-1}{T_{v_1}^v}\binom{N-1-T_{v_1}^v}{T_{v_2}^v} \ldots \binom{N-1-\sum_{i=1}^{k-1} T_{v_i}^v}{T_{v_k}^v} \prod_{i=1}^{k} R(v_i, T_{v_i}^v) \tag{5}$$

$$R(v, G_N) = (N-1)! \prod_{i=1}^{k} \frac{R(v_i, T_{v_i}^v)}{T_{v_i}^v!} \tag{6}$$

In (4), $R(v_i, T_{v_i}^v)$ can be recursively expanded, therefore, the number of permitted permutations for G_N rooted at v is calculated as (7).

$$R(v, G_N) = (N!) * \prod_{u \in G_N} \frac{1}{T_u^v} \tag{7}$$

When evaluating whether a node is a source, we consider not only the number of permitted permutations generated by a source, but also the probability that the source produces the permitted permutations. We use the propagation probability between nodes as the weight to measure the probability that permitted permutations will be generated. We call this model as the source detection model based on propagation probability.

In the proposed model, $R(v, G_N)$ is calculated as Eq. (8). In (8) the probability distance from source v to the root node v_i of each subtree can be seen as the weight to measure the probability of generating the permitted permutations $R(v_i, T_{v_i}^v)$. According to (8), $R(v_i, T_{v_i}^v)$ can be recursively expanded until the leaves of the tree is reached. The leaf subtrees have one node and one permitted permutation. Therefore, the number of permitted permutations for G_N rooted at v can be calculated as (9).

If we use (9) to detect the propagation sources of the linear network in Fig. 2, $R(v_9, G_N)$ equals $9 \times 0.8^{33} \times 0.2^3$ and $R(v_1, G_N)$ equals $9 \times 0.2^{15} \times 0.8^{21}$. $R(v_9, G_N)$ is significantly larger than $R(v_1, G_N)$, which is consistent with the estimation about the source in a real network.

$$PR(v, G_N) = (N - 1)! \prod_{i=1}^{k} \frac{PD(v, v_i)PR(v_i, T_{v_i}^v)}{T_{v_i}^v!} \tag{8}$$

$$PR(v, G_N) = (N - 1)! \prod_{i=1}^{k} \frac{PD(v, v_i)PR(v_i, T_{v_i}^v)}{T_{v_i}^v!} = N! \prod_{u \in G_n} \frac{PD(v, u)}{T_u^v} \tag{9}$$

If the propagation path between two nodes is long, $PD(v_i, v_j)$ will be a very small value. For the convenience of calculation, $PD(v_i, v_j)$ can be replaced with the distance $D(v_i, v_j)$, then we can obtain formula (10). For any infection graph G_N, the source is estimated as the node with the largest $R(v, G_N)$.

$$R(v, G_N) = N! \prod_{u \in G_N} \frac{1}{D(v, u) * T_u^v} \tag{10}$$

3 Experiment and Analysis

3.1 Experimental Data

We construct different underlying networks to evaluate the performance of the proposed algorithm. The underlying networks include small-world [12], scale-free network [13], and general tree network [13]. They are the most popular models for networks, which are often used to model computer network or social network.

Firstly we construct the underlying network according to parameter settings of different network models [12, 13]. In the experiments each underlying network contains

5000 nodes. We randomly set the information propagation probability between any two adjacent nodes. Next, we construct the infection network on the underlying network. We randomly generate a number between 0 and 1, if the number is bigger than the propagation probability between two nodes, information is transmitted to its neighbor. The source node is randomly selected. The model for information epidemics we select is the susceptible-infected (SI) model [14].

To objectively evaluate the performance of the source detection algorithm, we generated 500 infection networks for each underlying network. The description of the simulated networks is shown in Table 1.

Table 1. Description of the simulated networks

Type of network	Nodes in underlying network	Edges in underlying network	Average nodes in infection networks	Average edges in infection networks
Scale free	5000	21200	1034	5280
Regular	5000	13300	1089	3510
Small world	5000	31100	1267	8210

3.2 Evaluation Criteria

The location error is evaluated using the distance between the source detected by the algorithm and the real source. The distance is defined as the hops of the shortest path length between two nodes. In our work, we use the average location error to evaluate the performance of the source detection algorithms. We make 500 experiments for each type of networks, and the average location error is the average error of 500 experiments. The average location error is defined as (11).

$$\text{error}_{\text{avg}} = \left(\text{error}_1 + \text{error}_2 + \dots \text{error}_N\right)/N \tag{11}$$

3.3 Experimental Results

We simulated the information propagation process on different networks, and then detect the source using the source centrality model (SC) [4] and the model based on propagation probability (PSC), respectively. Table 2 shows the average location errors of two models.

Table 2. Average location errors of SC model and PSC model

Network type	Diameter of infection network	Average location error of SC	Average location error of PSC	Reduced error (SC-PSC)/SC
Scale free	12.6	2.944	2.708	8.0%
Regular	16.42	4.048	3.810	5.9%
Small world	10.9	2.108	2.068	1.9%

From Table 2, we can see that the average error of the PSC model is smaller than that of the SC model on all three types of complex networks, small-world network, regular network and scale-free network. The location error of PSC model is about 2%–8% lower than that of SC model.

We also take the linear network in Fig. 2 as an example to analyze why two models have different performances. It assumes that node v is the information source, and the number of infected nodes on the left of node v is n_1, and the number of infected nodes on the right of node v is n_2, where $n_1 = N - n_2$. For the source centrality model, when the product of T_u^v is the smallest, $R(v, G_N)$ has the biggest value (see (7)). Let $D_{\min}$ represent the minimum value of $\prod_{u \in G_N} T_u^v$, then $D_{\min}$ can be calculated as (12).

$$D_{\min} = \text{Min}(\{n_1 * (n_1 - 1) \ldots 2 * 1\} * \{n_2 * (n_2 - 1)..2 * 1\}) = \text{Min}\{n_1! * n_2!\} \quad (12)$$

$$f(x) = x! * (N - 1 - x)! \quad (13)$$

To obtain the minimum value of $D_{\min}$, we convert Eqs. (12) to (13), where x represents n_1. Calculating the derivative of (13) with respect to x, we obtain when $x = (N - 1)/2$, $D_{\min}$ has the minimum value. We can see the source node is the central node of the linear network.

However, in an actual network information is easy to be spread among nodes having close relationships, thus the lengths of the propagation paths are different. As shown in Fig. 2, node v_9 has close relationships with its neighbors. If v_9 is the source, the information can be spread far enough to v_1. If v_3 is the source, the length of the propagation path on the left of v_3 will be very short. This is mainly because the propagation probability between v_1, v_2, and v_3 is very small, the information is almost impossible to be propagated between them.

Due to the imbalance of information diffusion, n_1 is not always equal to n_2. The information source will deviate more from the center of the linear network as the difference between n_1 and n_2 increases. Because the source centrality model does not take into account the imbalance of information diffusion in the network, the accuracy of the source location is affected.

4   Conclusion

In this paper we propose the source detection model based on propagation probability. In the proposed model, we introduce the propagation probability into the complex network and use propagation probability to describe the capability of information propagation between network nodes. The proposed model aims to reduce the location error caused by the imbalance of information transmission in a network. We also simulate the propagation of information in different types of complex networks. The experimental results show that the probability model has a small location error, and the average location error is reduced by 2%–8% compared with the original model.

Acknowledgments. This work was partially supported by Scientific Research Foundation in Shenzhen (Grant No. JCYJ20160525163756635), Natural Science Foundation of Guangdong Province (Grant No. 2016A030313664), Key Laboratory of Network Oriented Intelligent Computation (Shenzhen).

References

1. Jalali, M., et al.: Information diffusion through social networks: the case of an online petition. Expert Syst. Appl. **44**, 187–197 (2016)
2. Ni, Y., et al.: Modeling and minimizing information distortion in information diffusion through a social network. Soft. Comput. **21**, 1–13 (2016)
3. Belák, V., Morrison, D., et al.: Phantom cascades: the effect of hidden nodes on information diffusion. Comput. Commun. **73**, 12–21 (2016)
4. Shah, D., Zaman, T.: Rumors in a network: who's the culprit? IEEE Trans. Inf. Theory **57**(8), 5163–5181 (2011)
5. Lokhov, A., et al.: Inferring the origin of an epidemic with a dynamic message-passing algorithm. Phys. Rev. E **90**(1), 12–19 (2013)
6. Zhu, K., Ying, L.: Information source detection in the SIR model: a sample-path-based approach. IEEE/ACM Trans. Netw. **24**(1), 408–421 (2016)
7. Dong, W., Zhang, W., Tan, C.: Rooting out the rumor culprit from suspects. In: IEEE International Symposium on Information Theory Proceedings (ISIT), pp. 2671–2675 (2013)
8. Chang, B., et al.: Information source detection via maximum a posteriori estimation. In: IEEE International Conference on Data Mining, pp. 21–30 (2016)
9. Nguyen, H., Roughan, M.: Improving hidden Markov model inferences with private data from multiple observers. IEEE Sig. Process. Lett. **19**(10), 696–699 (2012)
10. Wang, Z., et al.: Rooting our rumor sources in online social networks: the value of diversity from multiple observations. IEEE J. Sel. Topics Sig. Process. **9**(1), 663–677 (2015)
11. Wang, Z., Zhang, W., Tan, C.W.: On inferring rumor source for SIS model under multiple observations. In: IEEE International Conference on Digital Signal Processing (DSP), pp. 1001–1010 (2015)
12. Watts, D., Strogatz, S.: Collective dynamics of 'small-world' networks. Nature **393**, 440–442 (1998)
13. Barabasi, A., Albert, R.: Emergence of scaling in random networks. Science **286**, 509–512 (1999)
14. Bailey, N.: The Mathematical Theory of Infectious Diseases and its Applications. Griffin, London (1975)

Author Index

Printed in the United States
By Bookmasters